40 QUESTIONS ABOUT The Trinity

Matthew Y. Emerson
R. Lucas Stamps

Benjamin L. Merkle, Series Editor

40 Questions About the Trinity

Published by Kregel Academic, an imprint of Kregel Publications, 2450 Oak Industrial Dr. NE, Grand Rapids, MI 49505-6020.

This book is a title in the 40 Questions Series edited by Benjamin L. Merkle.

Italics in Scripture quotations indicate authors' added emphasis.

The Greek font, GraecaU, is available from www.linguistsoftware.com/lgku.htm, +1-425-775-1130.

ISBN 978-0-8254-4751-8

Cataloging-in-Publication Data is available from the Library of Congress.

Printed in the United States of America

25 26 27 28 29 / 5 4 3 2 1

"*40 Questions About the Trinity* is a splendid contribution to Kregel's 40 Questions series. Matt Emerson and Luke Stamps have once again teamed together to produce an excellent work that is grounded in Scripture and informed by leading thinkers throughout church history, and that engages the key questions and issues of our day. Students and church leaders will be blessed by this timely work that celebrates and affirms the conclusions from Nicaea on its 1,700th anniversary. I am thrilled to see the publication of this outstanding volume on the Christian doctrine of the Trinity. It is a genuine joy to recommend this thoughtful, readable, and faithfully orthodox work."

—David S. Dockery
President and Distinguished Professor of Theology
Southwestern Baptist Theological Seminary

"Christians often approach the doctrine of the Trinity with fear and trepidation, unsure where to begin and sometimes wondering why to even bother. Luke Stamps and Matthew Emerson offer us quite the gift in *40 Questions About the Trinity*. This book provides an excellent introduction to the center of Christian thought, the living God, as Stamps and Emerson's text orients readers to the history of this doctrine while also providing clear and precise explications of technical, Trinitarian terminology that is grounded in the exegesis of Holy Scripture. May we learn from them how to speak truly and faithfully about our God."

—Daniel Lee Hill
Baylor University

"These are the right questions to consider regarding the Trinity, and Emerson and Stamps are the right authors to consider these important questions. *40 Questions About the Trinity* is exemplary in showing how biblical and theological reasoning come together to articulate a faithful doctrine of God's triunity. Moreover, this book will be sure to serve readers well as Emerson and Stamps bring a myriad of Trinitarian conversations to an accessible level for students and church members alike. I will be utilizing this book with students for years to come and hope it gets the wide reading it deserves."

—Ronni Kurtz
Assistant Professor of Systematic Theology
Midwestern Baptist Theological Seminary

"Christians have several good questions about the Trinity, but sometimes even the most responsible theologians seem to be changing the subject or avoiding the questions. This book is the perfect matchup between the questions people are asking and the answers theology has to offer. Both responsive and responsible, *40 Questions About the Trinity* is a truly useful book."

—Fred Sanders
Torrey Honors College
Biola University

"In this well-organized and clearly written book, Luke Stamps and Matt Emerson offer a gift to students of Christian doctrine. They show how the doctrine of the Trinity is grounded in Holy Scripture; they trace the development of the doctrine through discussion of some of the major controversies and theologians within the tradition; and they provide a helpful re-articulation of one of the formulations found in that tradition. This book will serve as a helpful resource to both students and scholars."

—Thomas H. McCall
Timothy C. and Julie M. Tennent Professor of Theology
Asbury Theological Seminary

"The doctrine of the Trinity is central to the Christian faith, yet it can also be confusing. It is easy to get disoriented navigating the triune nature of God biblically, logically, and in the history of interpretation. What Christians need are trustworthy guides to help them along the way. I can think of no other book that covers so much ground in such a short space, clarifies the difficult questions, and introduces the history of thought. This will be one of the first books I give to people who have questions about the Trinity. My prayer is this book will continue the retrieval of historic Christian doctrine that has been championed by so many across the centuries."

—Patrick Schreiner
Associate Professor of New Testament and Biblical Theology
Midwestern Baptist Theological Seminary

"The doctrine of the Trinity may seem confusing and beyond our comprehension. Emerson and Stamps don't claim to solve the mystery—of course—but they clearly unpack the doctrine of the Trinity so that readers are able to grasp the elements. They demonstrate that the doctrine is grounded in Scripture and rooted in history. They also explicate the doctrine in systematic categories. Readers will find this book to be accessible, faithful, and one that will lead them to worship our triune God."

—Tom Schreiner
James Buchanan Harrison Professor of New Testament Interpretation
The Southern Baptist Theological Seminary

To the communion of the saints—the people of God, the body and bride of Christ, and the temple of the Holy Spirit—from whom we have learned the biblically rooted grammar of Trinitarian doctrine and for whom we hope this book serves as a small contribution to our ongoing transformation into the image of Christ

Contents

Part 4: The Trinity and Christian Doctrine

Abbreviations

IJST	*International Journal of Systematic Theology*
In Ioan.	*Commentary on John.* Thomas Aquinas.
JTS	*Journal of Theological Studies*
LHBOTS	Library of Hebrew Bible/Old Testament Studies
LXX	Septuagint
NIGTC	New International Greek Testament Commentary
NPNF[1]	*Nicene and Post-Nicene Fathers*, Series 1
NPNF[2]	*Nicene and Post-Nicene Fathers*, Series 2
NSBT	New Studies in Biblical Theology
NT	New Testament
OT	Old Testament
PNTC	Pillar New Testament Commentary
PPS	Popular Patristics Series
ST	*Summa Theologiae.* Thomas Aquinas, *Summa Theologiae, Prima Pars 1–49*, Latin/English ed. of the *Works of St. Thomas Aquinas*, trans. Laurence Shapcote (Steubenville, OH: Emmaus Academic, 2012).

Introduction

> Yet for us there is one God, the Father, from whom are all things and for whom we exist, and one Lord, Jesus Christ, through whom are all things and through whom we exist. (1 Cor. 8:6)
>
> There is one body and one Spirit—just as you were called to the one hope that belongs to your call—one Lord, one faith, one baptism, one God and Father of all, who is over all and through all and in all. (Eph. 4:4–6)
>
> Knowledge of the Trinity in unity is our whole life's fruit and goal. (Thomas Aquinas)[1]

The doctrine of the Trinity is not merely one discrete locus of theology. It is the sum and substance of the entire Christian religion. All other doctrines find their orientation in this supreme subject. Indeed, theology proper is precisely concerned with this grand topic: God himself is the Most Blessed Holy Trinity. Behind and above and underneath all other Christian doctrines stands the doctrine of Trinity in unity and unity in Trinity.

The triune God is the source, cause, end, and goal of created reality. Nothing exists apart from the creative and providential will of the God who is Father, Son, and Holy Spirit. The whole history of the cosmos is a grand drama of *exitus* and *reditus*: Everything comes forth from the triune God and everything (in its own way) returns to the triune God.

To make the point more concretely: You, our dear reader, exist for the sake of the Holy Trinity. You and I exist from the Father, through the Son, and by the Holy Spirit. Our very being is created by the God who is love. This infinite, tripersonal God knows you by name and loved you into being. Further, your only hope of salvation from sin's bondage and of restoration to friendship with God is made possible by the tripersonal God. The Father sent

1. Thomas Aquinas, *Sentences Commentary*, I d.2, q.1 a.5 exposition of the text. Cited in Gilles Emery, "God the Trinity," in *The Oxford Handbook of the Reception of Aquinas*, ed. Matthew Levering and Marcus Plested (Oxford: Oxford University Press, 2021), 629.

the Son for your reconciliation, and the Father and the Son sent the Spirit for your redemption. When the end comes and all things are consummated in Christ, the redeemed will spend eternity in the never-ending beatitude of beholding and glorifying the triune God. Nothing is more important, pressing, or far-reaching in its implications than knowing and loving the triune God.

This book is an introduction to the doctrine of the Trinity aimed at students, pastors, and thoughtful Christian readers. It intends to present the biblical and classical doctrine in an accessible way, showing its relevance for Christian exegesis, exposition, and experience. We have tried not to clutter the text with too many footnotes, but we do point readers to some of the most important primary and secondary literature. We are not breaking any new ground in this volume. Indeed, we intend not to. We echo the sentiment expressed so pointedly by the late Thomas Oden as one of the aims of his own systematic theology: "To make no new contribution to theology." Oden's "passion" was "in the closest possible adherence to the texts of classic Christian teaching."[2] Of course, old truths are always in need of new articulation and defense. New expressions, clarifications, and implications are still to be discovered. This must be done only in faithful response to the definitive Word of God once delivered to the saints and in conversation with other faithful responses of the Christian past.

The question-and-answer format of the book allows for some flexibility and freedom on the part of the reader to begin with his or her most pressing questions. However, there is a logical order to the four parts of the book. We begin in part 1 with some preliminary matters: What is the doctrine of the Trinity? Why is it so important? How do we go about studying it? From there, in part 2, we examine the foundational biblical teaching on the Trinity, working our way through each phase of the biblical canon. We approach this topic as two evangelical Baptist theologians who are committed to the supreme authority of Scripture. As we hope to demonstrate in this book, the doctrine of the Trinity that crystallizes in its creedal and conciliar form in the late fourth century is not an imposition on the biblical text but is rather a faithful summary of its teaching on the identity of God. The concepts and terms of the fourth century may be somewhat different, but the judgments they render are the same as the New Testament's.

The extensive biblical index at the end of the book should demonstrate that our concern throughout is primarily exegetical. The doctrine of the Trinity can be demonstrated from the Bible. The historical, dogmatic, and practical chapters are simply further reflections on the biblical revelation and its entailments. Part of our aim here is hermeneutical as well: We hope to lay bare the Trinitarian shape and content of the Bible so as to provide a

2. Thomas C. Oden, *Classic Christianity: A Systematic Theology* (New York: HarperOne, 1992), xiv.

hermeneutical framework for reading the Bible theologically. The reader may notice that we rely on some texts more often than others (e.g., Gen. 1; Prov. 8; John 5; Phil. 2). But this cluster of texts should be seen as a framework for reading the rest of Scripture in a Trinitarian fashion, and in that respect the chapters on different canonical corpora are instances of reading along the Bible's own Trinitarian grain. In this way, these biblical chapters are foundational for everything we have to say in the subsequent parts of the book.

In part 3 we survey the history of the doctrine of the Trinity from the second and third centuries, through the decisive fourth century and medieval and Reformation developments, to the modern era. The story of this doctrine is largely a story of heresy and orthodoxy, so, these chapters are crucial in order to understand how the biblical teaching on the Trinity was deployed and defended. We believe that the tradition of Christian orthodoxy is an indispensable hermeneutical tool for rightly interpreting, synthesizing, and defending the truth of Scripture. As Oden rightly asserts, "The history of classic Christianity is primarily a history of exegesis."[3] Therefore, to venture deeper into the Christian tradition is to take a step closer to, not further away from, the text of Holy Scripture.

In part 4 we integrate the biblical and historical material into dogmatic and practical conclusions. We seek to explain both the technical vocabulary of the doctrine (person, essence, relations of origin, perichoresis, etc.) and the contemporary and practical relevance of the doctrine (responding to controversies like eternal functional subordination and social Trinitarianism as well as articulating how the doctrine can be taught and applied).

The two of us have been conversing and writing together about the doctrine of the Trinity for more than a decade. While we worked together throughout and especially during the editing process, it should be noted that the chapters were drafted individually (Emerson drafted chapters 2, 4–12, 15, 26–27, 30–34, and 38; Stamps drafted chapters 1, 3, 13–14, 16–25, 28–29, 35–37, and 39–40). Despite any differences in style and disciplinary focus, we both fully endorse the completed product.

Doctrine is important because God is important, and no doctrine is more foundational than the doctrine of God himself. We approach this grand subject with fear and trembling, with full awareness of our inadequacy. Still, "we cannot but speak the things which we have seen and heard" (Acts 4:20, author's version). We are convinced that Jesus of Nazareth is the eternal and incarnate Son of God, who alone can save us from sin and reconcile us to God. We are convinced that the Holy Spirit of God has been poured into our hearts by faith to assure us of our adoption as beloved children of a loving Father. We are convinced that the mission of the church, the spiritual growth of individuals and families, and the hope of the nations are

3. Oden, *Classic Christianity*, xxv.

dependent upon a faithful response to God's revelation of himself as Father, Son, and Holy Spirit. And we are convinced that our eternal joy rests in our knowing, loving, and becoming one with the triune God. To this great end, we dedicate this volume to the communion of saints—the church of God in heaven and on earth—and pray that it might help even one person on their journey to eternal life in God's love.

PART 1

Introducing the Trinity

QUESTION 1

What Is the Trinity?

We begin with the simplest question: What is the Trinity? This question could be posed in a few different ways. We could ask about the *subject* of the Trinity, that is, God himself: the Father, Son, and Holy Spirit. We could also ask about the *revelation* of the Trinity: that is, God's disclosure of himself in redemptive history, culminating in the incarnation of the Son and the descent of the Spirit, as attested in Scripture. But we could also ask about the *doctrine* of the Trinity: that is, the traditional teaching about the Trinity that emerged in the earliest centuries of the church, which was formalized in the ancient creeds and councils and which still constitutes the benchmark for Christian orthodoxy. We will take each of these aspects of the question in turn. This chapter sketches out in summary form what the other chapters will spell out with more specificity.

The Subject of the Trinity

When Christians refer to the Trinity, most fundamentally they are referring to God himself, the one who exists eternally as Father, Son, and Holy Spirit. In short, the Trinity is the one true God. Though the Trinity is most clearly and finally revealed in the New Testament, God has always been a Trinity of persons. The triune God is the eternal one who exists independently from anyone and anything else. God is, as the Westminster Shorter Catechism puts it, "a Spirit, infinite, eternal, and unchangeable in his being, wisdom, power, holiness, justice, goodness, and truth" (Question 4). All perfections of goodness, truth, and beauty exist simply and eternally in him. Though he has no lack or deficiency, he created the universe out of the overflow of his goodness and for his own glory. God is the sovereign Creator and providential Lord of everything that is not God. He is the one who spoke the world into existence from nothing, and sustains and governs its every detail. In the revelation of his electing mercy, he is Yahweh, the covenant God of Israel, the God of Abraham, Isaac, and Jacob. Through the promises made and kept to Israel, he is also the God of all the nations and families of the earth. And, as we will see below, he is the God who discloses his triune nature definitively in the incarnate Son, indwelling Holy Spirit, and the benevolent Father whom they reveal.

So, again, the Trinity is simply the one true God. But to speak about this God as *Trinity* denotes particularly his three-in-oneness. In this sense, the Trinity is a way of naming the eternal splendor and beatitude of God's own being. God is not composed of parts; no one created him or put him together. But at the same time, mysteriously, this one true God exists from all eternity as Father, Son, and Holy Spirit. The three are *persons*, not *parts*, of God. The Christian church would eventually develop technical vocabulary to summarize and defend the biblical revelation of this three-in-oneness, and we will explain it much more in this volume. To wade into these waters a bit, we can say the Trinity indicates that there are processions (Latin, *processiones*, "goings forth," so to speak) and personal relations (*relationes*) in God. There is no growth or change in God, but that does not mean God is static. No, historically Christians have affirmed that God is pure act; there is no untapped potential in God. This means that God's eternal life is dynamic, not static. The effulgence of God's being eternally goes forth from the Father to the Son and from the Father and Son to the Spirit. The three are distinct from one another, not only in the ways that God reveals himself to creatures but also in God's own inner life. Each of the three persons is identical with the divine essence, and they are only distinguished from one another by these eternal personal relations. We will discuss these concepts in much greater detail throughout the book, but for now we highlight this: The Trinity is the one, all-glorious God in the eternal beatitude of his self-relatedness. As such, the Trinity is also the end of all creaturely existence. As God's image bearers, human beings in particular were made to know, love, obey, and finally to become one with this triune God. We find our own eternal beatitude in beholding the glory of the Holy Trinity.

The Revelation of the Trinity

So, in the proper sense, the Trinity is God himself. But how is this triune God revealed to us? What is the content of the revelation of the Trinity? As evangelicals, we might say that the Trinity is only revealed in Scripture. And to be sure, the Bible is the inspired, inerrant, and authoritative revelation of the triune God to us. But before the Bible had been completely written, there were the saving and revelatory events of God in history that would eventually be recorded in the New Testament: the incarnation, life, death, and resurrection of Jesus and the descent and indwelling of the Holy Spirit. In a recent treatment of the Trinity, evangelical theologian Fred Sanders speaks of the revelation of the Trinity as a threefold movement: The Trinity is revealed in the missions of the Son and Spirit, attested to in the New Testament, and adumbrated (or foreshadowed) in the Old Testament.[1]

The Trinity is revealed, most fully and properly speaking, in the saving missions (that is, the visible *sendings*) of the Son and Spirit.[2] The Father sends the Son for the salvation of the world, and the Father and Son send the Holy Spirit to dwell in and empower believers. In a sense, the definitive theophany, or manifestation of the Trinity, occurred at the baptism of Jesus in the Jordan River, an event the Eastern Christian tradition refers to as the theophany, or the manifestation of God. Again, God did not *become* Trinity at the baptism, but it was there that the Trinity was definitively *disclosed* in human history. The Son in his incarnate state is baptized, the benevolent voice of the Father echoes from heaven, and the Holy Spirit descends on Christ as a dove. The later events of the gospel and the descent of the Spirit at Pentecost constitute the fullness of the Trinity's revelation to humanity.

But for those of us who were not there at the baptism, on the Mount of Transfiguration, at the foot of the cross, in the veil of the empty tomb, or in the upper room at Pentecost, what access do we have to the revelation of the Trinity? In God's kindness, he has given us the authoritative, divinely inspired interpretation of these saving missions in Holy Scripture. It is to Scripture that we must turn to discover God's triune nature. We can know that God exists and that he is powerful through the things that God has made (Rom. 1:19–20). In other words, we can know certain things about God *by nature*, even if we distort and suppress those things because of sin (Rom. 1:18). However, there are some things that we can only know about God *by grace*, that is, by the special revelation of his word. The Trinity is among those truths known only by grace. We can know *that God exists* by seeing his handiwork in the seas, mountains, stars, and planets and by knowing the unique dignity of our own humanity. But we can only know *that God is Father, Son, and Holy Spirit* because of his condescension to teach us those things in the words of the Bible. The New Testament teaches us about the Trinity explicitly, while the

---

1. Fred Sanders, *The Triune God*, New Studies in Dogmatics (Grand Rapids: Zondervan Academic, 2016).
2. But we would not want to press this language so far as to deny a real revelation of the Trinity in the Old Testament itself. The identity of the God of Israel has always been triune, and we see ample evidence of this plurality in the Hebrew Scriptures themselves: God's creation through his word and Spirit, the plural pronouns in Genesis 1:26, the progressive revelation of the Messiah's divine identity (e.g., Ps. 45:6–7), the pervasive activity of the Holy Spirit in Israel's history, and the prosopological (personal) dialogues within the life of God (e.g., Ps. 110), to name a few. Still, there is a finality and fullness to the New Covenant missions and the apostolic Scriptures that testify to them, which brings clarity and context to the previous revelation.

Old Testament foreshadows that definitive New Testament revelation more implicitly and discreetly.

So, what does the Bible teach us about the Trinity? Many of the chapters in this book will seek to answer that question. But for now, we can summarize the teaching of Scripture on the Trinity under a few heads:

1. **God is one.** The New Testament (Mark 12:29; 1 Cor. 8:4, 6; 1 Tim. 2:5), no less than the Old Testament (Exod. 20:1–2; Deut. 6:4; Isa. 45:6), affirms that there is only one God. While there may be other spiritual beings (angels, demons, and human souls), there is—and can only be—one transcendent and immanent Creator and Lord of heaven and earth.
2. **Each of the persons is divine.** Once the first person, the Father, is distinguished in the New Testament, his deity is assumed throughout. The deity of the Son is demonstrated by the attributes, actions, names, titles, and worship of God that are ascribed to him. Similarly, the Holy Spirit is named as a distinct person alongside the Father and Son (e.g., Matt. 28:18–20; 2 Cor. 13:14), and his deity is likewise shown by his divine attributes, actions, names, and worship.
3. **The persons are distinct from one another.** The three are not simply successive manifestations or modes of revelation to humanity. They are simultaneously existing persons with real relations to one another (think of Jesus's baptism, Matt. 3:13–17). These distinctions are not merely ad hoc arrangements in redemptive history, but mark out real distinctions in eternity. These distinctions are made evident by the personal names given to each of the three in Scripture: Father, Son, and Holy Spirit. The Father is eternally the Father of the Son; the Son is eternally the Son of the Father; and the Holy Spirit is eternally the one "spirated," or breathed out, by the Father and Son. The three relate to one another and love one another in the eternal glory of God's own life (John 17:5). When the creedal tradition speaks of the eternal relations of origin—the eternal generation of the Son and the eternal procession or spiration of the Holy Spirit—it is simply following this biblical pattern of personal divine naming.
4. **Because God is one, he acts as one.** The three divine persons act as one in redemptive history. All of the actions of God in the world—creation, providence, redemption, and judgment—are attributed to all three persons. They are not three separate beings doing three separate but harmonious things. They each act in the others' actions. The Holy Trinity acts in an inseparable and indivisible manner. To pick just one example, consider the act of creation. The Father creates through his Word (John 1:1–3; cf. Gen. 1:3) and Spirit (Gen. 1:2).
5. **Some divine attributes or actions are appropriated to particular divine persons but not in such a way as to exclude the others.** So, for

example, we might say that the Father is our Creator, the Son is our Redeemer, and the Spirit is our sanctifier. But because of the previous point (that God acts in an indivisible way in all of his actions), this appropriation is only a manner of speaking. All three persons are the creator, redeemer, and sanctifier. The appropriation of a certain attribute to particular divine person only serves to highlight that person's unique personal identity. For example, the Son is referred to as the Word or Wisdom of God in Scripture, not because he alone possesses the divine attribute of wisdom but because this name highlights his unique personal property of *being from the Father*, as a word proceeds from a mind.

6. **Each person participates in the indivisible action of God in a manner that is appropriate to his personal identity.** In any act of the triune God in the world, there is only one action. But there are three modes of action fitting to each person. The Father acts as Father in the inseparable action of the Trinity, the Son as Son, and the Spirit as Spirit. The early church fathers, following the New Testament pattern, often spoke of these modes of action by means of distinct prepositions: The action of God comes from the Father, through the Son, and by the Spirit (see, e.g., 1 Cor. 8:6). And, of course, because the Son alone became incarnate, the actions that he carries out *humanly* are exclusive of the Father and Son (though the Father and Son remain with him). The point here is that everything that God does *divinely*, he does as Father, Son, and Spirit—in essentially indivisible but personally differentiated action.

The Doctrine of the Trinity

In many ways, the descriptions of the *subject* and the *revelation* of the Trinity already given in this chapter have included many features of the *doctrine* of the Trinity as it was historically developed. This overlap shows just how indebted the patristic doctrine of the Trinity was to the biblical teaching on God. And it also shows the indispensable role that historical, biblically derived doctrine plays in the interpretation and synthesis of the biblical material. We will return to matters of theological method in a later chapter, but for now it is sufficient to note that the tradition of Trinitarian thought should not be pitted against a high view of Scripture as the sole inspired and inerrant written revelation of God. So how should we summarize the doctrine of the Trinity? At the risk of oversimplification at this stage in the book, we can summarize the doctrine in three steps.

One divine essence/nature/being. As there is only one God, so there is only one divine essence or nature or being. As the doctrine developed, key terms in both Greek (*ousia*) and Latin (*essentia*, *substantia*, *natura*) became commonplace as descriptors for the oneness of God. There are three *whos* in the Trinity (see below), but there is only one *what*. The Son and Spirit share in the very same being that is the Father. Not three equal essences but one numerically singular divine essence. Everything that we would say about the essence of God (think here of all the divine attributes) are true equally and eternally of all three divine persons.

Two temporal missions that reveal two eternal processions. In the economy of redemption, God the Father sent God the Son for the salvation of the world, and the Father and Son sent the Spirit to indwell and empower the church. These temporal missions, relative to what God does in redemption, reveal the eternal processions—that is, who God is absolutely. More simply, what God does reveals who God is. The Son is *sent from* the Father because he *is from* the Father in his eternal generation. The Spirit is *sent from* the Father and Son because he *is from* the Father in his eternal procession. These eternal relations mark out three divine persons.

Three divine persons/hypostases. The persons are distinguished from one another both absolutely (as God is in himself) and relatively (as God acts in creation and providence). They are not merely three names or three modes of revelation for a God who is ultimately just one person. They are truly distinct persons. Just as with the oneness of God, key terms were developed to describe the threeness of God both in Greek (*prosopon*, *hypostasis*) and in Latin (*persona*).

In God's own inner life, the three persons are distinguished only by their eternal relations to one another—that is, by the processions mentioned above. These relations have been described as the *eternal relations of origin*. The Father is from no one; he is unbegotten. The Son is eternally begotten from the Father; and the Holy Spirit eternally proceeds from (or is "spirated," breathed out by) the Father and the Son. These eternal processions ("goings forth") are unique from creaturely processions (like a parent who has a child) in two important ways: (1) They are *eternal*, having no beginning or ending in time, and (2) they are *internal*, so to speak, in the life of God. They do not produce a second and a third God but take place within the one divine essence or nature.

In God's external activity, the persons are distinguished from one another not by distinct roles and functions but by distinct modes of action in the one inseparable action of God. Everything God does outside of himself he does indivisibly as Father, Son, and Spirit. But within this action, each of the divine persons acts in a manner fitting to his personal identity; the one act of God proceeds from the Father, through the Son, by or in the Holy Spirit.

All of this means that the three divine persons, while analogous to human persons in some ways, are utterly unique. The three divine persons are not three distinct beings (like three *people*) nor even three distinct centers of consciousness and will, but they are instead three distinct modes of being within the one being of God who mutually indwell and interpenetrate one another (*perichoresis*) in the one divine nature or essence. No analogies are truly fit for this, even if some analogies can capture a part of it. In the end, we are left only with wonder at the glory of the one true God, whose eternal being is revealed in his loving redemptive works.

Summary

What is the Trinity? We can ask this question in three different ways: the subject of the Trinity, the revelation of the Trinity, and the doctrine of the Trinity. The subject of the Trinity is the one true God himself as he exists eternally as Father, Son, and Holy Spirit. The revelation of the Trinity takes place in the saving missions of the Son and Spirit as they are testified to in the Scriptures of the Old and New Testaments. The doctrine of the Trinity as it developed in the early centuries utilized certain key terms in order to explain and defend this biblical teaching. God is one essence in three persons. We come to know this because of the two missions (of the Son and Spirit, respectively), which reveal the two eternal processions within God (the eternal generation of the Son and the eternal spiration of the Holy Spirit). The subsequent chapters in this book will explain in greater detail the specifics of this central and glorious Christian doctrine.

REFLECTION QUESTIONS

1. What aspects of the doctrine of the Trinity are most confusing to you? Which are the clearest?

2. What are you most excited to learn about regarding the doctrine of the Trinity?

3. How do you hope to grow in your spiritual life through learning more about the doctrine of the Trinity?

4. How is your prayer life reflective of your current understanding of the Trinity?

5. What biblical passages related to the doctrine of the Trinity are confusing to you right now?

QUESTION 2

Why Is It Important for Christians to Know the Doctrine of the Trinity?

The doctrine of the Trinity is central to the Christian faith because the triune God is the central object of our faith. In other words, we study this doctrine because we are trying to understand the God in whom we have faith, for whom we were made, and by whom we are saved. If you want to grow as a Christian, you need to understand the God who has made himself known to you in Jesus Christ. However, as important as this doctrine is, Christians often treat it as a theological hoop to jump through or a strange alleyway in an otherwise interesting and enlightening walk through the other major Christian doctrines. Let's begin by looking at a few reasons why Christians don't often believe this central doctrine is important to their life of faith.

Why Some Christians Think the Doctrine *Isn't* Important

Unfortunately, many Christians have mistaken notions about the doctrine of the Trinity that prevent or deter them from studying it. Sometimes Christians mistake this doctrine for another theological box they have to check in order to be considered "orthodox." In this scenario, the doctrine isn't something that makes a difference in their real life or ministry, but just something we must affirm to be called a Christian. So, often we'll say "yes" if someone asks if we believe the doctrine of the Trinity but only because we were taught it in a new members or confirmation class, not because it really makes a difference to us or to our faith.

A related mistaken notion is that the doctrine is unimportant specifically with respect to evangelism. Some of our popular gospel presentations include little, if any, reference to the doctrine of the Trinity or even to the fact that God is triune. The emphasis is squarely on our sin and need for a savior, a savior who has restored us to God through the crucifixion of

Jesus. Of course, we are sinners in need of a savior, and God did provide salvation for us in the death of Jesus on the cross. But these elements of the gospel presentation are so emphasized that they often lead to the exclusion of any explanation of who Jesus is as the Second Person of the Trinity in the flesh (or of the resurrection, Jesus's life, or the Holy Spirit, for that matter). Because many people come to saving faith in Jesus without understanding, much less hearing about, the doctrine of the Trinity, they think it is unimportant in comparison to other doctrines, in comparison to the kind of gospel presentation that led to their own conversion, and especially in comparison to "real life."

Finally, some Christians believe that the doctrine of the Trinity is only for academics. This notion comes in various forms, including those mentioned above, but here we want to focus on one particular version of this mistaken notion: that its academic focus is a result of it not being taught clearly in the Bible. If it were taught clearly in Scripture, more Christians would care about it. But since it isn't (so this objection goes), only those in ivory towers care deeply about something so esoteric and intellectual.

We will deal with each of these mistaken ideas in one way or another throughout the book. In this chapter we want to focus on four reasons that we *should* find the doctrine of the Trinity important and, in fact, central to our Christian faith and practice.

Why the Doctrine of the Trinity *Is* Important

The doctrine of the Trinity is important. In fact, it is absolutely crucial to Christian theology, to the church's worship, to evangelism, to the Christian life—to everything. This is because the doctrine of the Trinity is the doctrine of *who God is*—the God who made everything, the God who saved us by becoming one of us and dying for us in the person of his Son, the God who will make all things new when Jesus returns. Every single thing in existence—including other Christian doctrines, daily devotionals, corporate worship, and gospel presentations—owes itself to this one God, the triune God, Father, Son, and Holy Spirit, the God who has revealed himself to us in his incarnate Son, Jesus Christ, by his Holy Spirit.

So, other than this totalizing claim about all of reality, why is this doctrine so important? First, the doctrine of the Trinity is important because Scripture teaches it. Christian faith and practice must be derived from God's revealed, inspired, and inerrant word, the Bible. Anything that isn't taught in the Bible should not be taken as necessary for Christian belief and discipleship. But anything that is clearly taught in Scripture is required for the Christian life, and this includes the doctrine of the Trinity. We'll dive deep into how the Bible teaches the doctrine of the Trinity in part 2, but we want to say up front that this doctrine is thoroughly and explicitly biblical.

A second reason why this doctrine is important for Christians is because our study of it helps us obey the first commandment as well as the Greatest Commandment. In order to "have no other gods," we have to understand exactly who the One God is. And in order to love God with our whole mind, we have to grow in our knowledge of the triune God, Yahweh. The life of discipleship is not limited to gaining information, but it also cannot proceed without careful study of Scripture and its teachings about God, humans, creation, and salvation. In other words, we are not brains on a stick, but we should also not leave growth in our knowledge of God and his Word to the "professionals," whether they be pastors, professors, or Bible nerds.

Of course, our knowledge of God isn't intended to remain purely information; it is for transformation. Studying who God is leads us to worshiping him and submitting our lives to him. In this respect, a third reason that this doctrine is important is because studying it prompts us to pray and impacts our life of prayer.[1] Study of the Trinity leads to prayer because we cannot have any other proper response to contemplating who God is than to bow down before him. But it also should impact our prayer life, or the *way* that we pray. Understanding this doctrine helps us to understand that when we pray, we do not only pray to one of the divine persons but to the triune God.

Obviously Jesus commands to pray to "Our Father" (Matt. 6:9) and to ask "in my [Jesus's] name" (John 14:13), and there are numerous instances throughout Scripture where someone's prayer is described as "in the Spirit" (Eph. 6:18; Jude 20). So it is not as though we cannot or should not pray to the Father, in the name of the Son, and by the power of the Holy Spirit. But, as we will see later, while this formula is indicative of what is called Trinitarian *taxis*, or order, it does not mean that we only pray to one person at a time. Instead, we are always praying to the triune God, even if we direct some of our requests to one of the three divine persons.

More generally, the ultimate aim of our worship of the triune God—including prayer to him—is fellowship with the triune God. We think about and sing about and pray to God in order to dwell with God. We human beings, image bearers of the triune God, are made for this worshipful communion. This leads to a fourth reason that theology broadly, and study of the doctrine of the Trinity in particular, is important: because it is ultimately in service of this doxological purpose, this end goal for every human life.

Finally, the doctrine of the Trinity is important because without it we can't get the gospel right. You need to understand who God is as triune in

---

1. See Medi Ann Volpe, "Living the Mystery: Doctrine, Intellectual Disability, and Christian Imagination," *Journal of Moral Theology* 6 (2017): 87–102. I owe this reference to Nate Martin.

order to understand his Trinitarian work of salvation. It is the one God who saves us, who redeems us to himself. He does so in accordance with who he is: namely, the Father, Son, and Holy Spirit. The work of salvation, just like God's other external work—creation—is necessarily Trinitarian because God himself is triune. The Father sends the Son, the Son is sent by the Father, and the Holy Spirit is the agent of the Father's sending and the Son's sent-ness. The Father authorizes the incarnate Son's mission at his baptism, the incarnate Son pursues and fulfills his mission throughout his life and in his atoning death, and the Spirit anoints and empowers the incarnate Son for his mission. The Father hands the incarnate Son over to the Roman and Jewish authorities to be crucified, the incarnate Son lays down his life on the cross, and the Spirit sustains the incarnate Son in his crucifixion. And so on.

We will discuss this later in the book, but we need to be clear here that each person of the Trinity is not acting separately in these events. Instead, the one God is accomplishing the one act of salvation in Trinitarian fashion. This Trinitarian grammar for the doctrine of salvation is required if we are to understand the gospel rightly: It is the triune God who saves us, not only one of the divine persons.

But there is another reason why the doctrine of the Trinity is important for understanding the gospel rightly, a reason that was particularly emphasized in the early church. If each of the three divine persons are not fully God and one God, then the gospel isn't true. In fact, it can't be true. If the Holy Spirit or the Son isn't fully God, then it is impossible for either or both of them to ever bridge the gap between us and God that is caused by our sin. They must both be on the "God" side of the equation, so to speak (a concept to which we'll return later), in order to bring us away from our creaturely and sinful side of that same equation and back to God.

Summary

Understanding the Trinity rightly matters because it's taught in Scripture. If God has given us "all things that pertain to life and godliness" (2 Peter 1:3), if his words are eternal life (John 6:68), if in preaching the word of God we save both ourselves and our hearers (1 Tim. 4:16), if the word of God is living and active, and if the doctrine of the Trinity is taught in that same word, then it is something we should, we *must*, take seriously.

The reason why the Bible teaches this doctrine is because it concerns our ultimate purpose as human beings—to know and love the one true God. If we don't study the doctrine of the Trinity, our worship will suffer as we become unsure or even wrong about who the God we are trying to pray to and worship actually is. It will suffer as we become unsure or even wrong about the good news of the gospel. If each of the three persons isn't fully God, how could they ever bring us into right relationship with the one true God? For these reasons, we should take this doctrine seriously and doxologically.

REFLECTION QUESTIONS

1. Have you neglected the doctrine of the Trinity in your Christian walk? If so, why?

2. Which of the reasons for studying the doctrine of the Trinity above resonates with you the most? Why?

3. What are the dangers of neglecting this doctrine in your Christian walk?

4. What are the benefits of studying this doctrine for your prayer life?

5. How would you explain the doctrine's importance to someone who isn't convinced that it really matters?

QUESTION 3

How Should We Study the Doctrine of the Trinity?

The word 'Trinity' is not even in the Bible." Non-Trinitarians sometimes point out this fact as a way of undermining the doctrine of the Trinity. But many Christians themselves also wonder how their belief in the Trinity relates to their commitment to the ultimate authority of Holy Scripture. The *word* "trinity" may not be in the Bible, but can we find the *doctrine* or at least the *reality* of it there? Are the theological refinements of the ancient Christian creeds really necessary? Isn't the Bible sufficient? These questions are especially pressing for Protestants, who maintain that the Bible and the Bible alone is the sole and final authority in all matters of Christian faith and practice. Creeds, councils, and confessions may be more or less useful or faithful to the Bible, but they are not infallible. Only the Bible has that place in the matrix of Christian belief.

All of these considerations bring us to the important question of theological method. How do we go about studying the doctrine of the Trinity? To which sources should we turn? How can we be certain that our theological formulations are consistent with God's self-revelation in Jesus Christ as it recorded in Holy Scripture? What is the role of postbiblical Christian reflections on the teaching of Scripture? What authority does the Christian tradition possess in the system of Christian belief? Is Christian belief in the Trinity logically coherent? Is it consistent with Christian experience?

One helpful way of thinking through these questions is the so-called Wesleyan quadrilateral, which is associated with the founder of Methodism, John Wesley: Scripture, tradition, reason, and experience. Although Wesley himself never framed his thinking in this way exactly, it still summarizes a useful method that Protestant theology should aim for. To be sure, the four sides of the quadrilateral are not coequal sources of authority.[1] According to the Protestant principle of *sola Scriptura*, the Bible is the only infallible, written revelation of God. It is the *principium*, the principle and source, of all Christian doctrine. But in our interpretation and synthesis of Scripture, God has graciously given guides to the church. Tradition, as a representation of the consensus of Christian belief, shows us the ways the Spirit of God has illuminated the church across space and time. Reason, as the "handmaiden" of theology, helps us to test the logical coherence of our doctrinal formulations and explain and defend them in the face of challenges. Christian experience, the stage on which our Christian faith plays out, reminds us that doctrine is never merely an abstract and academic affair but is lived out in the context of the church and of the Christian life. In this chapter we will briefly explain how each of these factors—Scripture, tradition, reason, and experience—inform our study of this most crucial of Christian doctrines.

Scripture

The Trinity is most definitively revealed to humanity in the saving missions of the Son and the Spirit.[2] In other words, God's people come to know that God is triune because the Father sends the Son to be the Savior of the world and the Father and Son send the Holy Spirit to dwell in believers. These saving missions tangibly manifest to us the personal distinctions that exist in God himself. The Son is *sent from* the Father in history because he *is from* the Father in eternity. The Spirit is *sent from* the Father and Son in history because he *is from* the Father and Son in eternity. As St. Augustine argued, the temporal missions (these *sendings* in time) reflect and reveal the eternal processions (the relations that eternally exist between the divine persons).[3] So, the study of the Trinity has to begin with the saving events of the gospel: the incarnation, life, death, and resurrection of Jesus Christ, and the indwelling and empowering work of the Spirit that was inaugurated at Pentecost.

Obviously, believers today did not personally witness these historical events. We depend upon the testimonies to these events recorded in the New Testament. In other words, we depend upon the inspired and inerrant revelation of the Holy Trinity in Holy Scripture. So, a careful study of the New Testament—its language, literature, history, and theology—is

1. Albert Outler, "The Wesleyan Quadrilateral in John Wesley," *Wesleyan Theological Journal* 20 (1985): 7–18.
2. As we saw in question 1, Fred Sanders argues that the Trinity is revealed in the missions of the Son and Spirit, attested to in the New Testament, and adumbrated (foreshadowed) in the Old Testament. Fred Sanders, *The Triune God*, New Studies in Dogmatics (Grand Rapids: Zondervan Academic, 2016), 23.
3. Augustine, *The Trinity (De Trinitate)*, trans. Edmund Hill, ed. John Rotelle (Hyde Park, NY: New City, 1991).

necessary to discern what God has revealed about his triune nature. If the Trinity is only definitively revealed in the saving events of the gospel and in the New Testament witness to those events, then we must admit that the doctrine of the Trinity was not clearly articulated in the Old Testament. But that is not to say that the Old Testament is utterly silent about the Trinity or is unrelated to the Trinitarian revelation of the New Testament—far from it. Since the God of Israel has always been triune, it should not surprise us to find hints and foreshadows of the Trinitarian revelation that was to come. The two Testaments represent one unified revelation of God and must be read forwards and backwards, as it were.[4] The Old Testament is the necessary background and preparation for the New Testament, and the New Testament is only intelligible given the history and theological categories of the Old Testament. As the theologian B. B. Warfield argued, the Old Testament is like a chamber furnished but dimly lit.[5] In the light of the New Testament revelation we can go back to the Old Testament and see what was there all along, even if veiled until the mystery of the gospel was revealed.

Thus, any study of the Trinity must be firmly anchored in the study of the Bible. But how do we go about interpreting the Bible? A full treatment of a properly Christian hermeneutic lies beyond the scope of this chapter, but in brief, we would suggest a method that is theological, traditional, canonical, historical, and grammatical. Christian interpretation is *theological* in the sense that it begins, proceeds, and ends in Christian faith. All readers have presuppositions that they bring to the interpretive task. But this is a feature, not a bug, in interpretation. Presuppositions are not necessarily barriers to proper interpretation. Instead, they provide an initial cognitive framework that enables the interpretive enterprise to proceed. The question is whether or not we are willing to have our presuppositions shaped and reshaped by continued, close engagement with the biblical text in dialogue with the whole body of Christ. In this so-called hermeneutical circle, our understanding of Scripture's parts is informed by our understanding of the whole. Scripture's main message is clear—God and his gospel and this "rule of faith" helps to regulate our interpretation of the less clear or problematic passages.[6]

4. See Richard B. Hayes, *Reading Backwards: Figural Christology and the Fourfold Gospel Witness* (Waco, TX: Baylor University Press, 2016).
5. B. B. Warfield, "Trinity," in *International Standard Bible Encyclopedia*, ed. James Orr, 5 vols. (Chicago: Howard-Severance, 1915), 5:3012–22. Fred Sanders has formatted a helpful annotated version of Warfield's essay here: http://scriptoriumdaily.com/wp-content/uploads/2015/10/Warfield-Trinity Study Edition.pdf.
6. The notion of the rule of faith, or rule of truth, as an interpretive guide goes back at least to Irenaeus in the second century. See Irenaeus, *On the Apostolic Preaching*, trans. John Behr (Crestwood, NY: St Vladimir's Seminary Press, 1997), 41–42.

Christian interpretation of Scripture should also be *traditional* in the best sense of the word. The section below will have more to say about the role of tradition in the theological task, but for now it is sufficient to note that contemporary Christian interpreters are not beginning their work from scratch. We are not the first to read and interpret the Bible. We possess the distinct advantage of having two thousand years of interpretation to serve as a guide, a corrective, and an inspiration in our own interpretive efforts.

Christian interpretation is also *canonical* in the sense that the whole canon of Scripture provides the ultimate interpretive context for understanding any one particular text. To be sure, we ought to consider carefully the *historical* and *grammatical* features of any given text. Historical background is crucial for understanding the cultural milieu in which the Scriptures emerged. Grammatical, syntactical, and semantic tools help us to engage the text at a granular level. But the ultimate horizon of biblical interpretation is the whole Bible, read in terms of its redemptive-historical development and its climactic fulfillment in Jesus Christ.[7]

Other interpretive tools and strategies will be treated elsewhere in this book, but these are the broad parameters that guide our interpretation of Scripture.

Tradition

While Scripture is the supreme authority for Christian belief, it is not necessarily the only authority in the theological enterprise. Mature Christians recognize the need for teachers and more advanced readers of Scripture. Parents, pastors, friends, professors, books, and commentaries all guide us in our understanding and application of Scripture. It is in this sense that Christians can appeal to the "Great Tradition" of Christian reflection on the doctrine of the Trinity. As Protestants, we believe that the authority of tradition is *derivative* and *consensual*. Tradition is not equal to Scripture; any authority it possesses is derived from its conformity to the clear and demonstrable teaching of Scripture. Tradition is not an additional source of revelation alongside Scripture.[8] Instead, tradition should be viewed as the authoritative (even if fallible) guide to interpreting Scripture.

Another aspect of tradition's authority comes from the fact that it represents the consensus of the faithful across space, time, and denomination.

---

7. For more on the various "horizons" of biblical interpretation, see Richard Lints, *The Fabric of Theology: A Prolegomenon to Evangelical Theology* (Grand Rapids: Eerdmans, 1993).
8. Heiko Obermann distinguishes between Tradition I and Tradition II in this regard. Tradition I is the view presented here: that tradition serves as an interpretive guide to Scripture and thus is subservient to Scripture. Tradition II maintains that tradition is a second source of revelation alongside Scripture. See Heiko Obermann, *Forerunners of the Reformation: The Shape of Late Medieval Thought* (Cambridge: James Clarke & Co., 1966), 58.

The authority of tradition is not ultimately vested in a particular church office, institution, or council. Instead, it is vested in the entire body of Christ. To be sure, Christians have not reached consensus on every doctrine. In the history of Christian thought, there is a diversity of opinion on, say, theories of the atonement or the meaning and practice of the sacraments. On some doctrines we must speak in terms of a variety of *traditions*, plural. But on the doctrine of the Trinity, we can meaningfully speak about *the* tradition, singular; there is remarkable unanimity on the basic contours of the doctrine from the late fourth century (when the patristic doctrine of the Trinity reached maturity) to the present day among orthodox, Bible-believing Christians.

This singular tradition manifests itself at the broadest level in terms of the church's *creeds and councils* but is also evident in particular denominational *confessions of faith* (e.g., the Westminster Confession of Faith) and in the great *theological writers* of the past (e.g., Augustine, Aquinas, and Calvin).[9] The three ecumenical (that is, worldwide) creeds—the Apostles' Creed, the Nicene Creed, and the Athanasian Creed—have received wide support in the churches of the West, with the Eastern churches embracing the Nicene Creed as the summary of the faith. The seven ecumenical councils of the undivided church (that is, before the Great Schism of 1054 divided the Eastern Orthodox and Western churches) convened from the fourth to the eighth centuries in order to settle doctrinal debates related to the Trinity and the incarnation. These creeds and councils should still serve as signposts as contemporary theologians seek to discern the consensus of faithful Christian belief. Their doctrinal terms (such as "consubstantial" or "begotten before all worlds") are not infallible and could in principle be improved upon, but it would take a long time and a similarly broad consensus to establish any theoretical improvements. In sum, evangelical theologians today seeking to establish a doctrine of God should show significant deference to the wisdom of the ages, to what Spirit-indwelt Christians through the centuries have said about the triune nature of God.

Reason

Christian faith is reasonable. The Christian message can be presented in a "reasoned" way (Acts 18:19; 19:8). While human philosophy can be a source of demonic deceit (Col. 2:8), it can also be a kind of preparation for the gospel (Acts 17:28). All the treasures of wisdom and knowledge are hidden in Christ

---

9. On this threefold hierarchy of tradition (creeds, confessions, and theological luminaries), see Oliver D. Crisp, *God Incarnate: Explorations in Christology* (London: T&T Clark, 2009), 8–17. See also R. Lucas Stamps, "*Norma Normata*: The Role of Tradition in Analytic Theology," in *T&T Clark Handbook of Analytic Theology*, ed. James M. Arcadi and James T. Turner (London: T&T Clark, 2021), 45–54.

(Col. 2:3), who is the eternal Logos—Word, Wisdom, Reason—of God (John 1:1; 1 Cor. 1:24, 30).

Christian doctrine in particular is an exercise in created and redeemed reason, with the believing mind receiving the divine revelation and wrestling with its cognitive content. Following Augustine, Anselm, and others, we can speak of Christian theology as a "faith seeking understanding" enterprise. We accept Christian teaching by faith in the testimony of God: his Spirit-inspired Word as received by his Spirit-illumined church. But we then seek to convert, as it were, our faith to knowledge. What we receive by faith we come to conceive by reason. In this sense, philosophy or reason has come to be known as the "handmaiden" of theology (*ancilla theologia*). In theology, philosophy serves a ministerial role, not a magisterial role: it is the servant, not the master.

It is in this sense that reason can help to explicate the doctrine of the Trinity, demonstrate its logical coherence, and defend it against objections. The Christian doctrine of the Trinity is mysterious, but it is not illogical. If the doctrine of the Trinity could be shown to entail a logical contradiction, it would for that reason be untrue—not because God is somehow answerable to a standard of logic external to himself, but because God's own nature is logical and because his revelation is rational, reliable, and consistent. But, in point of fact, the doctrine is not illogical. To say that Father, Son, and Holy Spirit are identical in essence but distinct in person or relation may be incomprehensible, but it is not illogical. It may defy complete mastery by the human intellect, but it does not defy the laws of logic. Reason helps us to make this case by structuring conceptual models that elucidate the doctrine's reasonableness and coherence (see Question 37).

Experience

The final side of the quadrilateral is Christian experience. Experience is not so much a source of Christian doctrine as it is the soil in which doctrine grows and the fruit that it produces. The church's saving encounter with the only begotten Son of the Father gives rise to the need for some theological accounting of this experience. Who is this God with whom we have to do in the gospel of Jesus Christ? Take the metaphor of adoption that the New Testament uses to describe God's work of reconciliation. If we have been predestined in Christ for adoption as sons (Eph. 1:4), then what is the nature of the filial relationship between the Father and the Son that undergirds our own adoptive status? If we have received the Spirit of adoption by which we cry "Abba! Father!" then just who is this divine person we experience as both the Spirit of the Father and the Spirit of his Son (Rom. 8:10–11; Gal. 4:6)? To experience salvation in Christ by the Spirit is to raise precisely the questions that gave birth to the doctrine of the Trinity. Who is Jesus? Who is the Holy Spirit? Who is the Father? The answers to these questions that the church eventually discerned were in a sense forced upon it by its own experience of salvation. The Arian christ, for example, as a created being, cannot be the Christ the church encounters in salvation and worship. A mere creature cannot be the mediator of salvation since "salvation belongs to the LORD" (Ps. 3:8). A mere creature cannot be the object of worship, or else the church has been entangled in idolatry from the very beginning. In these ways, Christian experience—in salvation, worship, prayer, the sacraments, and so on—provides a test for the fittingness of Christian belief. Do our doctrines match and suit our Christian experience? *Lex orandi, lex credenda*: "The law of prayer is the law of belief." We pray what we really believe, but, equally true, we come to believe whatever it is that we pray.

Summary

So how should we study the doctrine of the Trinity? To pick up on the last point, we should study this doctrine prayerfully and worshipfully—in silent contemplation and joyful praise. Our experience of salvation in Christ by the Spirit gives rise to the questions that the doctrine of the Trinity answers. Our main source for these answers is the Bible, which infallibly testifies to the saving missions of the Son and Spirit. A right reading of Scripture ought to be theological, traditional, canonical, historical, and grammatical. The tradition in particular should guide our interpretation, as we learn from the exegetical and doctrinal "best practices" of the worldwide, historical church. Reason serves as a handmaiden in this task, helping to elucidate and defend the coherence of our doctrinal formulations. Finally, we are once again thrown back onto the experience of the triune God in prayer and worship. The study of the Trinity involves the exercise of our full intellectual capacities, but it is not a cold academic affair. Nothing less than our eternal beatitude is at stake as we contemplate the glory of the triune God.

REFLECTION QUESTIONS

1. The word "Trinity" is not in the Bible, but is the doctrine? If so, how?

2. What does it mean that our interpretation of Scripture should be theological, traditional, canonical, historical, and grammatical? Are any of these aspects more important than the others? Are any neglected more than the others?

3. What does it mean that the authority of tradition is derivative and consensual? How might our understanding of Scripture be hampered if we completely ignore the history of interpretation and seek to begin, as it were, from scratch?

4. Why is it important to demonstrate that Christian doctrines are not logically incoherent?

5. How does our Christian experience give rise to Christian doctrine? How does Christian doctrine, in turn, feed back into our Christian experience?

PART 2

The Trinity and Christian Scripture

QUESTION 4

What Strategies Did Christians Employ to Arrive at the Doctrine of the Trinity?

Christians confess the doctrine of the Trinity because the doctrine of the Trinity is taught in the Bible. However, it took the early church almost four centuries to confess it in the way that is now known as the classical doctrine of the Trinity. In this chapter we will summarize how the early church read the Bible and, eventually, articulated the doctrine of the Trinity as we describe it in this book and as it was confessed and taught throughout the medieval and Reformation periods.

We will use four categories to describe the early church's Trinitarian reading of the Bible: the Creator/creature distinction, the unity of the divine persons, the eternal relations of origin that distinguish the divine persons, and partitive exegesis, which distinguishes between the human and divine natures of Christ. These four categories are intertwined in the early church; they did not map them out or parse out their arguments into them. Rather, they employed them repeatedly and interconnectedly in answering opponents and constructing their doctrine of the Trinity.

There Is No God but YHWH

The first reading strategy employed by the early church is the Creator/creature distinction. This means that the early church saw in Scripture a stark contrast between God on the one hand and everything he created on the other. There is no "in between" in terms of what exists. One is either the Creator or one of his creatures. They turned to texts like Deuteronomy 10:14[1] and Nehemiah

1. "Behold, to the LORD your God belong heaven and the heaven of heavens, the earth with all that is in it."

9:6,[2] not to mention Genesis 1, to support this view. For all the earth to belong to God (Deut. 10:14), to be made by God (Gen. 1; Neh. 9:6), and to worship God (Neh. 9:6; cf. Phil. 2:10–11) means that God alone is God and everything else is "not God," that is, creature.

Additionally, the early church, along with ancient Israel, insisted that there is only *one* God, only one divine being on the Creator side of that distinction. This is one of the most central statements about who God is in Scripture (Deut. 6:4). There cannot be anything other than the one God on that side of the equation.

As we will see in our discussion of the next category, this distinction is crucial for identifying who Jesus is. If he shares in God's nature and actions (as he does), then he cannot be a mere creature. Again, there is no "in between" category here: One is either God or not-God. And if Jesus is identified as God (as he is), then he stands clearly on that divine side of the equation. The same goes for the Holy Spirit. But he and the Spirit also stand there not as second and third gods but with the Father as the one God. We will return to that insistence after discussing the ways in which the early church identified Jesus and the Spirit as God.

The Grace of Our Lord Jesus Christ, the Love of God, and the Fellowship of the Holy Spirit

In order to identify whether or not Jesus and the Holy Spirit stood on the divine or creaturely side of the equation, the early church commonly referred to four markers: appellations, attributes, actions, and adoration. (I, Matt, am a Baptist, so I have no choice but to alliterate these for my students.) First, in arguing that both Jesus and the Holy Spirit are divine, the early church noted that they share the same appellations, or names, as God. For instance, 1 Corinthians 8:6 identifies both the Father and the Son as possessors of the divine name.[3] Second, the early church noted that Jesus and the Holy Spirit also share the same divine attributes as God. For example, Jesus shares the attribute of possessing "life in himself" with the Father (John 5:26), and the psalmist identifies the Holy Spirit as omnipresent (Ps. 139:7–12). A third marker used by the early church to argue for Jesus's and the Holy Spirit's divinity is shared divine actions. Both Jesus and the Holy Spirit, along with the Father, create the world (e.g., Gen. 1:2; Ps. 32:6; John 1:1–3; Col. 1:15–17), judge (e.g., John 5:21–26), save (e.g., John 3:1–21), etc. Finally, the early church showed that Jesus and the Holy Spirit both receive the same adora-

2. "You are the Lord, you alone. You have made heaven, the heaven of heavens, with all their host, the earth and all that is on it, the seas and all that is in them; and you preserve all of them; and the host of heaven worships you."
3. On the exegetical warrant for this claim, see, for instance, Wesley Hill, *Paul and the Trinity: Persons, Relations, and the Pauline Letters* (Grand Rapids: Eerdmans, 2015), 112–19.

tion, or worship, as God, something the OT is clear only God should receive (e.g., Matt. 2:11; Mark 3:29; Rev. 1:17; cf. e.g. Exod. 20:3).[4]

Using these markers, the early church demonstrated that Jesus and the Holy Spirit are clearly on the divine side of the Creator/creature distinction. They cannot be creatures because they are called by names reserved for God, perform actions only performed by God, possess attributes only possessed by God, and receive worship proper only to God.

One final point is important in this regard. These three persons exist eternally and simultaneously. In other words, God isn't one of them at one point and another of them at another point; there has always been three persons: Father, Son, and Holy Spirit. The early church demonstrated this in a few different ways, including biblical events in which all three persons are present (cf. e.g., Jesus's baptism in Matt. 3:16–17); biblical statements in which all three persons are named together (e.g., Jesus's Great Commission in Matt. 28:19); and biblical passages in which two or more of the divine persons speak to one another (e.g., Ps. 110:1).[5]

The Father's Two Hands

As we've just seen, the early church clearly affirmed the full divinity of each of the three persons—Father, Son, and Holy Spirit—and that these three persons exist together eternally. They also affirmed that there is one and only one God. How can these two things be true at the same time—three persons, one God? The early church insisted that the persons *cannot* be distinguished from one another through differences in attributes (e.g., more power or authority for the Father), actions (e.g., only the Father creates), appellations (e.g., only the Father is Almighty), or adoration (e.g., only the Father receives ultimate glory). Instead, the early church argued as strongly as possible for the unity of the Godhead with respect to attributes, actions, appellations, and adoration. So, again, how are they distinguished from one another?

The early church argued that the Father, Son, and Holy Spirit are distinguished from each other through their eternal relations of origin. We will

---

4. These will be explored further in later questions. For examples of this kind of Trinitarian exegesis in the early church, see Athanasius and Didymus the Blind, *Works on the Spirit*, trans. Mark DelCogliano, Andrew Radde-Gallowitz, and Lewis Ayres, PPS 43 (Crestwood, NY: St Vladimir's Seminary Press, 2011); Augustine, *The Trinity*, 2nd. ed., trans. Edmund Hill, ed. John Rotelle. (Hyde Park, NY: New City, 2012); Basil of Caesarea, *On the Holy Spirit*, trans. Stephen Hildebrand, PPS 42 (Crestwood, NY: St Vladimir's Seminary Press, 2011); and Gregory of Nazianzus, *On God and Christ: The Five Theological Orations and Two Letters to Cledonius*, trans. Frederick Williams and Lionel Wickham, PPS 23 (Crestwood, NY: St Vladimir's Seminary Press, 2002).

5. This is called "prosopological exegesis" by contemporary biblical and theological scholars. See Matthew W. Bates, *The Birth of the Trinity: Jesus, God, and Spirit in New Testament and Early Christian Interpretations of the Old Testament* (Oxford: Oxford University Press, 2015), 27–40.

cover this topic again in a later chapter, so we will not belabor an explanation here. For now, it is important to understand that the early church saw in Scripture that the divine persons are distinguished from one another by, and only by, the manner in which they subsist in the divine essence. The Father is eternally unbegotten; he does not receive the divine essence from either of the other divine persons. The Son is eternally begotten, or generated; he eternally (without beginning or end) receives the divine essence from the Father. The Holy Spirit is eternally spirated, or eternally proceeds; he eternally (without beginning or end) receives the divine essence from the Father and the Son.

The early church looked to texts like Proverbs 8:22–31[6] and John 5:26; 15:26[7] to support this doctrine. This doctrine is in many ways a culmination of the previous two reading strategies; if God is one, and there are three divine persons, how does Scripture distinguish them? For the early church, the answer is the eternal relations of origin, as seen in those biblical texts and others like them.

Taking on the Form of a Servant

A final important reading strategy for the early church is today known as "partitive exegesis." This mode of reading distinguishes between statements about Jesus according to his humanity and statements about him according to his divinity. For the former, the early church identified passages where Jesus is said to be hungry, sleep, have human emotions, submit to the Father, and other such actions that are appropriate to his human nature. For the latter, the early church identified passages where Jesus is described in clearly divine ways (see chapters 12, 15, and 16 on these two patterns of reading). The biblical warrant for doing so, according to the early church, lies in Philippians 2:5–8:[8]

> Have this mind among yourselves, which is yours in Christ Jesus, who, though he was in the *form of God*, did not count equality with God a thing to be grasped, but emptied himself, by taking the *form of a servant*, being born in the likeness of men. And being found in human form, he humbled himself by becoming obedient to the point of death, even death on a cross. (emphasis added)

Notice that Jesus is described here with two "forms" or natures: divine and human. And he does not possess a human nature until the incarnation ("taking the form of a servant," "being born in the likeness of men," "he

---

6. See questions 11, 12, 14, 16, 27, and 28.
7. See questions 6, 12, 14, 16, 27, and 28.
8. See questions 8, 12, 14, and 16.

humbled himself," vv. 7–8). Thus, any action taken by Jesus that demonstrates or arises from this "humble state" is according to his humanity, or "the form of a servant," while any action taken by Jesus that demonstrates or arises from his "equality with God" is according to his divinity, or "the form of God."[9]

This was an incredibly important distinction for the early church, since the subordinationists and anti-Nicenes like Arius, Eunomius, and Asterius attempted to use the "form of a servant" passages to prove that Jesus wasn't truly, fully divine.[10] In distinguishing, then, between these two ways of describing Jesus in the Bible, the early church was, in accordance with Paul's words in Philippians 2:5–8, safeguarding Christ's full divinity and teaching his full humanity.

Summary

We end by emphasizing how extensively the early church relied on Scripture for its doctrine of the Trinity. We know there is only one God, and that he is totally distinct from his creation, from texts like Genesis 1:1, Deuteronomy 6:4, 10:14, and Nehemiah 9:6. We know that this one God exists in three persons—Father, Son, and Holy Spirit—each fully divine and coequal with one another, from texts like Psalm 110:1, Matthew 3:16–17, and Matthew 28:19. We know that these three persons are distinguished from one another *not* by differences in attributes, actions, appellations, or adoration but *only* by their eternal relations of origin, from texts like Proverbs 8:22–31, John 5:26 and John 15:26. And we know that Jesus is both fully God and fully man, and that we must carefully distinguish when Scripture speaks about Jesus according to either nature, from texts like Philippians 2:5–8. This doctrine is not important to the early church only because it was codified in the Nicene Creed. Nor did the early church state it in the way it did at Nicaea and Constantinople because they were too influenced by Greek philosophy. Instead, Christians throughout space and time confess this doctrine of the Trinity because it is taught clearly in God's revealed Word, the Holy Scriptures.

REFLECTION QUESTIONS

1. What are some typical ways in which you've heard the doctrine of the Trinity taught from the Bible?

2. How do the reading strategies above relate to how you read the Bible? What is similar? What is different?

---

9. See, e.g., Augustine, *On the Trinity,* I.4.7. This is the preferred way to explain texts like Mark 13:32.
10. See questions 13.

3. Which of the strategies above helped you in your understanding of how the Bible teaches the doctrine of the Trinity?

4. Which of the strategies above is/are still confusing to you?

5. Do any of the strategies above correct certain aspects of your understanding of the doctrine of the Trinity? Which ones? How so?

QUESTION 5

What Do the Synoptic Gospels Teach Us About the Trinity?

The gospels of Matthew, Mark, and Luke, commonly known together as the Synoptic Gospels, tell the story of Jesus of Nazareth. In and through their narration they also teach doctrine, and specifically they teach us who this Jesus is. That is, they teach us Christology. Of course, Christology is inherently linked to the doctrine of the Trinity, since in both orthodox Christianity and in the Synoptics Jesus is the Second Person of the triune God in the flesh. To say it differently, Jesus in the Synoptics is one with the one God and also distinct from his heavenly Father. The language of "person" and "triune" do not occur in the Synoptics (or in the rest of the Bible), but the Synoptics (and the rest of the Bible) teach us that there is one God who exists in three persons: Father, Son, and Holy Spirit.

In Matthew, Mark, and Luke, the narratives of Jesus focus primarily on his actions and attributes in order to identify him both as Israel's Messiah and the incarnation of Israel's true God. According to the Synoptic authors, Jesus of Nazareth does what only God does and is what only God is because in Jesus, Yahweh, the one and only true God, has come down to save Israel and the nations. In other words, Jesus is God because he acts as only God acts and possesses attributes reserved for God alone. And yet, Jesus is also distinct from his heavenly Father and from his Spirit (who is also the Spirit of his Father). Thus, the Synoptics give us the basic building blocks of Nicene Trinitarianism—the creator/creature distinction with Jesus and the Spirit firmly on the Creator side along with the Father, all three distinct from one another and yet one, the three persons of the one and only true God. And they do this through telling the story of Jesus as the fulfillment of the story of Israel and the world.

There Is No God But YHWH, Who Comes to Us in Jesus by His Spirit

The Synoptics share Israel's commitment to monotheism, the belief that there is only one true God. We see this repeatedly in the Synoptics, both in direct teaching and in narration. Perhaps the clearest example comes from the lips of Jesus, who responds to Satan in the wilderness with a citation of Deuteronomy 6:13: "Then Jesus said to him, 'Be gone, Satan! For it is written, 'You shall worship the Lord your God, and him only shall you serve'" (Matt. 4:10; cf. Luke 4:8). The Jewish leaders' rejection of Jesus is also fundamentally tied to their understanding of monotheism, as is evident by their response to Jesus in Mark 14:62–64:

> And Jesus said, "I am, and you will see the Son of Man seated at the right hand of Power, and coming with the clouds of heaven." And the high priest tore his garments and said, "What further witnesses do we need? You have heard his blasphemy. What is your decision?" And they all condemned him as deserving death.

This commitment left no room for a semi-divine, intermediary figure; one was either the one true God or not God.

We must bear in mind this commitment to the Creator/creature distinction as we turn to another set of Synoptic passages that teach us that Jesus is God. Again, these passages include both direct teaching and narration, although in the Synoptics the former do not appear nearly as much as they do in the gospel of John. One of the most obvious places in the Synoptics for Trinitarian reflection is Mark 4:35–41 (Matt. 8:23–27; Luke 8:22–25): Jesus calming the storm. In this story Jesus does what only God does in the OT; namely, he controls the elements. He is not portrayed as having enough faith to ask God to control the wind and the waves, like Elijah prays for fire at Mt. Carmel in 1 Kings 18:1–40 or for rain later in that same chapter. Instead, Jesus himself controls nature. In the OT, only Yahweh can do such a thing—and here in the NT Jesus is doing it. In fact, Mark's telling of this story even uses similar language as the description of Yahweh in Job 9:8 and 9:11.[1] In this passage, then, Jesus does what only God does. Along similar lines, Richard

---

1. On this passage (Mark 6:45–52), see Richard B. Hays, *Echoes of Scripture in the Gospels* (Waco, TX: Baylor, 2016), 70–73. Hays argues that Mark's description of Jesus intending to "pass by" the boat and walking on the sea is an allusion to Job 9 (LXX), in which YHWH "passes by (9:11 LXX)" and "tramples the sea (9:8 LXX)." If this is the case, then, according to Hays, "the story of Jesus's epiphanic walking on the sea, read against the background of Job 9, can be perceived as the signature image of Markan Christology" (72). This footnote comes from Matthew Y. Emerson, "Mark," in *The Trinity in the Canon: A Biblical, Theological, Historical, and Practical Proposal*, ed. Brandon D. Smith (Nashville: B&H Academic, 2023), 144; cf. also Ps. 89:9.

Bauckham observes that, in Mark (2:7; 4:41; 6:50; 10:18; 11:27–33; 12:37; and 14:62), Jesus exorcises demons, heals, forgives, "tramples the sea," and claims goodness reserved for God alone on his own authority and without reference to a further authority beyond himself.[2]

In addition to Jesus doing what only God does in the Synoptics, he also possesses attributes that lie clearly on the divine side of the Creator/creature distinction. The last example given by Bauckham above, that Jesus claims goodness reserved for God alone, is one way that the Synoptics display Jesus's possession of divine attributes. Jesus also possesses the same glory as the Father, as indicated in texts like Mark 8:38,[3] the transfiguration account (e.g., Mark 9:2[4]), and Matthew 21:9.[5] Another example of Jesus possessing divine attributes comes from Mark 2:6–8, where Jesus perceives that some in the crowd thought he blasphemed by claiming to be able to forgive sins.[6] Here, Jesus does something by his own power that only God can do—heal the paralytic and, more importantly, forgive his (and others') sins—but he also possesses an attribute that only God possesses, namely omniscience regarding others' thoughts and intentions. On this aspect of the story, John Chrysostom says, "He made public their secret thoughts before the demonstration which was concerned with the cure of the paralytic's body, wishing to prove to them the power of His Godhead. For that it is an attribute of God alone, a sign of His deity to shew the secrets of His mind, the Scripture saith 'Thou alone knowest men's hearts' (1 Kgs. 8:39)."[7]

The Great Commission of Matthew 28:18–20 also displays Jesus's divine attributes. Here Jesus claims to possess divine authority—"all authority in

2. Richard Bauckham, *Jesus and the God of Israel: God Crucified and Other Studies on the New Testament's Christology of Divine Identity* (Grand Rapids: Eerdmans, 2008), 265 n. 40 and n. 41. This sentence is adapted from Emerson, "Mark," in *The Trinity in the Canon*, 144.
3. See Basil of Caesarea, *On the Holy Spirit*, trans. Stephen Hildebrand, PPS 42 (Crestwood, NY: St Vladimir's Seminary Press, 2011), 41–42.
4. See John Chrysostom's comments in Chrysostom, *Eutropius, and the Vanity of Riches*, Homily 2 (*NPNF*[1] 9:258.
5. See Thomas Aquinas, Sermon 04: "Osanna Filio David," Another Sermon on Advent (December 1, 1269), in Thomas Aquinas, *The Academic Sermons*, The Fathers of the Church, Mediaeval Continuation, trans. Mark-Robin Hoogland (Washington, DC: Catholic University of America Press, 2010), 59–60 (Matt. 21:9). On the three passages mentioned in this sentence, see Emerson, "Mark," 127–28.
6. On this passage, see also Simon Gathercole, "The Trinity in the Synoptic Gospels and Acts," in *The Oxford Handbook on the Trinity*, ed. Gilles Emery and Matthew Levering (Oxford: Oxford University Press, 2011), 58–60.
7. John Chrysostom, *On the Paralytic* (*NPNF*[1] 9:218). Chrysostom goes on to say that this is not a reference to the Father alone knowing something, for "if the Father alone knows the heart, how does the Son know the secrets of the mind? 'For He Himself' it is said, 'knew what was in man' (John 2:25); and Paul when proving that the knowledge of secret things is a special attribute of God says, 'and He that searchest the heart' (Rom. 8:27), shewing that this expression is equivalent to the appellation 'God'" (218).

heaven and earth"—and also suggests his omnipresence—"behold I am with you always, even to the end of the age," even while he will ascend to his Father shortly thereafter. Further, these attributes are relational; his authority, which is all-encompassing, is also "given to" him. Other examples of Jesus exercising his divine authority in Matthew include 5:17–20; 7:28–29; 8:23–27; 9:1–8; 14:22–33; 18:18–20; and 26:64.[8]

The Great Commission also points to Jesus's divine identity in his command to baptize in the one divine name, a name of three persons—"Father, Son, and Holy Spirit." This indicates that each of the three persons shares the singular name, namely the name of the one true God of Israel, YHWH. Jesus and the Spirit thus possess the same divine appellations, or names, as the Father, indicating their complete equality with him as God. Given, additionally, the indications of divine authority in the Great Commission discussed above, it is clear that Matthew 28:18–20 is one of the key passages for the development of Nicene Trinitarianism and Chalcedonian Christology.

Finally, in the Synoptics Jesus receives divine adoration. He is worshiped by the magi (Matt. 2:11) and by the disciples after the calming of the storm (Matt. 14:22–33; cf. Mark 6:48).[9] He is identified by demons as the "Holy One of God"—the one who deserves their worship but against whom they instead rebelled (Mark 1:24).[10] Jesus in the Synoptics is no mere mortal adopted by God as his chosen vessel for salvation; instead, he is God the Son in the flesh, come to save Israel and the world.

Although the Gospels focus on the person of the incarnate Son, Jesus Christ, they also portray the Holy Spirit as fully God. As with Jesus, the Spirit's actions and attributes fall firmly on the divine side of the Creator/creature distinction. One of the crucial passages for demonstrating the Spirit's divinity falls under the category of adoration. In Mark 3:20–27 (Matt. 12:22–30), after the Pharisees accuse Jesus of casting out a demon by an unclean spirit, Jesus warns that blasphemy against the Holy Spirit is an unforgiveable sin. There are at least two things we can draw out of this passage. First, blasphemy is a sin that can only be committed against the one true God, YHWH. So, this text teaches us that the Holy Spirit *is* YHWH. Second, once again we have a relational element here—the Spirit who must not be blasphemed is Jesus's Spirit, the Spirit by which he casts out demons. This one true God, YHWH, is Jesus and is the Holy Spirit—and is the Father—in relation to one another.

---

8. On these passages and their relation to Jesus's divine authority, see Jonathan T. Pennington, "Matthew," in *The Trinity in the Canon*, 109.
9. On the Matthean passages, see Pennington, "Matthew," 111; on Mark 6:48, see Emerson, "Mark," 135.
10. See Emerson, "Mark," 134.

Not Three Gods, but Three Persons

This brings us to the final teaching of the Synoptics on the Trinity, which we have touched on throughout this chapter. The one true God of Israel, YHWH, is one God in three persons in the Synoptics. The Father is God but is not his Son Jesus or his Holy Spirit. Jesus is God in the Synoptics but is not his Father or his Holy Spirit. The Holy Spirit is God in the Synoptics but is not the Father or the Son. This gets us already to the very heart of Nicene Trinitarianism. Later doctrinal formulation in the fourth century is not an imposition of Greek philosophy but instead arises from the biblical text itself. Nicaea, Constantinople I, and Chalcedon do not add to the text but rather identify and properly use conceptual terms to make accurate theological judgments about patterns of biblical language.[11] In other words, *homoousios* and "eternally begotten" are not terms alien to Scripture but instead accurate reflections of Scripture's teaching.

Summary

The Father, the Son, and the Spirit are each God, and there is only one God—therefore they must be said to share the same divine essence. They each are fully God and yet are not one another, not through differentiation of attributes, actions, appellations, or adoration but only by their eternal relations of origin (again, something taught in Scripture). This is in the Synoptics, and it is in the rest of the NT, as we will see shortly in the subsequent chapters of this section.

REFLECTION QUESTIONS

1. What are ways that the Synoptics' talk of the Trinity can help your prayer life?
2. How does the Synoptics' teaching on the Trinity remind you of what the OT says about the triune God?
3. What is a passage in the Synoptics that has confused you but now seems clearer based on thinking through its teaching on the Trinity?
4. How should we understand Mark 13:32 given this chapter (and the previous one)?
5. What are one or two "go-to" texts for teaching the Trinity in the Synoptics?

---

11. See David S. Yeago, "The New Testament and the Nicene Dogma: A Contribution to the Recovery of Theological Exegesis," *Pro Ecclesia* 3 (1994): 152–64.

QUESTION 6

What Does the Gospel of John Teach Us About the Trinity?

The gospel of John has been the major source for Trinitarian doctrine since the earliest days of the post-apostolic church. It continues to hold—and, indeed, holds in this book—a prominent role in reflection on this central Christian belief. While the rest of the Bible teaches the doctrine of the Trinity, it is not an overstatement to say that much of classical Christian Trinitarianism can be built from the fourth gospel. This chapter will only be able to briefly explore the variety of rich, textured, layered ways in which the Beloved Disciple teaches his readers about the triune God. For the sake of brevity, three categories organize this survey, the first two of which we've discussed in Question 4: divine identity, divine relations, and direct statements.

Divine Identity

With respect to divine identity, we see the same kinds of statements in John as in the Synoptics. The evangelist ascribes to Jesus and the Holy Spirit actions, appellations, attributes, and adoration reserved for God alone. For instance, Jesus creates (1:1–3), judges (5:22, 27, 29), saves (3:15, 17), and has life in himself (5:26). John likewise clearly portrays the Spirit as divine (e.g., his saving work in 3:8). It would be a mistake to say that John teaches explicitly what the Synoptics do not, but it would also be a mistake to say that they teach in the same way. In John, we might speak of equating Jesus and the Spirit with aspects of divine identity as somewhat heightened and even more explicit than in the Synoptics (although we should be careful to continue to say that these are still clear and explicit in the Synoptics themselves). We might say that John spells out in narratorial asides what the Synoptics portray through the narrative itself.[1]

1. James Edwards, speaking of Mark's portrayal of Jesus walking on water, says this: "It is a divine epiphany in answer to their earlier bafflement when he calmed the storm, 'Who is

So, for instance, with respect to the claim that Jesus is the Son of God, Matthew 27:43 notes the response of the chief priests, scribes, and elders to Jesus's crucifixion: "He trusts in God; let God deliver him now, if he desires him. For he said, 'I am the Son of God.'" From Matthew's (and Mark's and Luke's) portrayal of Jesus, we can gather from the narrative that calling himself the Son of God was equating himself with God. But neither Jesus nor the Synoptic authors ever state that outright. John, on the other hand, makes this statement early in his gospel: "This was why the Jews were seeking all the more to kill him, because not only was he breaking the Sabbath, but he was even calling God his own Father, making himself equal with God" (John 5:18). All four Gospels make this clear, but only John does so in this explicit, narratorial fashion.

Another example of this kind of difference between John and the Synoptics[2] comes in John's opening lines. While the preexistence of the Son is narratively portrayed in the Synoptics, particularly through Jesus's "I have come" statements,[3] John states the Son's preexistence outright. "In the beginning was the Word, and the Word was with God, and the Word was God. He was in the beginning with God" (John 1:1–2). Further, while the Synoptics gesture toward the Son's authority over creation (e.g., Matt. 8:23–27; Mark 4:35–41; Luke 8:22–25), here John outright connects the Son's preexistence to his act of creation in v. 3: "All things were made through him, and without him was not any thing made that was made." Again, what the Synoptics portray through narrative (and, in this case, discourse embedded within a narrative), John teaches explicitly through his own narratorial introduction.

Divine Relations

Another way John builds on the Synoptics' portrayal of Jesus is through his heightened and multiplied reference to the divine relation between Father, Son, and Spirit. According to Scott Swain, in John, "Jesus's *relation* to his Father—his eternal divine *origin* from the Father (John 1:14, 18) and his eternal divine *orientation* toward the Father (John 1:1–2)—provides the most comprehensive framework for understanding Jesus's person and work (John 16:28)."[4] As

---

this?' (4:41). In this respect Mark's Christology is no less sublime than is John's, although John has Jesus *declaring* that he is the Son of God (John 10:36), whereas Mark has him *showing* that he is the Son of God" (*The Gospel according to Mark*, PNTC [Grand Rapids: Eerdmans, 2002], 199).

2. It is important to refrain from exacerbating the differences between the Synoptics and John, real and significant as they are. See, for instance, Richard Bauckham, "John for Readers of Mark," in *The Gospels for All Christians: Rethinking the Gospel Audiences*, ed. Richard Bauckham (Grand Rapids: Eerdmans, 1997), 147–71.
3. See Simon J. Gathercole, *The Preexistent Son: Recovering the Christologies of Matthew, Mark, and Luke* (Grand Rapids: Eerdmans, 2006).
4. Scott Swain, "John," in *The Trinity in the Canon: A Biblical, Theological, Historical, and Practical Proposal*, ed. Brandon D. Smith (Nashville: B&H Academic, 2023), 197, emphasis original.

Swain goes on to argue, the titles for Jesus—both those unique to him (e.g., *monogenēs*, "Son") and those he shares with the Father—the attributes he receives from the Father (e.g., in John 5), the actions he performs along with the Father (and the Spirit), and the honor he is due alongside the Father and the Spirit are all signs of his divinity demonstrated *in relation* to the Father.[5]

The same can be said of the Spirit's relation to the Father and the Son. The Spirit's divinity is seen in relation to the Father and the Son, with whom he shares titles, attributes, actions, and adoration. Additionally, the procession of the Spirit, like the name "only begotten" for the Son, is an indication of his divinity. In John, he is the Spirit who *proceeds from* the Father (15:26), and who is breathed out by the Son (20:22). He is the Spirit of the Father, and all that the Father has he has given to the Son, and so the Spirit is the Spirit of the Father and the Son, given by the Father and Son to the incarnate Son's disciples (16:12–15). This relational language throughout John's gospel indicates the intimate, mutual indwelling[6] of the Father, Son, and Spirit, and thus of their shared divinity.

As indicated by the language of the Father and Son "giving" or "sending" the Spirit, the eternal relations of origin that John identifies are reflected in the divine missions. The Father sends the Son into the world, and both the Father and the Son send the Spirit. These relational aspects of the divine missions, which are much more the focus in John (and in the Bible as a whole), teach us who God is in himself. Just as the eternal relations of origin indicate real distinction between the persons in their relation to one another but not between them with respect to essence, so too the external missions indicate distinction in person in their relation to one another while also affirming equality in and unity of essence. The Son is not different from the Father *essentially* because the Father sends the Son, even if this sending does indicate a difference between them *relationally*. The same is true of the Spirit.[7] The

---

Earlier in the chapter, Swain also notes the same fourfold demonstration of Jesus's divinity in John as we find in the Synoptics and as we've summarized several times, namely that, in John, "1) Jesus shares the divine name(s), . . . 2) Jesus possesses divine attributes, . . . 3) Jesus performs divine works, . . ." and "4) Jesus is worthy of divine honor" (195–96).

5. Swain, "John," 195–96.
6. Swain, "John," 204.
7. Emphasis original. As Swain notes, "(1) While the relation between the Father and the Son is *asymmetrical* when it comes to Jesus's mission (i.e., the Father sends, the Son is sent, not vice versa), Jesus's mission involves *no disparity in authority*. Quite to the contrary, the one who comes in his Father's name, comes as one who shares his Father's authority (John 3:35; 5:22–23, 27; 10:18; 12:13; 13:3; 17:2). (2) While the Father's sending of the Son exhibits a *real*, rather than a merely *metaphorical, distinction* of persons, it involves *no separation of persons*: 'He who *sent* me is *with* me. He has not left me alone' (John 8:29; 16:32). (3) While the Son's mission effects *a new mode* of his personal presence among us as one of us, whereby he takes on the form of our mortal flesh and our troubled souls (John 1:14; 12:27; 13:21), it involves *no spatial movement on the part of his person*. He ever remains 'at

"sending" language of John is thus another way that the fourth gospel teaches us about the Trinity through emphasizing the eternal relations between the divine persons.

Direct Statements

We have already talked about, or at least mentioned, three of the primary passages in this category: John 1:1–3, 5:18, and 5:26. It is worth mentioning at least one more, in John 8:58–59:

> Jesus said to them, "Truly, truly, I say to you, before Abraham was, I am." So they picked up stones to throw at him, but Jesus hid himself and went out of the temple.

Although the phrase in Greek (*egō eimi*) can simply be a declarative statement about personal identity or action (e.g., "I am a carpenter"; "I am going"), in this context Jesus clearly means much more. The Pharisees, to whom he is speaking, grasp his full import and try to stone him for blasphemy. This is because Jesus means to invoke the divine name, YHWH, "I AM," when he uses the phrase "I am" in John 8:58.

The context makes this clear, not only from the Pharisees' reaction but also in the lead up to the statement itself. The whole chapter relates Jesus's attempt to explain who he is to the Pharisees, even though they continually refuse to understand. He uses the phrase "I am" two other times in the previous verses (vv. 24, 28), but the ESV translates the Greek phrase "I am he," instead of simply "I am." Again, this is a plausible translation on the face of it, but given the force of the statement in v. 58, it is reasonable to conclude that John records this conversation between Jesus and the Pharisees in a way that highlights the threefold repetition of "I am," culminating in the climactic instance of v. 58.

In the previous two instances, Jesus refers to himself as "I am" in the context of the divine missions. In v. 24 he says, "I told you that you would die in your sins, for unless you believe that I am he [literally, "I am"] you will die in your sins." And in v. 28 he tells the Pharisees, "When you have lifted up the Son of Man, then you will know that I am he, and that I do nothing on my own authority, but speak just as the Father taught me." Thus, up to the point of the final argument in vv. 48–59, Jesus's use of the phrase centers on his coming accomplishment of atonement for sin through his impending crucifixion. But in v. 48 and following, the conversation turns from how the Pharisees (and the world) can be saved through the sacrifice of the Son of Man to the

---

the Father's side,' ever turned toward his Father's face, to which he directs the entirety of his incarnate mission (John 1:1, 18; 5:19–20; 13:3; 16:28; 20:17; cf. 3:13)" (Swain, "John," 206–7).

ultimate origin of the Son. Whereas the Pharisees charge Jesus with being the son of a Samaritan and a demon, Jesus claims that he is the Son of the Father in heaven. And not just an earthly Son adopted by the Father but the eternal Son, the only begotten Son of the Father who has existed from the beginning. "Before Abraham was, I am." This is the force of Jesus's statement: to claim the name of the God of Israel; the God of Abraham, Isaac, and Jacob; the God who revealed his name to Moses in the burning bush, as his own. And in claiming that name, he claims equality—indeed, unity in identity—with the God of Israel. The Pharisees know exactly what he means, and they try to stone him accordingly.

Of course, Jesus is not claiming singular status as the God of Israel—he is the God of Israel with his Father, from whom he comes both in eternal procession and external mission. Throughout the passage Jesus distinguishes between himself and his Father, teaching us that the God of Israel is Father and Son and, later in the Farewell Discourse, also Spirit. John's Trinitarianism is thus narratively portrayed and taught through narratorial asides, but it is also crucially given to us on the lips of Jesus himself through direct statements, both here in John 8:12–59 as well as elsewhere (e.g., John 5:26; 15:26; cf. also 1:1–3).

Summary

As in the Synoptics, Jesus in John is fully God, as are the Father and the Spirit. They each equally possess the same divine attributes, perform the same divine actions, share the same divine names, and receive the same glory that only God deserves. They are the one God in three persons, distinct only via their eternal relations of origin. This Trinitarian grammar is thoroughly biblical, and the gospel of John provides a large portion of the evidence for that fact.

REFLECTION QUESTIONS

1. What are some ways that John's talk of the Trinity helps your prayer life?
2. How does John's teaching on the Trinity remind you of what the OT says about the triune God?
3. What is a passage in John that has confused you but now seems clearer after thinking through his teaching on the Trinity?
4. How should we understand the "sending" language in John given this chapter (and the previous two)?
5. What are one or two "go-to" texts for teaching the Trinity in John?

QUESTION 7

What Does the Book of Acts Teach Us About the Trinity?

In the book of Acts, Jesus's mission to the world, given to him by the Father, continues through the gift of Spirit. This, in a nutshell, is how Acts teaches us about the Trinity: namely, through the narrative of the gospel going to the ends of the earth. The incarnate, risen, ascended Lord Jesus, sent to the world by the Father, now sends his Spirit to his church to proclaim the good news of his death and resurrection to the Jew first and then to the Gentile. Acts is thus a continuation of the divine act of redemption, in which the now-accomplished work of Christ is proclaimed and applied from Jerusalem to Judea and Samaria and to the ends of the earth.

As in the previous chapters, we will focus our attention on divine identity and divine relations. Regarding the former, Acts, like the Gospels, associates Jesus and the Spirit with attributes, appellations, and adoration reserved for God in the OT. Acts also demonstrates the intra-Trinitarian relations between the divine persons through its description of the divine missions, and particularly in narrating the growth of Christ's church through the gift of his Spirit.

Divine Identity

In terms of divine identity, once again we find the Son and Spirit described as performing actions alongside the Father, possessing attributes and appellations, and receiving adoration reserved for God and God alone in the OT.

Divine Actions

For instance, in Acts Jesus forgives sins (Acts 5:31), an act clearly reserved for God alone in the OT (e.g. as summarized in Mark 2:7).[1] And, as we saw in our

1. Adonis Vidu, *The Same God Who Works All Things: Inseparable Operations in Trinitarian Theology* (Grand Rapids: Eerdmans, 2021), 18.

discussion of this act in question 5, the religious leaders clearly understood what Jesus was claiming about himself in the Synoptics when he forgave sins (in, e.g., Mark 2). Likewise, Peter's description of Jesus in Acts 2:34 as having "poured out" the Spirit he received from the Father on the church is an act reserved for God alone. Only God possesses his Spirit, and so only God can pour out his Spirit (e.g. Joel 2:28–32). Jesus both possesses the Spirit, through receiving him from the Father, and pours out his Spirit onto his people.[2]

The Spirit's activity, especially in directing and sending the early church's leaders, is also noteworthy. The Holy Spirit directs Philip in his conversation with the Ethiopian eunuch (Acts 8:29) and later carries him away to Azotus (vv. 39–40). Notice in Acts 8:29 that not only does the Spirit direct Philip, but we also hear him speak directly to Philip: And the Spirit said to Philip, "Go over and join this chariot" (v. 29). Luke thus narrates this story in such a way that shows the Spirit to be personally distinct from the Father and the Son and also equal to him in his actions, directing a divinely appointed conversation and taking Philip from one geographic location to another.[3]

Similarly, the Holy Spirit prevents Paul from preaching the gospel in Asia but directs him to speak in Macedonia (16:6–10).[4] Notice that Luke uses three parallel phrases in this passage: "the Holy Spirit" who prevents Paul from "speak[ing] the word" in Asia, the "Spirit of Jesus did not allow them" to go into Bithynia, and "God" called them to "preach the gospel" to the Macedonians. The same God who calls Paul and his companions to preach to the Macedonians also prevented them from speaking the word in Asia or going into Bithynia. That is, the way these phrases are parallel to one another in this passage indicates that the Holy Spirit is the Spirit of Jesus and is God, and he is the one who both prevents speaking the word to or even going into one place while calling the apostle to preach the gospel somewhere else. Notice also that the middle phrase, "Spirit of Jesus," indicates the intra-Trinitarian relations—the Holy Spirit is the Spirit of the Son. We will return to this point later.

A related passage is Acts 13:2: "While they were worshiping the Lord and fasting, the Holy Spirit said, 'Set apart for me Barnabas and Saul for the work to which I have called them.'" The Spirit again speaks and directs here, indicating both personal distinction from the Father and the Son and divine action with respect to directing the church's mission. The Spirit can and does lead, guide, and direct the apostolic church in their mission to the ends of the earth. His choosing "Saul and Barnabas for the missionary task described in Acts is thus an indication of his divinity."[5]

---

2. Vidu, *The Same God Who Works All Things*, 31–36.
3. Robert Letham, *The Holy Trinity: In Scripture, History, Theology, and Worship* (Phillipsburg, NJ: P&R, 2004), 60.
4. Letham, *The Holy Trinity*, 60.
5. Letham, *The Holy Trinity*, 77.

Divine Attributes

Regarding shared divine attributes, we have already seen that both Jesus and the Spirit share divine authority and share it equally with one another and with the Father. With respect to Jesus, in Acts 2:33–35 Peter twice says that Jesus shares authority with the Father. First, in verse 33 Jesus is "exalted to the right hand of the Father." This spatial language indicates that Jesus shares divine authority with the Father. Peter's quotation of Psalm 110:1 two verses later is a similar indication. In this instance of prosopological exegesis,[6] Peter reads the psalm in such a way that indicates the Father and Son share authority, authority acknowledged by the Father in his communication to the Son ("The Lord [the Father] said to my Lord [the Son]").[7] Jesus is also seen at God's right hand (Acts 5:31), again indicating that Jesus shares authority with the Father.

Divine Appellations

Along with actions and attributes, both Jesus and the Spirit (along with the Father) share divine appellations, or names. This is one of the more unique aspects of Acts's contribution to the doctrine of the Trinity—the association of the divine name with more than one divine person, and especially with the crucified and risen Lord Jesus. This association happens in a few ways. First, when Luke tells us of Paul's conversion in Acts 9:1–22, he equates the name of the Lord Jesus with "the Lord," the name upon which he and other Christ followers call on to be saved (Acts 9:14, 21; 22:16).[8] This intricate web of naming in Acts 9 moves back and forth between "the Lord"—the Hellenized version of the divine name—and "the Lord Jesus," thus associating Jesus's name with the name of Israel's God, the one true God, YHWH. Additionally, it is on this name that Paul and other believers call for salvation, which is only true of God, YHWH, in the OT (e.g., Peter's summary comment in Acts 2:21).

Another instance like this comes in two of the early occasions of apostolic preaching, Acts 2:21 and Acts 4:12. In Acts 2:17–21 Peter quotes Joel 2:28–32, a passage about the promised eschatological day of the Lord. In that OT text, YHWH promises to return to Israel, pour out his Spirit, and save "everyone who calls on the name of the Lord" (Acts 2:21). A few verses later, at the conclusion of his sermon and in response to the crowd's question as to how they should respond, Peter tells those listening to, "Repent and be baptized every one of you in the name of Jesus Christ for the forgiveness of your sins, and you will receive the gift of the Holy Spirit" (2:38). As we noted earlier, here Jesus

6. This term refers to two divine persons conversing with one another in a particular biblical passage. See the definitions and brief discussions in questions 3 and 15.
7. Matthew W. Bates, *The Birth of the Trinity: Jesus, God, and Spirit in New Testament Early Christian Interpretations of the Old Testament* (Oxford: Oxford University Press, 2015), 153–55, 160–61; cf. also his discussion of Ps. 2:7 (162–63).
8. Letham, *The Holy Trinity*, 47.

does what only YHWH does, and what he promises to do in Joel 2:28–32, namely forgive sins and pour out his Holy Spirit. But notice also that Peter instructs the crowd to be baptized "in the name of Jesus Christ." The name of YHWH is associated with Jesus in Acts 2. We also see this equation of the name of Jesus with the name of God in Acts 4:12, a much briefer speech by Peter that carries the same point.

Divine Adoration

Finally, in Acts Jesus and the Spirit both receive adoration reserved for God. With respect to Jesus, Stephen prays to him in Acts 7:59–60, where the proto-martyr asks Jesus to receive his spirit. Interestingly, this prayer mirrors Jesus's prayer to the Father on the cross in Luke 23:46.[9] Rather than this being an indication that Jesus isn't really God, it is instead both an instance where we see Jesus doing what only God does, namely being prayed to, and also an instance that reminds us of Jesus's true humanity. Thus Luke in both his gospel and his sequel teaches that Jesus is one man with two natures, human and divine. With respect to the Holy Spirit, he also receives adoration reserved for God. As in reference to blaspheming the Holy Spirit in the Synoptic Gospels, Luke in Acts teaches this through narrating a story about the Holy Spirit being sinned against. In Acts 5:3–4, Peter says that lying to the Holy Spirit is lying to God[10]:

> But Peter said, "Ananias, why has Satan filled your heart to lie to the Holy Spirit and to keep back for yourself part of the proceeds of the land? While it remained unsold, did it not remain your own? And after it was sold, was it not at your disposal? Why is it that you have contrived this deed in your heart? You have not lied to man but to God."

Jesus and the Spirit in Acts receive the same adoration that God does in the OT, adoration reserved for God in the OT (Exod. 20:1–3).

Divine Relations

With respect to divine relations, we move canonically from an emphasis on the relation between Father and Son in the gospel of John to an emphasis on the Father's and Son's relation to the Spirit in Acts. Throughout the book, and namely as the gospel goes into each new territory from Jerusalem and Judea to Samaria to the ends of the earth, the Spirit is called the "gift," or "gift of God," in conjunction with the apostolic preaching (Acts 2:38; 8:20; 10:45;

9. Letham, *The Holy Trinity*, 47.
10. Letham, *The Holy Trinity*, 61.

11:17).[11] This indicates that he comes *from* God as the Spirit *of* God. Much like we can say about the incarnation with respect to the Father sending the Son, the gift of the Spirit is God sending God.

Related to this economic pattern of sending is the relation between Jesus and the Spirit in the post-ascension narratives of Acts. In the Gospels, it is the Spirit anointing and empowering the incarnate Jesus, and it is this same Spirit who is given to the church by the resurrected and ascended Jesus.[12] This once again teaches about the shared divinity of Father, Son, and Spirit, since God the Spirit anoints the incarnate Jesus who then pours out his Spirit, the Spirit of the Father and the Son,[13] on his people after his ascension. But it also once again teaches us about the two natures of Christ, since it is according to his humanity that he is anointed and empowered by God the Spirit.

Summary

Thus, the book of Acts teaches us about the Trinity in similar ways to what we have already seen in the Gospels. This is namely through identifying Father, Son, and Holy Spirit as God through attributing to them actions, attributes, appellations, and adoration reserved for God and God alone in the OT. The book also emphasizes the divine relations between Father, Son, and Spirit, giving us the language for what would later become known as the eternal relations of origin, in its narration of the divine missions and particular the sending of the Spirit.

REFLECTION QUESTIONS

1. Who have you typically thought about as the "main character" of Acts? How does seeing the Trinity in Acts impact your answer to that question?

2. What are some ways that John's talk of the Trinity helps your prayer life?

3. How does Acts' teaching on the Trinity remind you of what the OT says about the triune God?

4. What is a passage in Acts that has confused you but now seems clearer based on thinking through its teaching on the Trinity?

5. What are one or two "go-to" texts for teaching the Trinity in Acts?

---

11. R. B. Jamieson and Tyler R. Wittman, *Biblical Reasoning: Christological and Trinitarian Rules for Exegesis* (Grand Rapids: Baker Academic, 2022), 121.
12. Vidu, *The Same God Who Works All Things*, 33, 248–49, 266; cf. also 257; Acts 2:33.
13. As we saw earlier, the Spirit is named "the Spirit of Jesus" in Acts 16:7.

QUESTION 8

What Do Paul's Letters Teach Us About the Trinity?

Paul's letters mark a shift in the NT canon, from story to letter, or from narrative to epistle. Rather than the Gospels and Acts telling us what happened, Paul and the other NT epistolary authors apply what happened in God's economy of salvation to specific congregations in the various parts of the Roman Empire in the first century. Despite this shift in genre, though, the letters of Paul (and James, Peter, John, and Jude) assume the narrative substructure of the NT. God's Son, Israel's Messiah, Jesus of Nazareth, was sent by God the Father through God the Spirit to live the life that we can't; to die the death we deserve for the forgiveness of sins; to descend into the place of the dead, the enemy's stronghold, to declare his victory over sin and death; and to rise from the dead three days later as king over all things, including death, hell, and the grave. He ascended into heaven and sits at the right hand of the Father, ruling and reigning over all things until he returns on the Last Day to judge the living and the dead, to restore God's creation, and to dwell eternally with his people in the new heaven and new earth. This story is assumed and even referenced in the letters of the NT, including Paul's, and informs their instruction to the churches to whom they are writing.[1]

As in the previous chapters, we will focus our attention on divine identity and divine relations. Regarding the former, Paul's letters, like the Gospels and Acts, associate Jesus and the Spirit with attributes, actions, appellations, and adoration reserved for God in the OT. Paul's letters also demonstrate the intra-Trinitarian relations between the divine persons through its description

1. See Fred Sanders, "Pauline Epistles," in *The Trinity in the Canon: A Biblical, Theological, Historical, and Practical Proposal*, ed. Brandon D. Smith (Nashville: B&H Academic, 2023), 245–47.

of the divine missions, and particularly in narrating the growth of Christ's church through the gift of his Spirit.

Divine Identity

In terms of divine identity, once again we find the Son and Spirit, alongside the Father, described as performing actions, possessing attributes and appellations, and receiving adoration reserved for God and God alone in the OT.[2]

Divine Actions

Jesus is identified as the Creator in Colossians 1:15–20 and 1 Corinthians 8:6. In the former text, Paul comprehensively describes the Son's responsibility for creation, since "by him all things were created, in heaven and on earth, visible and invisible, whether thrones or dominions or rulers or authorities—all things were created through him and for him. And he is before all things, and in him all things hold together."[3] The Son who became incarnate in the person of Jesus of Nazareth is the same Son who created, sustains, and is before all things. In the latter text, Paul again attributes everything in creation to the Son but uses the phrase "through whom are all things." This is because he is attributing creation to both the Father and the Son at the same time—creation is from the Father and through the Son.[4]

Paul also identifies Jesus as the judge in 1 Thessalonians 3:13; 5:23; 2 Thessalonians 1:7–10; and 1 Corinthians 5:10.[5] As we've discussed in our chapter on the gospel of John, and as we will see in the chapter on the OT, this activity is reserved for God and God alone in the OT. And yet Paul repeatedly attributes it directly to Jesus. The same is true of the term "Savior," which is one of Paul's most used titles in reference to Jesus. As Robert Letham notes, "Since salvation is a work of God himself, the apostle Paul's consistent description of Jesus as Savior implicitly attributes deity to him (Titus 2:11–13; cf. Titus 1:4; 3:6; Phil. 3:20; 2 Tim. 1:10; for Peter, see 2 Peter 1:11). Moreover, in Titus 2:11–13 Paul expressly calls Jesus Christ 'our great God and Savior.'"[6]

Regarding the Holy Spirit in Paul's letters, the Third Person of the Trinity also does what only God does. He gives spiritual gifts (1 Cor. 12:4–6; "the same Spirit") along with the Father ("the same God") and the Son ("the same Lord"); he raises Jesus from the dead and will raise believers from the dead

---

2. One of the most detailed and exegetically rigorous treatments of this topic can be found in Richard Bauckham, "Paul's Christology of Divine Identity," in *Jesus and the God of Israel: God Crucified and Other Studies on the New Testament's Christology of Divine Identity* (Grand Rapids: Eerdmans, 2008), 182–232.
3. Robert Letham, *The Holy Trinity: In Scripture, History, Theology, and Worship* (Phillipsburg, NJ: P&R, 2004), 44.
4. Letham, *The Holy Trinity*, 44.
5. Letham, *The Holy Trinity*, 45.
6. Letham, *The Holy Trinity*, 46.

at the last day (Rom. 8: 9–11), the day of judgment; he is grieved over our sin (Eph. 4:30); and he seals us for the day of redemption (Eph. 1:13; 4:30).[7]

Divine Attributes

One of the most prominent ways we see divine attributes attributed to the Son in Paul's letters is in references to preexistence. For instance, in Philippians 2:5–7, there is a clear movement from the Son "in the form of God" to him taking on the "form of a servant," "being born in the likeness of men." However one adjudicates the meaning of "form of God," it is clear that there is a temporal point in time in which the Son, who was not previously incarnate, becomes incarnate.[8] Likewise, the "sending" language of Romans 8:3 and Galatians 4:4, in which the Father sends the Son in the incarnation, indicates the Son's preexistence (and, thus, his divinity). This is analogous to the sending language we saw in John.[9]

The Spirit, too, possesses divine attributes according to Paul. Perhaps the most obvious indicator of the Spirit's divinity in terms of attributes is found in 1 Corinthians 2:10–13, in which Paul declares that only the Spirit knows the mind of God and expresses it to humanity in God's revelation of himself to us. A related passage, 1 Corinthians 12:1–3, teaches us that it is only through the Spirit of God that we can speak the truth, namely the truth that "Jesus is Lord!"[10]

Divine Appellations

In addition to divine actions and attributes, Paul also uses names reserved for God alone for the Son and Spirit. The most obvious example of this comes in 1 Corinthians 8:4–6:

> Therefore, as to the eating of food offered to idols, we know that "an idol has no real existence," and that "there is no God but one." For although there may be so-called gods in heaven or on earth—as indeed there are many "gods" and many "lords"—yet for us there is one God, the Father, from whom are all things and for whom we exist, and one Lord, Jesus Christ, through whom are all things and through whom we exist.

Notice that Paul quotes the OT text, Deuteronomy 6:4—"there is no God but one" (1 Cor. 8:4)—and then glosses it to include both the Father and the Son—"there is one God, the Father . . . and one Lord, Jesus Christ." We have

7. Letham, *The Holy Trinity*, 60.
8. See Letham, *The Holy Trinity*, 48–49 for discussion and citation of alternate views. I (Matt) agree with Letham's interpretation of the passage, including the fact that this is a plain statement about the Son's preexistence and therefore his divinity.
9. Letham, *The Holy Trinity*, 48–49.
10. Letham, *The Holy Trinity*, 60–61.

already discussed this passage above in its attribution of the divine act of creation to both the Father and the Son, but Paul also is attributing the name of God, YHWH, to both the Father and the Son through glossing the main OT text about the oneness of God and his name.[11]

Paul also attributes the names of "God" and "YHWH" to Jesus in Romans 9:5 and Philippians 2:9–11, respectively. In the former passage, Paul says, "To them belong the patriarchs, and from their race, according to the flesh, is the Christ, who is God over all, blessed forever. Amen." The phrase "who is God over all" is a clear reference back to "the Christ," the nearest singular nominative noun to which the relative pronoun can refer. In Philippians 2:9–11, Paul says that Jesus has been given "the name that is above every name," which is again a clear reference to the divine name, YHWH, a name reserved for God and God alone.[12] Additionally, we could point to the fact that Paul's nearly constant use of *kyrios* ("Lord") as a title for Jesus appears to be a deliberate ascription of the Tetragrammaton ("YHWH") to Jesus.[13]

With respect to the Spirit, Paul frequently includes the Spirit in what Letham calls triadic patterns. "Most obvious of all in Paul's letters," he argues, "is his apostolic benediction in 2 Corinthians 13:14 (v. 13 in Greek), where he associates 'the fellowship of the Holy Spirit' with 'the grace of our Lord Jesus Christ' and 'the love of God [the Father].'"[14] We can also include other Pauline texts—such as Romans 15:30, 1 Corinthians 12:4–6, Galatians 4:4–6, Ephesians 2:18, Colossians 1:3–8, 2 Thessalonians 2:13–14, and Titus 3:4–7—that name the Holy Spirit alongside the Father and the Son.[15] These triadic patterns clearly link the name of the Holy Spirit with the names of the Father and the Son, thus putting him on equal footing—divine footing—with the first and second persons of the Trinity.

Divine Adoration

Finally, Paul ascribes worship, reserved for God alone, to Jesus. His prayer of "*maranatha*" in 1 Corinthians 16:22 alludes to Jewish worship practices of the period and would have been understood as a prayer to God.[16] Paul also uses doxological phrasing in Colossians 1:15–20, Philippians 2:5–11, and 2 Timothy 2:11–13, which is most likely an indication that these passages

---

11. See on this passage R. B. Jamieson and Tyler R. Wittman, *Biblical Reasoning: Christological and Trinitarian Rules for Exegesis* (Grand Rapids: Baker Academic, 2022), 97–98; and Wesley Hill, *Paul and the Trinity: Persons, Relations, and the Pauline Letters* (Grand Rapids: Eerdmans, 2015), 112–22.
12. Letham, *The Holy Trinity*, 41–42.
13. Letham, *The Holy Trinity*, 43, cf. in particular the biblical references in n. 25. As Letham notes here, in Greek translations of the OT, *kyrios* ("Lord") is used to translate "YHWH."
14. Letham, *The Holy Trinity*, 60.
15. Letham, *The Holy Trinity*, 61.
16. Letham, *The Holy Trinity*, 43; cf. also 47.

were adapted from hymns sung in corporate worship. These passages about Jesus contribute to the idea that early Christians viewed these hymnic biblical texts as attributing adoration reserved for God alone to Jesus.[17] Additionally, there are at least two passages that appear to be doxologies addressed directly to Christ: Romans 9:5 and 2 Timothy 4:18.[18] Even more direct are Paul's offerings of prayer to Jesus in both 2 Corinthians 12:8–9 and 1 Thessalonians 3:11–12.[19] Finally, Letham argues that corporate worship is the most likely context for confessing Christ as *kyrios* ("Lord") in, for example, Romans 10:9–13, 1 Corinthians 12:1–3, and Philippians 2:9–11.[20] Each of these passages indicate that the earliest Christians worshiped Jesus in corporate gatherings, prayed to Jesus, confessed Jesus as Lord in the context of public worship, and thus viewed him as divine.

Divine Relations

In addition to these markers of divine identity, Paul also speaks of the three persons of the Godhead relationally and in ways that indicate their shared, singular, and equal divinity. Wesley Hill has thoroughly demonstrated this aspect of Paul's Trinitarianism, and in key texts that we've discussed above in relation to divine identity: Philippians 2:5–11 and 1 Corinthians 8:6. Hill also exegetes 1 Corinthians 15:24–28 in relation to 1 Corinthians 8:6. Hill's basic argument is that, yes, Jesus does what only God does according to Paul, but Paul's letters also speak of God *as God* in a relational sense. The Father is the Father because he is the Father of the Son. The Son is the Son because he is the Son of the Father. The Spirit is the Spirit because he is the Spirit of the Father and the Son. These names, indicative of relations within the Godhead, are not historical accidents happening in time for Paul but are the way that God exists eternally. God is who he is precisely because he is Father, Son, and Spirit.[21]

In addition to the texts Hill exegetes, we can also note a few other ways that Paul speaks of God's existence as triune using relational terms. In Colossians 1:15, for instance, Paul says that Christ is "the image of the invisible God." As Steven Duby notes, this language of image both intricately ties the Son to the Father relationally (and eternally) and also distinguishes between Father and Son. The Son is the image of the Father, and image means exact representation (cf. Heb. 1:3). But image also means distinction, in that the image is relationally distinct from the image's source. This language of the Son as the Father's image thus affirms both the Son's full divinity and his distinction from

17. Letham, *The Holy Trinity*, 46.
18. Letham, *The Holy Trinity*, 47.
19. Letham, *The Holy Trinity*, 47.
20. Letham, *The Holy Trinity*, 47.
21. Hill, *Paul and the Trinity*, e.g., 99–103 for the Son in relation to the Father and 135–66 for the Spirit's relation to the Father and the Son.

the Father at the same time.[22] The same kind of equality-in-distinction occurs with the language that Paul uses about the Holy Spirit, naming him the "Spirit of God" and "Spirit of Christ" in Romans 8:9–10 and Galatians 4:6. In both texts, the Spirit dwells within the believer *as the presence of God*.[23] Notice also in Romans 8:9–10 that Paul alternates between the phrases "Spirit of God" and "Spirit of Christ," thus all at once affirming the equality of Christ with God, the Spirit's procession from the Father and the Son, and the Spirit's full divinity. This relational language that Paul uses is full of teaching about the Holy Trinity.

Summary

Once again in Paul's letters we see the same kind of Trinitarian teaching that we've seen in other biblical books. Paul affirms that Father, Son, and Holy Spirit are each God based on their shared divine attributes, actions, appellations, and adoration. They also are the one God together, via their eternal relations of origin. While Paul does not use this exact language, his teaching in his letters give warrant to this pattern of language that articulates the doctrine of the Trinity.

REFLECTION QUESTIONS

1. How does the story of the Bible inform how we understand the doctrine of the Trinity?

2. How might your prayer life be supported, challenged, or changed given how Paul speaks about the Trinity?

3. How does Paul's teaching on the Trinity remind you of the ways in which the OT speaks about the triune God?

4. What is a passage in Paul's letters that has confused you but now seems clearer based on thinking through his teaching on the Trinity?

5. What are one or two "go-to" texts for teaching the Trinity in Paul's letters?

---

22. Steven Duby, *Jesus and the God of Classical Theism: Biblical Christology in Light of the Doctrine of God* (Grand Rapids: Baker Academic, 2022), 56.
23. Adonis Vidu, *The Same God Who Works All Things: Inseparable Operations in Trinitarian Theology* (Grand Rapids: Eerdmans, 2021), 33–34.

QUESTION 9

What Do the General Epistles Teach Us About the Trinity?

At this point, we have trodden a well-worn biblical-theological path, charted by Holy Scripture and made plain to us by the early church theologians who read the Bible in light of the revelation of God through his Son Jesus Christ by the power of the Holy Spirit. In the Gospels, Acts, and Pauline Epistles, we have seen that both the Son and the Spirit, alongside the Father, are known by divine appellations, perform divine actions, possess divine attributes, and receive divine adoration. They also are described in ways that indicate their eternal relations of origin. This pattern continues in the latter portion of the NT, first in the General Epistles and then in the book of Revelation. In this chapter we will follow this Trinitarian exegetical path through the epistolary works of Peter, James, John, Jude, and the writer to the Hebrews.

Divine Identity

With respect to divine identity, the authors of the General Epistles describe the Son and Spirit in ways that identify them as divine along with the Father. As with our earlier chapters, the means by which they do so include names used, actions described, attributes considered, and worship received.

Divine Appellations

Regarding divine names, the writer of Hebrews quotes Psalm 45:6–7 to describe God the Son incarnate. As Letham notes, "this psalm distinguishes God from God," and thus "God who occupies the throne is anointed by God." It is therefore fitting to conclude that "Hebrews considers that the Son is the anointed and enthroned king who is also God."[1] Letham also notes that the

1. Robert Letham, *The Holy Trinity: In Scripture, History, Theology, and Worship* (Phillipsburg, NJ: P&R, 2004), 42.

binitarian naming patterns found in James (1:1) and Peter (1 Peter 1:17–21; 5:10; 2 Peter 1:1, 2) associate God with Jesus Christ through the double naming of "God and Father" with "Lord" to refer to Jesus.[2] John, "on the other hand," Letham goes on to comment, "sticks to the terms that Jesus used" in John's gospel—"Father/God and the Son/Jesus Christ (1 John 1:1–2:1), the Father and the Son (1 John 2:22–24), and God and his Son (1 John 5:20)." Second John also repeats this naming scheme (2 John 3, 9). Jude twice refers to God/the Father and the Lord/Jesus Christ (Jude 1, 4), while at the end of the letter he "addresses his doxology to God our Savior through Jesus Christ our Lord (Jude 24–25)."[3] All of these patterns clearly couple the name "God," typically used in association with "the Father," and the name "Lord," typically used in association with "Jesus Christ," thus associating the divine name of God with the name of God's incarnate Son, Jesus Christ.

Likewise, the Spirit's naming in the General Epistles indicates his shared divinity with the Father and the Son. In 1 Peter 1:11 he is "the Spirit of Christ," thus associating his identity, his nature, with the nature of the incarnate Son.[4] Indeed, throughout the first chapter of Peter's first letter, the Holy Spirit is included in a triadic pattern. Again, quoting Letham,

> Peter's introduction to his first letter is triadic. He calls his recipients "elect exiles . . . according to the foreknowledge of God the Father, in the sanctification of the Spirit, for the obedience of Jesus Christ" (1 Peter 1:1–2). His first main paragraph has a triadic structure, referring to the God and Father of our Lord Jesus Christ (v. 3), Jesus Christ (vv. 3ff.), and the Spirit of Christ and the Holy Spirit (vv. 11–12).[5]

As we will see below, this triadic naming pattern links not only the names of Father, Son, and Spirit but also their actions.

Divine Actions

As we have seen in previous chapters, the primary actions associated with divinity and attributed to the Son and Spirit along with the Father are creation and redemption. This pattern continues in the General Epistles, and espe-

2. Letham, *The Holy Trinity*, 54.
3. Letham, *The Holy Trinity*, 54.
4. For the implications of this phrase with respect to the eternal relations of origin, see Steven J. Duby, *Jesus and the God of Classical Theism: Biblical Christology in Light of the Doctrine of God* (Grand Rapids: Baker Academic, 2022), 194–95 as well as the surrounding section. See also Letham, *The Holy Trinity*, 61.
5. Letham, *The Holy Trinity*, 67.

cially with respect to Jesus. In the opening paragraph of Hebrews,[6] the writer identifies Jesus as the one "through whom" God created the world (Heb. 1:2) and the one who "upholds the universe by the word of his power" (Heb. 1:3).[7] Hebrews 1:10–11 is perhaps even more explicit than this, since here the author quotes Psalm 102:25–27 in reference to Jesus:[8]

> Of old you laid the foundation of the earth in the beginning,
> and the heavens are the work of your hands;
> they will perish, but you remain;
> they will all wear out like a garment,
> You will change them like a robe, and they will pass away,
> But you are the same,
> and your years have no end.

Here, the Son is the one who creates the entire world *and* who is eternal ("But you are the same, and your years will have no end").[9] We should also note that, in this text, the writer names the Son "Lord" (*kyrios*), and in the OT text the term "Lord" (*kyrios*) is clearly a reference to YHWH, God himself. This gives further credence to the idea that when we see "Lord" used as a name for Jesus in the NT, it is no mere honorific—it is an indication of his shared divinity with the Father and the Spirit. Thus Hebrews 1:11–12, in applying Psalm 102:25–27 to the Son, attributes to the Son divine actions (creation), divine attributes (eternality), and divine appellations ("Lord").

Peter also attributes salvation to the Son and does so by naming him both "God" and "Savior" in 2 Peter 1:1.[10] As we saw in the last chapter, "Since salvation is a work of God himself," the use of the title "Savior" and attribution of salvation to the work of the Son "implicitly attributes deity to him."[11] Notice also that Peter uses two divine names for Jesus in this same sentence: "God" and "Savior."

The Holy Spirit is also described in the General Epistles as performing divine actions, namely revealing who God is to humanity. This is described in various ways and especially in both Peter's and John's letters. In 1 Peter

---

6. On the Trinitarian character of the opening chapter of Hebrews, see C. Kavin Rowe, "The Trinity in the Letters of St Paul and Hebrews," in *The Oxford Handbook on the Trinity*, ed. Gilles Emery and Matthew Levering (Oxford: Oxford University Press, 2011), 45–47.
7. Letham, *The Holy Trinity*, 44.
8. Letham, *The Holy Trinity*, 42.
9. Or, to put it as Jamieson and Wittman do, "He is intrinsically superior to angels *as their creator and sustainer* (Heb. 1:3, 10–12)" (emphasis added). R. B. Jamieson and Tyler R. Wittman, *Biblical Reasoning: Christological and Trinitarian Rules for Exegesis* (Grand Rapids: Baker Academic, 2022), 174.
10. Letham, *The Holy Trinity*, 46.
11. Letham, *The Holy Trinity*, 46.

1:11–12, it is "the Spirit of Christ," also called "the Holy Spirit" in the same passage, who first gives to the OT prophets the predictions and prophecies concerning the coming of Israel's Messiah and then is given to the church to preach "the good news" of the gospel at Christ's advent. Similarly, in 2 Peter 1:16–21 Peter concludes his teaching on the superiority of the prophetic word by stating that "no prophecy was ever produced by the will of man, but men spoke from God as they were carried along by the Holy Spirit." Prophecy is closely connected to God's divine knowledge, in that the future is only known by God and thus can only be revealed to creatures by God (Isa. 46:9–10). For the Spirit to give prophecy to the OT prophets, then, is an indication of his divine knowledge and therefore of his divine nature.[12] In the Johannine Epistles the Spirit performs a related function in that he and he alone (as the Third Person of the one God) distinguishes truth from error (1 John 4:1–6) and testifies to our true knowledge of the Son whom the Father has sent (1 John 4:13–15; 1 John 5:6–12).[13] The gift of revelation, particularly in prophecy, can only be given by God who reveals himself, and only God can give us the gift of discernment between good and evil, truth and error. Peter and John attribute these divine activities particularly to the Holy Spirit.

Divine Attributes

As with the Pauline Epistles, the Son's preexistence is the primary way that the General Epistles attribute divine attributes to the Son. We have already seen this in Hebrews 1:2–3, where the Son is the one "through whom" God creates all things. In 1 Peter 1:20, Christ is "foreknown before the foundation of the world," which in context is more likely a reference to his preexistence than it is to simple divine foreknowledge of his existence in time. More explicitly, John makes plain the preexistence of Christ in the prologue of his first letter and especially through its connections to similar affirmations in the fourth gospel.[14]

Divine Adoration

Finally, the Son and Spirit receive worship reserved for God alone and alongside the Father in the General Epistles. To return to a passage we've already considered multiple times, Hebrews 1:2–3 says that the Son shares in the glory of the Father and is in fact the "exact representation of his being." This is a relational statement as well, but for now it is simply important to note that the Father and Son possess the same glory and therefore deserve the same worship. In 2 Peter 3:18 Peter concludes his second letter with a very clear benediction directed to Christ, and which also attributes divine names to

12. Letham, *The Holy Trinity*, 67.
13. Letham, *The Holy Trinity*, 67.
14. On each of these passages, see Letham, *The Holy Trinity*, 48.

Christ ("God" and "Savior"): "But grow in the grace and knowledge of our Lord and Savior Jesus Christ. To him be the glory both now and to the day of eternity. Amen."[15] To state the obvious, Peter ascribes glory directly to the incarnate Son in this text.

Two other texts are worth mentioning here. First, in Hebrews 1:6, the writer cites two texts at once, Deuteronomy 32:43 (LXX) and Psalm 97:7: "All angels are to worship him." This is a remarkable statement in that both OT texts are clearly referring to YHWH, who alone should receive worship. It is also remarkable in that both OT texts are intended to place all other "gods" under YHWH's feet. Given the OT's, and especially Deuteronomy's, insistence on exclusive worship of YHWH (Deut. 6:1–4), the writer of Hebrews attribution of this to the Son is incredible. The only explanation is that the Son is YHWH just as the Father who sent him is.[16] Finally, Jude 20–21 directs believers to "pray in the Holy Spirit." As we saw in the last chapter regarding the term "*maranatha*," to pray was and is an act of worship, and so to pray to, or, in this case, "in," a person is to consider them divine and to worship them in prayer.[17]

Divine Relations

In addition to these markers of divine identity, we also find in the General Epistles texts that indicate God's eternal relations of origin. First, to return yet again to Hebrews 1:3 and also to recall what we said in the last chapter about Colossians 1:15, the term "image" or "exact representation" serves both to affirm the Son's full divinity and to distinguish the Son from the Father. The Son as "image" means that the Son is God in relation to the Father, and vice versa. Other language of divine relation occurs regarding the Spirit in the General Epistles. The Father sends, or gives, the Holy Spirit, both in the Petrine (1 Peter 1:12) and Johannine (1 John 3:21–24) Epistles.[18] As we saw in the chapter on the gospel of John, the language of giving or sending is an indication of divine missions, which in turn reveal the eternal processions in the inner life of God. The Spirit who is sent by the Father in the economy of redemption is the same Spirit who proceeds from the Father and the Son in his eternal relation.

Summary

As we have seen in previous chapters, the General Epistles affirm that Father, Son, and Holy Spirit are each equally God. They each share the same divine attributes, appellations, actions, and adoration, and they are the one God together via the eternal relations of origin. While not possessing this later sys-

---

15. Letham, *The Holy Trinity*, 46–47.
16. Letham, *The Holy Trinity*, 42.
17. Letham, *The Holy Trinity*, 67.
18. Letham, *The Holy Trinity*, 67.

tematic language, they each contribute biblical teaching that is the source of this Trinitarian grammar.

REFLECTION QUESTIONS

1. How does the doctrine of the Trinity help you read the General Epistles well, both theologically and spiritually?
2. What are ways that the General Epistles' talk of the Trinity helps your prayer life?
3. How does the General Epistles' teaching on the Trinity remind you of the ways in which the OT speaks about the triune God?
4. What is a passage in the General Epistles that has confused you but now seems clearer based on thinking through its teaching on the Trinity?
5. What are one or two "go-to" texts for teaching the Trinity in the General Epistles?

QUESTION 10

What Does the Book of Revelation Teach Us About the Trinity?

Revelation joins and culminates the biblical chorus about the triune God. John's description of God as the one God of Israel who exists as Father, Son, and Holy Spirit echoes and builds on the rest of the biblical witness's description. Revelation, like the rest of the Bible, affirms that there is one and only one God, the God of Israel, YHWH. And again, like the rest of the Bible, John affirms that this one true God exists in three persons, each fully God and distinct from one another. Further, the Apocalypse uses the language of divine identity and divine relations to do so, as we have seen in other parts of Scripture. As Brandon Smith puts it,

> It is clear from the text that John grappled with the implications of Jesus's and the Holy Spirit's relationship to YHWH, and in the end he does not hesitate to apply divine titles and characteristics of YHWH to the Son and Spirit, nor does he downplay clear worship of the persons even as they stand next to God.[1]

Divine Identity

John uses the same strategies of applying divine attributes, actions, appellations, and adoration to the Son and Spirit alongside the Father. He also utilizes relational language to identify Father, Son, and Holy Spirit as equally divine and as the three persons of the one God. We begin with aspects of divine identity.

1. Brandon D. Smith, *The Trinity in the Book of Revelation: Seeing Father, Son, and Holy Spirit in John's Apocalypse*, Studies in Christian Doctrine and Scripture (Downers Grove, IL: IVP Academic, 2022), 31.

Divine Attributes

As with Paul and the General Epistles, John primarily applies preexistence to the Son in terms of divine attributes. In Revelation 1:17, for instance, Jesus appears to John and tells him, "I am the first and the last." The language of "first" is indicative of preexistence, someone who "comes before" all things.[2] Heightening this interpretation is the fact that the phrase is also connected to both divine worship ("I fell at his feet as though dead") and divine names in Revelation, namely "Alpha and Omega," both of which we will explore below. For now, it is important to note that "first and the last" is used with both "Alpha and Omega" and "beginning (*archē*) and the end" by Jesus to refer to himself in Revelation 22:13. This is another indication that Jesus means "first and the last" in both instances to indicate preexistence.[3]

Revelation 3:14 also indicates preexistence. Here Jesus refers to himself as "the beginning of God's creation."[4] While this may sound like it posits creaturehood to Jesus, the Greek word for "beginning" (*archē*) simply means "That which is first," and that primacy can be "either in time or in rank and authority."[5] Shifting the interpretive balance toward "authority" is that masculine form of the noun (*archōn*), which carries the "basic meaning" of "'ruler,' 'lord,' or 'prince'"[6] and is used of Jesus in Revelation 1:5 ("ruler of the kings of the earth"). Jesus is thus in Revelation 3:14 the "beginning" of God's creation in the sense of being its head, or ruler, associating the temporal aspect of "beginning" with Christ's rule over creation rather than with him having been created in time. Either way, if he is the "first" of creation, at the very least he existed prior to his incarnation, and being head over creation ought to be understood as indicating that he was not yet another created being, first among equals, but creation's head as the Creator.

Likewise, the Son's divine authority is emphasized in at least three other ways throughout the book. First, he has the authority to judge in Revelation. We will see this in his actions as well, but in terms of possessing attributes, it is the Son specifically who has the "book of life" (Rev. 3:5; 13:8; 17:8). This is an indication of his authority over the last judgment.[7] Similarly, the Son's being seated on the throne (5:1–14; cf. also 20:11–15, especially in connection to the "book of life") is an indication of his divine authority, specifically his authority to judge the living and the dead.[8] Finally, in Revelation 1:10–11 Jesus is said

---

2. Robert Letham, *The Holy Trinity: In Scripture, History, Theology, and Worship* (Phillipsburg, NJ: P&R, 2004), 48
3. Letham, *The Holy Trinity*, 48.
4. Letham, *The Holy Trinity*, 48.
5. Randall Merrill, "Authority," in *Lexham Theological Wordbook*, ed. Douglas Mangum et al., Lexham Bible Reference Series (Bellingham, WA: Lexham, 2014).
6. Merrill, "Authority."
7. Smith, *The Trinity in the Book of Revelation*, 108.
8. Smith, *The Trinity in the Book of Revelation*, 112–24.

to have "a voice like a trumpet," mostly likely an allusion to YHWH's voice to Israel in Exodus 19:16. Bolstering this connection is the fact that John, Israel (Exod. 20:18), and Moses (Deut. 7:11) "see" God's voice in these passages.[9]

The Spirit is also seen possessing divine attributes in Revelation, namely through his ability to enable John's visions, particularly his vision of divine worship in the throne room of God. As Smith notes,

> The fact that the Spirit is enabling the vision of this center of worship indicates the Spirit's divine power and authority to bring John into the "throne room" where God dwells and where worship is received. Put another way, John's emphasis is not about the Spirit as the *means* of a trance or heavenly transportation but the Spirit's *mediation* into the divine presence, which, in combination with the Son's place on the throne, lends itself towards a Trinitarian understanding of the Spirit.[10]

Only God can reveal God, and it is the Spirit who does so in Revelation.

Divine Actions

In Revelation, one of the most important indicators of the Son's equality with the Father in terms of divinity is that prophecy comes from Jesus. In both the introduction (1:1–16) and also the letters to the churches (1:17–3:22), the Word of God comes directly from the mouth of the incarnate, ascended Lord.[11] As Smith notes, the purpose of the book of Revelation is to *reveal* who God is and what he has done in Christ, and this task is proper to God alone.[12]

We also find Jesus exercising judgment throughout the book. This is one of the primary indicators of his divine authority and thus of his divine nature. In Revelation 2:18 Jesus introduces himself as "the Son of God" and uses phrases from Daniel's Ancient of Days to describe himself. He then goes on to say in verse 23 that, regarding Jezebel, he "will strike her children dead" (*kai ta tekna autēs apoktenō en thanatō*). As Smith notes, "The Greek phrase [*apoktenō en thanatō*] ['strike dead' or 'kill'] compares to Ezekiel 33:27 (LXX), which is followed by the phrase 'and they will know that I am the Lord' (Ezek 33:29 LXX)." In other words, Jesus's indication that he will "strike dead" the followers of Jezebel is an example of his status as the divine Judge.[13] Similarly, Jesus's authority to open the seals of judgment in Revelation 6:15–17[14] and the

9. Smith, *The Trinity in the Book of Revelation*, 99.
10. Smith, *The Trinity in the Book of Revelation*, 167–68.
11. Letham, *The Holy Trinity*, 47; Smith, *The Trinity in the Book of Revelation*, 91.
12. Smith, 93–96.
13. Smith *The Trinity in the Book of Revelation*, 106–7.
14. Smith, *The Trinity in the Book of Revelation*, 130.

statement that "he judges in righteousness" show his divine status as the Judge of the universe and therefore his ontological equality with God the Father.[15]

Regarding the Holy Spirit, it is he who guides John through the vision, and who is thus the agent of Jesus's Revelation to John. As we saw with the Son above, revealing God's person and work is proper to God alone, and so the Spirit is performing divine activity when he personally reveals and guides John through the vision given by Jesus.[16]

Divine Appellations

Divine naming of the Son is frequent in Revelation. The phrase "Alpha and Omega" is an indication of the Son's eternality and also used in conjunction with the Father.[17] Similarly, the term "Almighty" appears to be used by the Son to refer to himself in Revelation 1:8. This term is also probably an allusion to the Tetragrammaton (YHWH), and, if so, is one of if not the most explicit case of Jesus being referred to—and, in fact, referring to himself as—the God of Israel by name.[18] The names "the holy one" (Rev. 3:7)[19] and "Lord of lords and King of kings" (17:14)[20] are also phrases that indicate the divine status (and thus divine nature) of the incarnate Son. The name "seven spirits" for the Holy Spirit is also an indication of the Spirit's divinity. The number seven is known to represent perfection in antiquity, and so this is one way to indicate not just any spirit but the perfect Spirit, namely the Spirit who is God.[21]

In addition to the individual names for Father, Son, and Spirit in Revelation, there are also a number of triadic patterns in the book. One such pattern is found in Revelation 1:4–5:

> John to the seven churches that are in Asia:
>
> Grace to you and peace from him who is and who was and who is to come, and from the seven spirits who are before his throne, and from Jesus Christ the faithful witness, the firstborn of the dead, and the ruler of kings on earth.

As Letham notes, this triadic formula links directly the Father ("him who is and who was and who is to come"), the Spirit ("the seven spirits who are

---

15. Smith, *The Trinity in the Book of Revelation*, 125–26.
16. Smith, *The Trinity in the Book of Revelation*, 151–52.
17. See the discussion in Smith, *The Trinity in the Book of Revelation*, 94.
18. Smith, *The Trinity in the Book of Revelation*, 97–99.
19. Smith, *The Trinity in the Book of Revelation*, 108–9.
20. Smith, *The Trinity in the Book of Revelation*, 128–30.
21. Smith, *The Trinity in the Book of Revelation*, 151–65. See also Richard Bauckham, *The Theology of the Book of Revelation*, New Testament Theology (Cambridge: Cambridge University Press, 1993), 110.

before the throne"), and the Son ("Jesus Christ the faithful witness, the firstborn from the dead, and the ruler of kings on earth"). John beginning with "Grace to you and peace from . . ." and linking it to each of those names lends credence to the idea that each of these persons is divine.[22] That opening phrase is used elsewhere in the NT, and especially by Paul, in reference to greetings from God himself. It is typically articulated as "Grace to you and peace from God our Father and from the Lord Jesus Christ."[23] Thus Revelation contains one of the most explicit Trinitarian formulations in the Bible in this opening greeting to the seven churches in Asia.

Divine Adoration

Finally, both the Son and the Spirit, along with the Father, receive divine adoration in Revelation. For instance, in the verses immediately following the ones quoted above, the Son is ascribed "glory and dominion forever and ever" (Rev. 1:6).[24] Perhaps even more explicit is Revelation 5:8–10, in which the Son is worshiped both in action (falling down, praying; Rev. 5:8–9) and in word ("Worthy are you," Rev. 5:10).[25] In Revelation 14:14 the Son is seen "seated on the cloud one like a son of man, with a golden crown on his head, and a sharp sickle in his hand." This occurs after he is seen receiving worship from the 144,000 in Revelation 14:1–5 and is also most likely an allusion to Isaiah 19:1 where YHWH is depicted seated on his throne.[26] He also receives priestly acts of worship in Revelation 20:6,[27] and John prays to him in Revelation 22:20.[28]

Divine Relations

The above picture gives plenty of evidence that the persons mentioned, Father, Son, and Spirit, are who they are in relation to one another. One of the most obvious examples of this is in Revelation 3:1–6, in which Jesus begins his letter to Sardis by saying, "And to the angel of the church in Sardis write: 'The words of him who has the seven spirits of God and the seven stars.'" It is clear from this text that Jesus possesses both the Spirit ("the seven spirits of God") and the angels ("the seven stars"). But this is not to equate the Spirit with the angels, since at the end of the letter Jesus says to Sardis, "He who

22. Letham, *The Holy Trinity*, 67–68.
23. On the connection between Revelation's epistolary opening and the other NT epistles, see Matthew Y. Emerson, *Christ and the New Creation: A Canonical Approach to the Theology of the New Testament* (Eugene, OR: Wipf & Stock, 2014), 143–44.
24. Smith, *The Trinity in the Book of Revelation*, 102–3.
25. On the Trinitarian character of Revelation 4–5, in addition to Smith's work, see Scott R. Swain, *The Trinity and the Bible: On Theological Interpretation* (Bellingham, WA: Lexham Academic, 2021), 97–120.
26. Smith, *The Trinity in the Book of Revelation*, 104.
27. Smith, *The Trinity in the Book of Revelation*, 134.
28. Smith, *The Trinity in the Book of Revelation*, 46–47.

has an ear, let him hear what the Spirit says to the churches." The angels do not speak God's Word to the churches but deliver it. The Spirit, on the other hand, speaks God's revelation to God's people. Thus the "and" of verse 1 is not epexegetical (thus making "the seven spirits of God" synonymous with "the seven stars") but merely conjunctive (thus distinguishing "the seven spirits of God" from "the seven stars"); Jesus possesses the Spirit eternally by virtue of their eternal relations of origin, and he possesses the angels by virtue of his creation in time of them.[29]

Summary

Revelation ends the canon with clear Trinitarian teaching, both in its narrative and in its declarations about who God is. Father, Son, and Spirit are together and in equal measure the one God who was and is and is to come. Each does what only God does, is named with names that only God has, possesses attributes which only God possesses, and is worshiped as only God deserves. And they are God in relation to one another: The Son is the Son of the Father, and the Spirit is the Spirit of the Father and the Son. Revelation thus provides a fitting end to the Bible, not only in terms of its conclusion to the biblical narrative but also with respect to its Trinitarian doctrine.

REFLECTION QUESTIONS

1. When you think about the book of Revelation, what is the first doctrine that comes to mind? If it's not the Trinity, how does the doctrine you thought of relate to the doctrine of the Trinity in Revelation?

2. What are ways that John's talk of the Trinity helps your prayer life?

3. How does Revelation's teaching on the Trinity remind you of the ways in which the OT speaks about the triune God?

4. What is a passage in Revelation that has confused you but now seems clearer based on thinking through its teaching on the Trinity?

5. What are one or two "go-to" texts for teaching the Trinity in Revelation?

---

29. Smith, *The Trinity in the Book of Revelation*, 107–8.

QUESTION 11

What Does the Old Testament Teach Us About the Trinity?

It might seem odd to end our exploration of the biblical data about the Trinity with the Old Testament. In the history of salvation, the progress of revelation, and, of course, the order of canonical writing, the OT comes first. And, we should hasten to add, the whole Bible, including the OT, is a Trinitarian book—written by the triune God to reveal himself and his saving work to his people. There is more to say in this regard, but here the point is that placing the chapter on the OT after the chapters on the NT is not an indication of its theological importance or revelatory character. The OT teaches the Trinity because it reveals the Trinity and is written by the Trinity.

The Old Testament Is a Trinitarian Text

In the progress of revelation and the history of salvation, though, God most clearly and fully reveals himself as Father, Son, and Spirit in the person and work of the incarnate Son, Jesus Christ, sent by the Father and anointed and empowered by the Holy Spirit. Thus, when we read the OT as Christians, we do so with this Trinitarian lens already in place. We have, as Christians, already put our faith and trust in this triune God, the one who saved us through coming for us in the person of Jesus, God the Son in human flesh. We do not "turn off" our faith when we read the OT. Instead, we are, by our very nature as Christians, Trinitarian readers.

But as we read in Trinitarian fashion, we do so as those who already understand how the OT's promises have been fulfilled in Christ. This is a fundamentally different scenario than the original audience. Israel waited with expectation for the person and time of the Messiah to be revealed (1 Peter 1:10–14), whereas we now know that Jesus, God the Son in the flesh, is the long-awaited Savior of Israel and the world. This latter knowledge, which creates the lens by which we read the OT, is given to us by the NT. So, to come back to where we started, we don't start with the NT in Trinitarian discussions because it is better than the OT, or because it reveals the Trinity and the OT doesn't. It is simply because what is promised in the OT has already been revealed to us in the NT, and we cannot help but read with that lens in place.

With these foundational commitments in mind, we'll explore how the OT reveals the Trinity to us. They fit with what we say about Scripture and the Trinity in other chapters, including the chapters on the Trinity in the NT and the chapter on how early Christians read the Bible in Trinitarian fashion. In what follows, we will explore these similar textual features under two categories: Trinitarian pressure points and exegetical examples.

Trinitarian Pressure Points

We could proceed by working through the categories we reference elsewhere: the full divinity of each of the three divine persons as seen through their shared attributes, actions, appellations, and adoration; the relational identity of the persons seen through prosopological exegesis; and distinguishing between Christ's human and divine natures seen through partitive exegesis. But these reading strategies are primarily used by the early church to prove that the already revealed Christ is fully God and that his Spirit is also fully God. Since we already confess this reality as Christians, this kind of "apologetic" strategy is secondary to reading the OT as it is intended to be read—as the revelation of the triune God, Yahweh, the God of Israel. So, instead of retreading the formula used in our chapters on the NT, we will here show that there are already Trinitarian pressure points in the OT,[1] pushing readers to see that the God of Israel, Yahweh, the one and only true God, exists in three persons.[2]

An example of this pressure comes in Daniel 7. In this passage we first encounter the Ancient of Days sitting on his throne (vv. 9–10), judging the monstrous, bestial rulers who wreak havoc on the earth (vv. 1–8). In his judgment he casts down these wicked beasts and destroys the leader, demonstrating his total dominion and authority (vv. 11–12). In the next two verses, though, we are introduced to another figure, "one like the Son of Man," who is given by

---

1. The language of "pressure" in relation to the biblical data and Trinitarian hermeneutics is most notably attributed to C. Kavin Rowe in his seminal essay, "Biblical Pressure and Trinitarian Hermeneutics," *Pro Ecclesia* 11 (2002): 295–312.
2. For a fuller treatment of the Trinity in the Old Testament, see Heath A. Thomas, "Old Testament," in *The Trinity in the Canon: A Biblical, Theological, Historical, and Practical Proposal*, ed. Brandon D. Smith (Nashville: B&H Academic, 2023), 61–82. See also Christopher Seitz, "The Trinity in the Old Testament," in *The Oxford Handbook on the Trinity*, ed. Gilles Emery and Matthew Levering (Oxford: Oxford University Press, 2011), 28–40. Seitz has also reflected on the Trinitarian character of the OT elsewhere. See, most notably and recently, his *The Elder Testament: Canon, Theology, Trinity* (Waco, TX: Baylor University Press, 2021).

the Ancient of Days "dominion and glory and a kingdom." And this is not just creaturely dominion or glory or kingdom but "an everlasting dominion" and indestructible kingdom—that is, the kind of dominion and kingdom that only God, the Ancient of Days, possesses. To press the connection between the Son of Man and the Ancient of Days even further, Daniel 7:27 says, "the kingdom and the dominion and the greatness of the kingdoms under the whole heaven shall be given to the people of the saints of the Most High; his kingdom shall be an everlasting kingdom, and all dominions shall serve and obey him." The kind of language used about the Son of Man in verses 13–14 is now used about the Most High, or Ancient of Days, in verse 27. What was conceptually connected in verses 9–10 and 13–14 is now linguistically connected in verse 27. The Son of Man possesses the same dominion and kingdom and therefore sits on the same throne as the Ancient of Days, the Most High, and yet he is also distinct from the Ancient of Days (v. 13, "the Son of Man . . . was presented before him").

The same kind of unity and distinction is found in another Trinitarian pressure point, Psalm 110:1. Here, David begins the psalm with this line: "The LORD says to my Lord: 'Sit at my right hand, until I make your enemies your footstool.'" Here David's God, *Yahweh* (LORD), addresses David's God, *Adonai* (my Lord), and also gives him authority ("Sit at my right hand") and dominion ("until I make your enemies a footstool"). Once again we see unity of divinity, both in terms of shared names and shared authority, but also distinction in both speech and order.

Another text that may provide Trinitarian pressure is Genesis 1.[3] Normally when we think about this topic in relation to the Bible's opening chapter, we point to the phrase "let us make man in our image, after our likeness" (Gen. 1:26). This is a highly contested claim among biblical scholars these days, and many do not believe that phrase is warrant for a Trinitarian reading. Regardless of how we take Genesis 1:26, though, there are other ways in which Genesis 1 provides Trinitarian pressure. For instance, already in verse 2 we see a distinction between God and the Spirit of God. The latter is not subordinated ontologically or functionally in the text. Instead, the Spirit is active ("hovered") and present as God creates. We could also discuss what it means for God to create through something distinct from him—his words. But even though the text distinguishes between God and his words, these words still are the agent by which God brings forth his creation. What does it mean for God to be distinct from his Spirit and his words, but for his Spirit and his words to be present with him at and bring forth his creation? This is the kind of question that is caused by Trinitarian pressure points in the OT.

3. On a Trinitarian reading of Genesis 1, see Francis Watson, *Text, Church, and World: Biblical Interpretation in Theological Perspective* (Grand Rapids: Eerdmans, 1994), 137–53.

Exegetical Examples

In addition to the Trinitarian character of the OT as a whole and certain Trinitarian pressure points, there are also specific exegetical examples of Trinitarian texts. Here we will discuss three of those, but, as with Trinitarian pressure points, this is not exhaustive or comprehensive. Our first example comes from the book of Psalms.[4] In the introduction to the book, Psalms 1–2, the psalmist portrays a wise man who delights in God's law and does not walk in the way of the wicked (Ps. 1). This man is also portrayed as God's Son, his king who rules the nations and breaks those who resist him with a rod of iron (Ps. 2). These opening psalms are eschatological in that they are looking for a wise man dwelling with God in a garden who also rules over all the nations—a man who doesn't exist yet, as is evident from Psalm 3 (and Ps. 78, and a host of other psalms). This eschatological outlook remains throughout the rest of the book, as seen, for example, in the royal psalm that ends Book 2 (Ps. 72) and the resurrection psalm that ends Book 3 (Ps. 89). But the climax of the book of Psalms comes at the end of Book 5 (Pss. 146–150). Using the same language Psalms 1–2 use to describe the wise king who will rule the nations, Psalms 146–150 describe Yahweh himself ruling the nations, breaking them with a rod of iron. Elsewhere, I (Matt) have put it like this:

> In these final psalms, it is YHWH who executes justice (Ps. 146:7; cf. 72:1–2), who loves the righteous (146:8; cf. 1:6) and destroys the wicked (Ps. 145:20; cf. Ps. 1:6), who calls kings and peoples of the earth to praise him (148:11; cf. 2:1, 2, 10, 11), who is praised in his sanctuary, on his holy hill, in all his holiness (150:1; cf. 2:6). Notice that, *in these texts, what the Son of God* will *do in Psalm 2,* namely rule over the kings and peoples of the earth with justice and holiness on the holy hill of YHWH, *is what YHWH* is doing *in Pss. 145–150.* In other words, *the Son is YHWH himself, the LORD's presence on earth.*[5]

---

4. The following is a summary of the teaching of Dr. Robert L. Cole, formerly of Southeastern Baptist Theological Seminary. Many of the exegetical insights can be found in the following: Robert L. Cole, *Psalms 1–2: Gateway to the Psalter*, Hebrew Bible Monographs (Sheffield: Sheffield Phoenix, 2013); Robert L. Cole, *The Shape and Message of Book III (Psalms 73–89)*, LHBOTS 307 (Sheffield: Sheffield Academic, 2000); and Robert L. Cole, *Why Psalm 23 Is Not about You: Reading Psalm 23 in Context*, 2nd ed. (Athens, GA: College & Clayton, 2020). If by chance one of these insights is not published in one of the books listed above, then I owe it either to (1) his Old Testament 2 course notes or (2) conversation and correspondence over the last sixteen years.
5. Matthew Y. Emerson, "Reading the Psalms Theologically: Part II," *Credo Magazine*, January 25, 2021, https://credomag.com/2021/01/reading-the-psalms-theologically-part-ii/, emphasis original.

The psalms have a Trinitarian shape, or order, to them, where God's Son in Psalms 1–2 does what Yahweh does in Psalms 146–150.

Another example of Trinitarian exegesis comes from Proverbs 8:22–31. In this text, Lady Wisdom describes herself as having been "brought forth" before creation (vv. 25–26), as being present with God as his "master workman" during creation (vv. 27–30), and as God's "delight" who rejoices in him daily (vv. 30–31). We will be necessarily brief here: There are two sets of choices for the identification of Lady Wisdom. First, she is either created in time or she is eternal (i.e., "brought forth" in v. 25), and second, she is either the personification of one of God's attributes or she is a metaphor for God the Son. Regarding the former, we can say simply that it makes no sense for God at any point to be without his Wisdom. If Wisdom is created in time in verse 25, then God does not possess all of his attributes from eternity. This is just nonsensical—especially with respect to wisdom!

That leaves us the question of exactly who Lady Wisdom is in Proverbs 8. Is she merely a personification of one of God's attributes, or is she a metaphorical depiction of God the Son? Although this question remains debated, I lean heavily toward the latter interpretation, for a number of reasons. First, and perhaps most importantly, Paul says in 1 Corinthians 1:24 that Christ *is* the wisdom and power of God. Who else could this be besides the preincarnate Son? Second, the poem distinguishes between God and his Wisdom over and over again. Wisdom is next to, is the delight of, and is brought forth by God. This proverb of Solomon is obviously making a personal distinction between Yahweh and Yahweh's Wisdom. Finally, the term "brought forth" in verse 25 has to mean something in this scenario where Wisdom is eternal. What else can it mean in that case besides the fact that God the Father eternally begets God the Son, his Wisdom? This interpretation has a long and important history in the development of Nicene Trinitarianism, and, more importantly, makes the most sense out of the text.[6] In Proverbs 8:22–31, then, we have another exegetical example of reading the OT in Trinitarian fashion.

A final example comes from the names used in the OT, and specifically the name, "Spirit of the LORD." Much like Wisdom in Proverbs 8, this name for the Holy Spirit—used throughout the OT—indicates a distinction between God and his Spirit. Once again, like with Wisdom in Proverbs 8, we do not want to interpret this as God having "parts" or some entity outside of himself. Instead, we see this name as relational, and namely indicating a relation between God and God's Spirit. This kind of relational naming will be

6. On reading Proverbs 8 in Trinitarian fashion, see Matthew Y. Emerson, "The Role of Proverbs 8: Eternal Generation and Hermeneutics Ancient and Modern," in *Retrieving Eternal Generation*, ed. Fred Sanders and Scott R. Swain (Grand Rapids: Zondervan Academic, 2017), 44–66.

picked up later in the NT, and especially by the apostle Paul, to reference both the singular Godhead and his tripersonal nature.[7]

Summary

The OT reveals the same God as the NT—the one and only God, the God of Israel, Yahweh, who exists in three persons: Father, Son, and Holy Spirit. While the revelation of this one God is most fully seen in the person and work of Jesus Christ, sent by his Father and anointed by his Spirit, the OT does not reveal a different God or only one person of the triune God, but the whole Trinity. It does so by indicating that God is who he is as being-in-relation. He possesses both Word/Wisdom and Spirit, equal to him yet distinct from him.

REFLECTION QUESTIONS

1. Do you read the OT references to God as referring to the Trinity? Why or why not?
2. How has this chapter supported, challenged, or changed the way you read the OT's references to God?
3. What are ways that the OT's talk of the Trinity helps your prayer life?
4. What is a passage in the OT that has confused you but now seems clearer based on thinking through its teaching on the Trinity?
5. What are one or two "go-to" texts for teaching the Trinity in the OT?

---

7. See Wesley Hill, *Paul and the Trinity: Persons, Relations, and the Pauline Letters* (Grand Rapids: Eerdmans, 2015).

PART 3

The Trinity in Christian History

SECTION A

The Trinity in the Early Christian and Medieval Periods

QUESTION 12

What Did Second- and Third-Century Christians Believe About the Trinity?

During the first two centuries of the church's post-apostolic existence, the doctrine of the Trinity was implied but not yet fully articulated. Words like *homoousios* ("same essence") and *hypostasis* ("person") were not used in theological writing about God (or at least not in a way that was agreed upon by all Christians). Nevertheless, what we find in the second and third centuries are theologians who begin to build the framework for what will later become Nicene Trinitarianism, and they do so by interpreting the biblical data that teaches Nicene Trinitarianism.

The Apostolic Fathers

In the second century AD, the first one hundred years or so after the New Testament was completed and the last apostle, John, died, Christian leaders primarily focused on exhorting their congregations to faithfulness in the midst of temptation and persecution. Christians faced pressure from both Jewish and Greco-Roman opponents to turn away from faith in the risen Christ. Pastors, bishops, and leaders like Ignatius, Polycarp, and Clement urged their readers to remain steadfast in their hope in God through his work of salvation in the person of Jesus Christ by the power of his Spirit. While these exhortations vary in impetus and in strategy, they all have that ultimate goal in common. Whether the temptation is to apostatize in the face of Roman imperial or local governmental persecution or to turn back to Jewish dietary restrictions or to give in to Greco-Roman cultural norms related to religion, sex, class, and money, each of these writings reminds readers that they have been redeemed through Jesus's death and resurrection and therefore should remain faithful to him.

In the midst of these exhortations, the writers use language that relies on biblical patterns and that also provides the building blocks for what will later become Nicene orthodoxy. Specifically, they speak of the Father, Son, and Holy Spirit in ways that place them squarely on the divine side of the Creator/creature divide, and in similar ways and using similar categories to what we have already seen in the biblical data. For instance, in 1 Clement both the Holy Spirit and Jesus are identified as the speaker of OT texts—words from Israel's God, YHWH, to his people. In 1 Clement 13:1, it is the Holy Spirit who speaks in Jeremiah 9:23–24 (cf. also 1 Sam. 2:10 LXX; 1 Cor. 1:31; 2 Cor. 10:17), and, in 1 Clement 22:1–7 Clement introduces a quotation of Psalm 34:11–17, 19 by saying that "[Christ] himself through the Holy Spirit thus calls us." In both instances, Clement identifies the Spirit and the Son, respectively, as the distinct personal agents of Scripture's words to Israel in the OT, and in the latter text it is the Son who speaks *through* the Spirit.

Clement also demonstrates adoration of the Son alongside the Father, ascribing to him glory and honor, as in 1 Clement 21:11–12: "All these things the great Creator and Master of the universe ordered . . . especially abundantly to us who have taken refuge in his compassionate mercies through our Lord Jesus Christ, to whom be the glory and the majesty for ever and ever. Amen."[1] We even find Trinitarian patterns of naming, as in 1 Clement 58:2: "For as God lives, and as the Lord Jesus Christ lives, and the Holy Spirit (who are the faith and the hope of the elect)."[2] These examples could be multiplied throughout the rest of the corpus known as the Apostolic Fathers.[3] For now, it is important simply to note that the earliest Christians in the post-apostolic period spoke of the Father, Son, and Holy Spirit in ways that mirror the biblical language and thus provide the framework for subsequent theological reflection.

The Apologists

When we come to the middle of the second century and the first half of the third century, we encounter a group known as the apologists. Typically, in historical theology, three apologists receive most of the attention: Justin Martyr, Irenaeus of Lyons, and Tertullian. Regarding Justin Martyr (100–165), his *First Apology* and *Second Apology* are written to defend Christianity against pagan detractors, while his *Dialogue with Trypho* is an apologetic directed toward Jewish opponents to the gospel. In the latter, Justin focuses on identifying Jesus as the object of OT prophecies and the speaker of OT texts. For

---

1. Citations from 1 Clement are from Michael W. Holmes, ed., *The Apostolic Fathers: Greek Texts and English Translations*, 3rd ed. (Grand Rapids: Baker Academic, 2007).
2. In Greek, this phrase even more clearly makes parallel the three persons through the combined use of the singular demonstrative participle in naming and the singular relative pronoun in the participial phrase at the end: ζῇ γὰρ ὁ θεὸς καὶ ζῇ ὁ κύριος Ἰησοῦς Χριστὸς καὶ τὸ πνεῦμα τὸ ἅγιον, ἥ τε πίστις ἡ ἐλπὶς τῶν ἐκλετῶν.
3. This is typically understood to include the letters of Ignatius and Polycarp, the Martyrdom of Polycarp, 1 and 2 Clement, the Epistle of Barnabas, the Epistle to Diognetus, the Didache, and the Shepherd of Hermas.

Justin, these are clear evidence that Jesus is not just another human being but the incarnate Son of God, sent from the Father. In the apologies, Justin argues against pagan philosophy, especially Stoicism. In each of these works and in his other writings, I (Luke) have said elsewhere:

> [Justin] represented a movement that has come to be known as Logos Christology. In confrontation with pagan philosophy (especially Stoic philosophy), Justin and other theologians such as Clement of Alexandria emphasized the Johannine notion of the Son's identity as the Logos, the eternal Word of the Father. The Stoics maintained that there is a universal principle of reason, the Logos, which permeates all of reality and gives to it its rational shape and purpose. In an apologetic maneuver, the Logos Christologians emphasized that this Logos is a distinct divine power, which is revealed in Jesus of Nazareth. Justin maintained that the Logos is eternally inseparable from the Father. He writes, "This power [the Word] is indivisible and inseparable from the Father, just as they say that the light of the sun on earth is indivisible and inseparable from the sun in the heavens" (*Dialogue with Trypho*, 128). There is reason to believe that, for Justin, the Logos is, in a sense, subordinate to the Father. Indeed, there are hints of subordinationism that run throughout the Fathers of the second and third centuries, tinges that will be erased and corrected in the fourth-century pro-Nicene doctrine. But for the present purposes, it is worth noting a principle that lays the groundwork for the more mature doctrine of the Trinity: the Father is never without his Word/Reason/Wisdom.[4]

This emphasis on Word and Wisdom brings us to another apologist of the era, Irenaeus of Lyon (c. 120–c. 200). Like Justin, Irenaeus labored to demonstrate that all of Scripture pointed to Christ, and he does so most particularly in *Demonstration of the Apostolic Preaching*. But he also, like Justin, labors against pagan opponents of Christianity. In his arguments against the Gnostics in *Against Heresies*, Irenaeus famously notes that the Son and Spirit are active in creation along with the Father, summarizing this Trinitarian work as the Father creating via his "two hands."[5] For Irenaeus, this image indicates both the divinity of the Son and Spirit—they create, something only God does—and the relational argument both for the Son's and Spirit's divinity and

---

4. R. Lucas Stamps, "The Trinity," in *Historical Theology for the Church*, ed. Jason G. Duesing and Nathan A. Finn (Nashville: B&H Academic, 2021), 49.
5. See, for instance, *Against Heresies* 4.20.1.

for the Trinity itself. The Father is never without his two hands, or, to recall Justin's language, his Word and Wisdom, indicating that the Father is who he is *in relation to* the Son and the Spirit. Likewise, because the Son and Spirit are the Father's hands, they are equal to him in essence *via their relation to him*. While this is not a full-fledged articulation of Nicene Trinitarianism (which would obviously be an anachronistic characterization), we do see how it provided a foundation for the later judgments of the fourth century.

Finally, Tertullian (c. 155–c. 240) provided important exegetical, theological, and conceptual foundations for the later judgments of Nicaea I and Constantinople I. As I (Luke) have noted elsewhere, Tertullian "is well-known for coining the term 'Trinity' (Latin, *Trinitas*) as well as the key Latin terms that would remain in use into the fourth century and beyond: God is one in substance (*substantia*) and three in persons (*personae*)," particularly in his work *Against Praxeas*."[6] Contra to his ideological opponent, who presented a kind of modalistic and monarchical view of God,[7] "Tertullian argued that there are indeed three distinct divine persons that can be detected in the biblical narrative: the persons are distinct but inseparable and inseverable."[8]

The Alexandrian

A final figure we need to mention in the second and third centuries is Origen of Alexandria (c. 185–c. 255). Origen was a prolific thinker and author, producing works of textual criticism, philosophy, hermeneutics, biblical commentary, and the first truly systematic theology. Regarding the latter, in his *On First Principles*, Origen very clearly articulates the doctrine of the eternal generation of the Son:

> And how can one, who has learnt to know and think piously about God, think or believe that the God and Father ever existed, even for a single moment, without begetting this Wisdom? For he would either say that God was unable to beget Wisdom before he begot her, so that afterwards he begot into being her who formerly did not exist, or else that he was able to but, what is impious even to say about God, unwilling to beget; both alternatives, as is patent to all, are absurd and impious, that is, either that God advanced from a

6. Stamps, "The Trinity," 51.
7. "Modalism" refers to the heretical view that God is only one person, revealed as Father, Son, and Spirit at different times but never all three at one and the same time as the one God. "Monarchical" refers to the subordinationist heresy, in which the Son and Spirit are said to be ontologically inferior to the Father. In other words, they are not "as divine" as the Father is.
8. Stamps, "The Trinity," 51.

> condition of being unable to being able, or that, while being able he hid this and delayed the begetting of Wisdom.
>
> Therefore we acknowledge that God is always the Father of his only-begotten Son, who was indeed born of him, and derives from him what he is, but without, however, any beginning, not only that which may be distinguished by periods of time, but even that which intellect alone is accustomed to contemplate within itself or to contemplate, if we may thus speak, with the bare intellect and reason. Wisdom is thus believed to be begotten beyond the limits of any beginning that we can speak of or understand.[9]

Origen goes on to speak, more than anyone else thus far but in the same vein as Tertullian, of the eternal generation of the Son. His argument is rooted in the biblical data and in theological questions arising from the biblical text.

Despite the positive contributions of these theologians, there are strains of subordinationism throughout, particularly in Origen. As I (Luke) have said elsewhere, "he sees the Son occupying a mediating position between the Father and the created world."[10] There are, in other words, statements in second- and third-century theologians that seem to place the Son as somehow less than the Father. We should hasten to say again, though, that in all of these instances they are coupled with the insistence that the Son is fully divine. It is the lack of clarity on this question, namely how the Son is equal to the Father and also *Son*, that leads to the great debate of the fourth century and the judgments at Nicaea and Chalcedon.[11] On the one hand, Arius and other subordinationists found supposed support in Origen for their view that the Son is "less than" the Father. On the other hand, Athanasius and other pro-Nicenes relied on Origen's explication and defense of the eternal generation of the Son to argue for his complete equality with the Father. We turn to this debate in the next two chapters.

Summary

The second- and third-century theologians follow the biblical authors in worshiping the Son and Spirit alongside the Father. In that sense, they are already expressing liturgically what they will later clarify theologically. They do not answer every theological question about the doctrine of the Trinity, nor do

9. Origen of Alexandria, *On First Principles*, vol. 1, ed. and trans. John Behr (Oxford: Oxford University Press, 2017), 41, 43.
10. Stamps, "The Trinity," 52.
11. On the development of the doctrine of the Trinity in the second and third centuries, and especially regarding the pivotal role of Origen in the subsequent watershed fourth-century debates, see John Behr, *The Way to Nicaea*, vol. 1 of *Formation of Christian Theology* (Crestwood, NY: St Vladimir's Seminary Press, 2001).

they always speak clearly on the issue, but they do provide the postbiblical foundation for subsequent clarification and conversation on the topic.

REFLECTION QUESTIONS

1. What are ways that the second- and third-century theologians' talk of the Trinity helps your prayer life?

2. How does the second- and third-century theologians' teaching on the Trinity remind you of the Bible's teaching on the Trinity?

3. How do the questions asked and answers given by the second- and third-century theologians remind you of questions you've asked about the Trinity while reading the Bible?

4. What is a passage in Scripture that has confused you but now seems clearer based on thinking through the second- and third-century theologians' teaching on the Trinity?

5. What is one teaching strategy from the second- and third-century theologians that could help you explain the Trinity to someone else?

QUESTION 13

What Were the Major Trinitarian Heresies in the Early Church?

Scripture is not a systematic theology encyclopedia. Its stories, poems, laws, proverbs, historical narratives, epistles, and apocalypses must be interpreted and synthesized. Its theological referents must be wrestled with and puzzled over and finally surrendered to and adored. This is not to suggest that the biblical materials are somehow underdeveloped and deficient, waiting for the theologian to craft something coherent from them. No, what we have suggested in the biblical chapters of this book is that the biblical witness is clear and consistent, even if variegated and diverse. The biblical material places an interpretive "pressure" upon its readers to draw certain conclusions about the central actors in the biblical drama: the Father, Son, and Holy Spirit.[1] These conclusions have theological entailments for the identity of the biblical God, who lies above and under and beyond the drama of redemptive history. And wrestling with these conclusions and entailments through careful and prayerful attention to Scripture constitutes the church's encounter with the divine. But in this Spirit-infused process of exegesis, reflection, and encounter, sometimes things misfire. Sometimes readers mishear the voice of God in Scripture, or misconstrue the pressures of the biblical text. Sometimes readers venture out on their own, apart from the consensus of the faithful, and end up drawing the wrong conclusions and teasing out the wrong entailments. Human fallenness sometimes results not just in error but in heresy.

1. C. Kavin Rowe, "Biblical Pressure and Trinitarian Hermeneutics," *Pro Ecclesia* 11, no. 3 (2002): 295–312.

Defining Heresy

Heresy, then, requires some definition.[2] Heresy is not just any disagreement among Christians regarding biblical interpretation. Heresy is sometimes too flippantly or hastily thrown out in theological debate. As we are using it here, *heresy is a willful departure from the clear teaching of Scripture, as it has been interpreted by a consensus of the church throughout space and time, on a matter of primary importance*. Each facet of this definition deserves some comment. First, heresy involves a willful departure. The Greek word for heresy (*haeresis*) and its cognates signify a *choice*, a decision to divide into a sectarian group (Acts 5:17; 1 Cor. 11:19; cf. Titus 3:10; 2 Peter 2:1). Heresy, in this sense, is not an accident. It is not merely a function of being insufficiently taught. It is a deliberate decision in favor of false doctrine.

Second, heresy concerns the clear teaching of Scripture. Heresy may be diagnosed according to certain creedal summaries of Scripture (more on this in the next point), but the source of authority that ultimately determines the truth of a theological position is Scripture itself. By underscoring the *clear* teaching of Scripture, we are expressing our commitment to the Protestant belief in Scripture's perspicuity. The Westminster Confession of Faith summarizes well what this belief means and what it does not mean:

> All things in Scripture are not alike plain in themselves, nor alike clear unto all; yet those things which are necessary to be known, believed, and observed, for salvation, are so clearly propounded and opened in some place of Scripture or other, that not only the learned, but the unlearned, in a due use of the ordinary means, may attain unto a sufficient understanding of them. (1.7)

As some have put it, we might say that *the main things are the plain things* (and the plain things are the main things). The Bible is sufficiently clear that there is only one God and that Father, Son, and Holy Spirit each are, mysteriously, identified with this one God. The Bible clearly identifies these persons with one another and yet distinguishes them according to their relational names. Heresy departs not from some esoteric extrabiblical apparatus but from the plain teaching of the Bible itself.

Third, this plain teaching of Scripture is confirmed in the history of Christian interpretation. As we argued in Question 3, the tradition is not to be equated with Scripture nor seen as a second source of revelation alongside Scripture. Nevertheless, the tradition does serve as a derivatively authoritative guide to interpreting Scripture, because the tradition represents a consensus

---

2. See Allister McGrath, *Heresy: A History of Defending the Truth* (New York: HarperOne, 2009).

of what Spirit-illuminated readers have seen in Scripture. This authority is vested ultimately in Scripture itself but is mediated instrumentally through what Thomas Oden called the "consensual tradition," or the consensus of the faithful across time and location.[3]

Finally, heresy is demarcated by its departure from Scripture on a primary doctrine. It would be a mistake to flag something as heresy on a relatively minor doctrine. All doctrines contained in or implied by Scripture are important, but not all are central or integral. Some doctrines are like primary colors (red, yellow, and blue) that are reducible to nothing else. Other doctrines are more like secondary or tertiary colors that are formed from these primary colors and their mixtures with other colors. So, for example, divergent views on the millennium of Revelation 20 or even of certain aspects of the order of salvation would typically not rise to the level of heresy. These doctrines are derivative of more integral truths and are sometimes several steps removed from the core of the Christian faith. Primary doctrines are those that, if they were denied, would change the very essence of the Christian faith. Therefore, denying the Trinity or the deity and humanity of Christ would be considered heresy.

Early Trinitarian Heresies

Early Trinitarian heresies can be grouped into three main types: dynamic monarchianism, modalistic monarchianism, and Arianism.[4] Monarchianism was a broad category of views that located the unity of God in the person of the Father and viewed the Son and Spirit either as distinct instruments or simply manifestations of the Father (monarchianism comes from *mono*, "alone" + *archein*, "to rule"). Dynamic monarchianism, then, describes a position that identified the Father alone as God. Jesus Christ, in this view, was a mere human being in whom God's power (*dunamis*) was mightily at work. The Son was the authoritative instrument through which God's loving and saving rule was administered to the world, but he was not viewed as a distinct divine person coequal to and coeternal with God the Father. The Holy Spirit, on this view, was seen as a description of God's

---

3. Oden uses this term throughout his systematic theology. See Thomas C. Oden, *Classic Christianity: A Systematic Theology* (New York: HarperOne, 2009).
4. The literature on Trinitarian heresy and orthodoxy in the early centuries is (blessedly) vast. Introductory resources include: Khaled Anatolios, *Retrieving Nicaea: The Development and Meaning of Trinitarian Doctrine* (Grand Rapids: Baker Academic, 2011); Lewis Ayres, *Nicaea and Its Legacy* (Oxford: Oxford University Press, 2004); and John Behr, *The Nicene Faith: Part I* and *The Nicene Faith: Part 2*, vols. 1 and 2 of *Formation of Christian Theology* (Crestwood, NY: St Vladimir's Seminary Press, 2004). See also Leo Donald Davis, *The First Seven Ecumenical Councils (325–787): Their History and Theology* (Collegeville, MN: Liturgical, 1990); Justin S. Holcomb, *Know the Heretics*, Know Series (Grand Rapids: Zondervan, 2014).

power or activity, not as a distinct person. The early Ebionites, for example, held that Jesus was the Messiah and Savior but balked at the idea that he was a distinct divine person consubstantial (of the same essence) with the Father and Spirit.

Another type of monarchianism was the kind espoused by Noetius and Sabellius: namely, modalism. In this view, the Son and Spirit are simply distinct manifestations of the Father. The three are not distinct persons who exist in real relations with one another from all eternity. They are, instead, distinct and successive manifestations of a God who is intrinsically one person. They are simply distinct modes of revelation. This view has some parallels with modern Oneness or "Jesus-Only" Pentecostalism.

The final category of early heresy can be grouped under the general heading of "Arianism." This term should be used somewhat loosely. The actual views of the fourth-century priest Arius of Alexandria have been obscured by the destruction of all but a few of his writings. Later, pro-Nicene theologians such as Athanasius sometimes used the epithet "Arian" to describe a range of views that can only be applied anachronistically to the historical Arius. Arius's condemnation at the Council of Nicaea in 325 made association with him a liability, which is why figures like Athanasius were so quick to apply the label to later heretics like Eunomius of Cyzicus. The gist of Arius's own view can be summarized in one of his favored slogans: "There was once when he was not."[5] In other words, there was a time when the Son of God did not exist. For Arius, the Son was the first and greatest of God's creatures through whom God made everything else, but the Son is not coeternal with God. This view has some close parallels with contemporary Jehovah's Witnesses, who likewise view the Son as a creation of God the Father.[6]

The Arian heresy prompted the Trinitarian controversies of the fourth century. Arianism was formally condemned at the Council of Nicaea in 325, but its influence persisted throughout the century. Later theologians like Eunomius continued to deny the full deity and eternality of the Son. Nicaea's insistence that the Son is consubstantial (*homoousios*) with the Father was rejected, and several alternatives were proposed. Eunomius and his followers can be classified as *Heteroousians*: They maintained that the Son and Father are different (*hetero*) in being and substance. The Homoians suggested that the Son was "like" (*homoi*) the Father but not the *same* (*homo*) as the Father.

5. For some of the most important documents of the early Trinitarian debates, see William G. Rusch, trans. and ed., *The Trinitarian Controversy* (Minneapolis: Fortress, 1980).
6. See, for example, the statement on Jesus from the Jehovah's Witnesses website. "We follow the teachings and example of Jesus Christ and honor him as our Savior and as the Son of God. (Matthew 20:28; Acts 5:31) Thus, we are Christians. (Acts 11:26) However, we have learned from the Bible that Jesus is not Almighty God and that there is no Scriptural basis for the Trinity doctrine." Jehovah's Witnesses, "What Do Jehovah's Witnesses Believe?" https://www.jw.org/en/jehovahs-witnesses/faq/jehovah-witness-beliefs/.

The *Homoiousians* were even willing to say that the Son is "like according to essence" with the Father but stopped short of affirming Nicaea's stronger claim: *homoousios*. Pro-Nicene theologians such as Athanasius were unwilling to compromise on this point and continued to insist on the Nicene doctrine.

The error of the Macedonians can be considered an extension of the Arian heresy as the controversy turned more explicitly to the identity of the Third Person, the Holy Spirit. Macedonius, bishop of Constantinople, and his followers maintained that the Holy Spirit was created by the Son and was subordinated to the Father and Son. Those who held this heresy were also called Pneumatomachians: "fighters against the Spirit." Athanasius called these heretics *Tropici* because of the "tropes," or interpretations, they utilized to undermine the Spirit's full deity. Athanasius as well as the Cappadocian Fathers opposed the Macedonians no less than the Arians and Eunomians. The final edition of the Nicene Creed, adopted at the Council of Constantinople in 381, explicitly repudiated Macedonianism by speaking of the Spirit as the "Lord and Giver of life," who "with the Father and Son is worshiped and glorified."

Summary

In sum, "heresy" is not a term to be thrown around lightly. It does not apply to tertiary or even secondary matters of biblical interpretation. Instead, it connotes a willing departure from the clear teaching of the Bible on a matter of first importance. In the early centuries of the church, several kinds of Trinitarian heresy arose. Many of these heresies can be classified as "Monarchianism" because they taught that the Father alone is the "monarch" or ruler of all. Dynamic Monarchianism maintained that Jesus was merely a man in whom the power of God was uniquely manifested. Modalistic Monarchianism denied that Father, Son, and Holy Spirit are distinct divine persons and taught instead that they are merely three distinct modes of divine revelation. Finally, Arianism as a broad category (including the similar positions held by Eunomianism and Macedonianism) taught that the Son and Spirit were created by the Father and therefore are not God or equal with the Father. Each of these ancient heresies have manifestations today as well, which is why it is so crucial to understand the development of early Christian orthodoxy: that is, right teaching on God's being and works.

REFLECTION QUESTIONS

1. Why is "heresy" so important to define?

2. Have you taken heresy seriously in your own Christian life? Why or why not?

3. How do you distinguish between "primary" doctrines and "secondary" or "tertiary" ones?

4. How does your church think about which doctrines are "primary," "secondary," and "tertiary"?

5. How does understanding Trinitarian heresies help your prayer life?

QUESTION 14

What Happened at the Council of Nicaea?

We return in this chapter to our historical survey, begun in question 12, with the first few generations of the post-apostolic period. We ended that chapter with a summary of the growing divide in the late third century between "subordinationists," or those who denied the full divinity of the Son, and those who affirmed the full divinity of the Son. This divide led to a crisis point, which we will explore in this chapter: the Council of Nicaea.

The early church meeting that would come to be recognized as the first ecumenical council convened in 325 in the city of Nicaea. Though its decisions were disputed, its key terminology left largely undefined, and its disciplinary dictates short-lived, the meeting of some 250–300 bishops over the summer of 325 stands apart as the foundational "Great and Holy Synod" of the Christian church. Thereafter, the subsequent ecumenical councils would appeal not only to Scripture but also to the "holy fathers" of the Nicene Council. Citing Hilary of Poitiers on the significance of the council and its creed, T. F. Torrance refers to Nicaea as "'an unalterable determination (*imperturbata constitutio*) of the Church', or a great irreversible event in the life of the Church, second only to the one foundation which Christ himself had laid in the apostles and prophets, but serving it, building on it, and in some sense sharing in its unrepeatable character."[1] To be sure, Nicaea's theological conclusions are not on the same plane as Holy Scripture, the only inspired and infallible written revelation of God, but they have been received by all branches of Christian theology, including Protestantism, as a faithful interpretation and synthesis of the biblical teaching on the being and works of the triune God. In this chapter we will consider the background, the proceedings and decisions, and the theological significance of the Council of Nicaea.

1. Thomas F. Torrance, *The Trinitarian Faith: The Evangelical Theology of the Ancient Catholic Church*, 2nd ed. (London: T&T Clark, 1997), 13.

Background

A comprehensive consideration of the ecumenical councils must consider both the political and theological developments that led to their convening.[2] In terms of the Council of Nicaea's political background, the conversion of Constantine in 312 looms large. For the first three centuries, Christianity was a growing but persecuted minority in the Roman Empire, spreading especially in urban areas. For a time, the Roman policy of persecution was localized, but by the mid-third century imperial pressure on Christianity had become a more formal and systemic policy. The Roman emperor Decius issued a decree in 250 that required worship of the gods and the cult of the Caesar, leading to a short-lived but severe persecution of Christians. A half-century later, the so-called Great Persecution was initiated by Diocletian in 303 and lasted until 311 when the emperor Galerius fell ill and sought to appease the Christian God by issuing an edict of toleration for the Christians. The next year, Galerius's successor Constantine was famously converted at the Battle of Milvian Bridge when he allegedly saw a vision of the cross in battle and heard the words, "In this sign you will conquer." In 313 Constantine issued the Edict of Milan, permanently providing toleration for Christianity. Persecution continued in the eastern part of the empire, but in 324 Constantine defeated the eastern emperor Licinius. As the uncontested emperor, Constantine set out to unify the empire, and with the Arian controversy threatening that unity, he called the Council of Nicaea in 325 to resolve the dispute.

In one sense, the theological background of the council could include the entirety of the church's Trinitarian reflection in the first three centuries: Irenaeus's early reflections on the persons in the economy, Justin's Logos Christology, Tertullian's Trinitarian grammar (*trinitas*, one *substantia*, three *personae*), Origen's development of the concept of immanent processions, and the errors of modalism and subordinationism were all important stages in the lead up to the council. But it was the teaching of the Egyptian priest Arius that provided the spark for the controversy. As we discussed in the previous chapter, Arius taught that the Son was a creature; there was a time when he did not exist. The Son was the first and greatest creation of the one true God, who is absolutely transcendent and indivisible. The Arians equated "begotten" with "created," and so to speak of the Son as the eternally begotten Son is to speak of him as a created being. Like the Sabellians and subordinationists,

2. On the history of the debates in this period, see, for example, Khaled Anatolios, *Retrieving Nicaea: The Development and Meaning of Trinitarian Doctrine* (Grand Rapids: Baker Academic, 2011); Lewis Ayres, *Nicaea and Its Legacy* (Oxford: Oxford University Press, 2004); and John Behr, *The Nicene Faith: Part I* and *Part 2*, vols. 1 and 2 of *Formation of Christian Theology* (Crestwood, NY: St Vladimir's Seminary Press, 2004). See also Leo Donald Davis, *The First Seven Ecumenical Councils (325–787): Their History and Theology* (Collegeville, MN: Liturgical, 1990), 33–80. The narration of events here follows Davis's concise account.

the Arians maintained that a distinction of persons entails a distinction of substance.[3] The Sabellians took that assumption to mean that there are no real distinctions of persons. The subordinationists and the Arians took it to mean that the persons are distinct but ordered in a hierarchy of being.

Arius came under fire for his beliefs about the Son's creation at the hands of his bishop, Alexander of Alexandria. In 320, Alexander convened a synod of the Egyptian and Libyan bishops to address the problem, and a supermajority of the bishops voted to condemn and exile Arius. Arius fled first to Caesarea and Nicomedia, where he was received by a pair of bishops who shared the name Eusebius, both of whom would figure prominently in somewhat different ways in the debates that persisted throughout the fourth century. A synod that met at Nicomedia exonerated Arius and condemned Alexander. Arius published his teachings in verse in a work called *Thalia* ("Banquet" or "Abundance"). Once Constantine became the sole emperor in 324, he set out, through his principal ecclesiastical advisor Ossius of Cordoba, to resolve the conflict between Arius and Alexander. The controversy came to a head when Constantine called a council to meet in Nicaea, a city east of the capital that would be more accessible to the western bishops.

Proceedings and Decisions

Accounts of the council set the number of bishops who met at Nicaea somewhere between 220 and 318. Alexander and Arius were the main opponents, but each had prominent bishops in their corner. Eustathius of Antioch, Marcellus of Ancyra, and Macarius of Jerusalem stood against Arius. Eusebius of Caesarea, Eusebius of Nicomedia, and several others stood with him. Western bishops were also represented, with Ossius chief among them. Accounts are uncertain, but Nicholas of Myra, who would give rise to the Santa Claus legends, may have also been present.[4] Constantine himself presided over the council and participated in the debates, thought it appears that he did not cast a vote.

As the debate ensued, condemnations were cast from both sides. Eusebius of Nicomedia proffered an Arian creed, which the bishops rejected. Eusebius of Caesarea then suggested the baptismal creed of his own see (episcopal seat of church governance), which the emperor and the bishops approved. But the version that came to be accepted as the council's official creed was based on a Syro-Palestinian creed, and it more forcefully excluded the views of Arius. The final creed reads as follows:

---

3. Thomas Joseph White, *The Trinity: On the Nature and Mystery of the One God* (Washington, DC: The Catholic University of America Press, 2022), 136.
4. The story of Nicholas punching Arius after his blasphemous speech is almost certainly apocryphal, however one might wish it were true (if only for the Christmas memes).

> We believe in one God the Father Almighty, Maker of all things visible and invisible; and in one Lord Jesus Christ, the Son of God, begotten of the Father, only-begotten, that is, from the substance of the Father, God from God, Light from Light, True God from True God, Begotten, not made, of one substance with the Father, through Whom all things were made. Who for us men and for our salvation came down and became incarnate, and was made man, suffered and rose on the third day, And ascended into heaven, And is coming with glory to judge the living and dead, And in the Holy Spirit.

After the creed, the following anathemas were appended:

> But those who say, There was when the Son of God was not, and before he was begotten he was not, and that he came into being from things that are not, or that he is of a different hypostasis or substance, or that he is mutable or alterable—the Catholic and Apostolic Church anathematizes.

The Nicene Creed as we know it was only completed at the Council of Constantinople in 381 (which included a fuller statement on the Holy Spirit), but the core of the creed was present here. The creed excluded Arianism with its clear distinction between creation and begottenness. The Arians were happy to admit that the Son was eternally begotten, but they meant by this that he was created from nothing by the Father before the world was created. The creed makes clear that the Son was *not created* from nothing but was *begotten* from the Father. The creed's most significant phrase also proved to be its most disputed: "of one substance" (*homoouios*, Latin *consubstantia*) with the Father. Did this phrase mean that the Father and Son were the same kind of being, that they were made from the same kind of stuff? Or did it mean that the Father and Son were numerically identical, one in being (although distinct in relation to one another)?[5] Athanasius, Alexander's assistant at Nicaea and his successor as bishop of Alexandria, and other "pro-Nicene" theologians would argue for the latter meaning of the phrase, but a diversity of opinions existed even at the time of the creed's acceptance.[6] Some seemed to affirm the *homoousion* with the first sense in view. Others, like Marcellus of Ancyra, could sign onto the numerical identity sense of the *homoousion* but with a more modalist interpretation. The precise meaning of the term would be debated throughout the better part of the century.

---

5. Davis, *The First Seven Ecumenical Councils*, 61.
6. Lewis Ayres develops the notion of "pro-Nicene" theology in his *Nicaea and Its Legacy*. For more on these disputes, see question 15.

The council's anathemas also made clear the condemnation of Arius. The Son did not come into being. He was eternally begotten from the Father's being. As such he is not a different being from the Father. Note that Nicaea equated the terms *hypostasis* and *ousia*. Over the course of the century, the two terms came to be distinguished, with *hypostasis* developing into the term denoting the three persons and *ousia* their shared essence. In any event, Arian interpretations of the Son's identity and origin were formally anathematized at the council. The council also included a number of canons, or ecclesiastical rules, which dealt with matters such as qualifications for clergy, the liturgical calendar, and the readmission of those who had lapsed during persecution.

Theological Significance

From an immediate ecclesiastical perspective, the effects of the council were short-lived. Just a few short years after the council, Arius was recalled from his exile and Athanasius, now bishop of Alexandria, was pressured to receive him back into fellowship, which he refused to do, resulting in his own exile! The disputed term *homoousios* continued to be disputed. Rival terms emerged. Theologies reminiscent of Arianism were ascendant, gaining favor in the imperial court. We will return to the reception of Nicaea in the next chapter, but for now we note several important theological advances that emerged from the Great Synod.

First, the council affirmed that the Father and Son are one in being or essence. The Son was not created *ex nihilo* the way that "all things visible and invisible" were. He stands on the divine side of the ledger. He was not created but begotten from the very substance of the Father. As such he is *homoousios* with the Father and cannot be treated as a distinct substance or being from the Father. Against Arianism and all other previous forms of subordinationism, Nicaea affirms the absolute equality and unity of the Father and Son.

Second, the council affirmed a real distinction between the Father and Son. Though they are identified in being, they are distinguished in relation. The Father begets, and the Son is begotten. Being begotten from the Father's substance ensures that the Son is consubstantial with the Father, but it also underscores a real distinction between the two. The Son is the same being as the Father, but he is that one being in a distinct mode: His being is from the Father. The two are equal, but the Son stands in a relation of "derived equality."[7] The persons are distinguished not in being, will, or action but in terms of eternal relations of origin. The eternally unbegotten Father eternally begets the Son, and so the two are one in being but distinct in person or relation.

Third, the council left open the identity of the Holy Spirit and his relation to the other divine persons. The controversy that led to the Council of Nicaea was specifically about the identity and origin of the Son in relation to

7. White, *The Trinity*, 129.

the Father. Later in the fourth century, debates would arise about the person of the Holy Spirit, and the second ecumenical council would address these concerns, as we explore in the next chapter. But for now, the Spirit's identity is simply inserted as a kind of placeholder at the end of the creed: "And the Holy Spirit." Still, the threefold nature of the rule of faith remains intact; the church confesses belief not just in Father and Son but in the Holy Spirit as well.

Summary

The teachings of Arius prompted enormous controversy in the fourth-century church that forced the church to articulate more clearly its biblical doctrine of the Trinity. Arius taught that there was time when the Son did not exist—that the Father created the Son. The church convened its first ecumenical council in 325 in the town of Nicaea in order to address this error. The council fathers decided against Arius and in favor of his opponents (especially Alexander and his allies) in affirming that the Son is "not made" but begotten of the Father. The key term in the council's creed that would become the benchmark of Trinitarian orthodoxy was *homoousios*: The Son is "of the same nature" as the Father. The council's immediate reception was mixed, as theologians continued to debate Arianism and the meaning of the creed's terms, but the theological bombshell had been dropped. Ever after, Nicaea would stand as a turning point for Christian orthodoxy. Later theologians would look back upon the decisions of the council's "holy fathers" as a momentous accomplishment.

REFLECTION QUESTIONS

1. What have you heard or been taught about the Council of Nicaea and its importance previously?
2. How does learning about the events of the Council of Nicaea help you better understand the doctrine of the Trinity?
3. How do Nicaea's conclusions on the doctrine of the Trinity remind you of the Bible's teaching on the Trinity?
4. How do the questions asked and answers given by Nicaea remind you of questions you've asked about the Trinity while reading the Bible?
5. What is a passage in Scripture that has confused you but now seems clearer based on thinking through the Council of Nicaea's conclusions on the Trinity?

QUESTION 15

What Was the Trinitarian Contribution of the Pro-Nicenes?

The Trinitarian heresies in the early church and the confrontation of the arch-heresy, subordinationism, at the Council of Nicaea at root were issues of biblical interpretation. The contribution of Athanasius of Alexandria thus lies primarily in his defense of the judgments of Nicaea as thoroughly biblical. Although it is a common sentiment that the Nicene doctrine of the Trinity is a product of Hellenistic philosophy, the reality is that the controversy over subordinationism in the fourth century was primarily about hermeneutics. In fact, as we will see in this chapter and the next, the fault of the subordinationists, *not* the pro-Nicenes, is to subject scriptural statements to Hellenistic philosophical categories. The years after the first Council of Nicaea were filled with political maneuvering related to theological debate. In the end, the argument came down to how to read the Bible. As I (Luke) have summarized elsewhere,

> The council, in other words, did not settle all disputes. Other theological trajectories, especially those associated with the two Eusebians—Eusebius of Caesarea (263–339) and Eusebius of Nicomedia (d. 341)—exerted influence in both ecclesiastical and imperial contexts. Within just a few years after the council, Arius was recalled from his enforced exile and readmitted to communion with the church. Athanasius, who succeeded Alexander as bishop of Alexandria, refused to acknowledge Arius's readmittance and found himself on the losing end of the emperor's dictates. For his defense of Nicaea's *homoousios* and his own strict interpretation of it (along with some other political accusations against him), Athanasius experienced exile five different times for a total of seventeen

> years over the course of the mid-fourth century. Athanasius produced some of the most important "anti-Arian" writings of the century, including his important *Defense against the Arians* (350). In the West, Hilary of Poitiers (d. 367) took up a similar cause of defending Nicaea, primarily through exegesis rather than any sophisticated philosophical reasoning. His ten-volume *De Trinitate*, written during his own exile, stands as his most lasting contribution to the defense of the Nicene settlement against Arian and semi-Arian opponents.[1]

The years between Nicaea (325) and Constantinople (381) were thus filled with controversy, in particular controversy over how to understand specific texts in Scripture. The issues of Nicaea, and especially that of whether *homoousios* was an appropriate extrabiblical term to describe the teachings of the Bible about God, came down to hermeneutics.

Subordinationist Hermeneutic

The Nicene controversy was so heated, and its conciliar decisions debated so vigorously afterward, in part because the various parties held much in common. Although the controversy included many more positions than just two, it is helpful for our purposes to speak of two main parties: the pro-Nicene party and the subordinationist party.[2] The former held that the decisions at Nicaea, including the adoption of the Nicene Creed, were biblically faithful and theologically accurate. The latter held that Nicene decisions were wrong, specifically because the Son was not *homooousios* with the Father; rather than equal in essence, he (and, by implication, the Spirit) was subordinate to the Father in both essence and, therefore, function.

One area of commonality between the two parties was their insistence on exegetical arguments. It is not the case that one party worked purely from Hellenistic philosophy while the other only paid attention to the Bible; both groups frequently referred to biblical texts to defend their respective positions. Both parties also held in common an acknowledgement of their devotion to Jesus (and the Spirit) in the various aspects of corporate worship. Arius and other subordinationists did not hold that Jesus was *merely* a man but saw him as something more than that, something—someone—worthy of reverence and devotion. Of course, they also did not hold that he was fully God in the way that the Father is, and so the Son (and the Spirit) occupied some kind of

---

1. R. Lucas Stamps, "The Trinity," in *Historical Theology for the Church*, ed. Jason G. Duesing and Nathan A. Finn (Nashville: B&H Academic, 2021), 53–54.
2. On the complexities of the debate, its historical setting, and defining the parties involved (including the use of the term "pro-Nicene"), see Lewis Ayres, *Nicaea and Its Legacy* (Oxford: Oxford University Press, 2004).

middle space between God the Father and creation. According to them, that was enough to warrant reverence and devotion in corporate worship. Finally, both parties considered themselves to be "Trinitarian": Again, the subordinationists held that the Son and the Spirit were unique and associated with divinity in some way but not in exactly the same way as God the Father. They were thus each "god" while only the Father is the one God of the Bible. Both sides could therefore claim to be exegetical, liturgical, and Trinitarian.[3]

As should be evident from this description, though, these commonalities existed predominantly on the surface. With respect to exegesis, subordinationist interpretation tended toward isolating individual passages from the rest of Scripture and reading those individual passages at a surface level. While they did sometimes connect different passages of Scripture together (e.g., Prov. 8:22–31and 1 Cor. 1:24), this often was only meant to support their pre-determined conclusion that the Son was not equal to the Father. They were, in other words, committed "to find texts that supported the distinction between the Father and Son and to cite them together."[4] This commitment was rooted in a more fundamental one, namely a commitment to "distinguishing between the undivided Monad and all other beings. For Arius especially, this Platonic view of the deity led him to distinguish God the Father, as the Monad, from what was derived from him. The idea of a Trinitarian deity unified in essence is therefore antithetical to Arius', and others', fundamental beliefs about the nature of the divine being."[5] As we noted above, this means that, for the subordinationists, "the Father exists as Monad, while the Son (or Logos) and Spirit exist as mediatory beings between Creator and creation who were nevertheless worshiped as divine."[6] Thus their project was intent on identifying texts that made, on their readings, sharp distinctions between Father and Son. In the next chapter, we will see that Eunomius and Asterius continued the subordinationist hermeneutic of Arius and the two Eusebiuses with respect to the Holy Spirit, albeit from slightly different starting points.

These commitments, to a Platonist conception of God that allowed only for God's oneness to be defined as numerically singular ("Monad") and their corresponding commitment to find biblical texts that demonstrated a distinction between Father and Son, determined their understanding of the liturgical devotion to Christ and also the term "Trinitarian." Regarding the former, they acknowledged that the church expressed devotion of and reverence

---

3. On the exegetical nature of the debates, see, for instance, John Behr, *The Nicene Faith: Part I*, vol. 2 of *Formation of Christian Theology* (Crestwood, NY: St Vladimir's Seminary Press, 2004), 124–25, 208–15.
4. Matthew Y. Emerson, "The Role of Proverbs 8: Eternal Generation and Hermeneutics Ancient and Modern," in *Retrieving Eternal Generation*, ed. Fred Sanders and Scott R. Swain (Grand Rapids: Zondervan Academic, 2017), 50.
5. Emerson, "The Role of Proverbs 8," 50.
6. Emerson, "The Role of Proverbs 8," 50.

toward the Son but without equating him to the Father. With respect to the latter, their use of "Trinitarian" obviously varied widely from the pro-Nicene definition. It is safe to say that they were alike in name only.

Pro-Nicene Hermeneutics

Pro-Nicene interpreters also held precommitments, but, in contrast to subordinationists, these precommitments arose from the biblical text itself.[7] We discussed some of these hermeneutical presuppositions in an earlier chapter, but it will be helpful to revisit them here and also add a few others in order to contrast them with the hermeneutic of the subordinationists. Perhaps the most important of these is the Creator/creature distinction. This commitment, arising from texts like Genesis 1, Deuteronomy 10:14, Nehemiah 9:6, and Romans 1:25, says, "Anything that is uncreated is God, while anything that is created is not God. This necessarily excludes any sense of a divine but created mediatorial being."[8]

Additionally, and considering this distinction, pro-Nicenes were committed to reading Scripture according to its own economy, or shape. In particular, they differentiated between texts that speak of the Son according to his divinity from those that speak of the Son according to his humanity. Like the Creator/creature distinction, this distinction between "form of God" and "form of a servant" texts arises from the biblical text itself, and namely from Philippians 2:6–8. A third hermeneutical pre-commitment held by the pro-Nicenes is that Scripture interprets Scripture. In some ways, this is merely an application of the first two precommitments. If the Son (and Spirit) is identified as divine, then, according to texts like Deuteronomy 6:4, 10:14, and Nehemiah 9:6, he must be fully divine since there is only one God and no "middle man" between him and his creation.[9] And if that is the case, then passages that speak about the Son's submission to the Father or his human traits like hunger and tiredness must be speaking about him "in the form of a

---

7. Of course, a subordinationist might respond that their commitment to God's numerically singular oneness is from the Bible (e.g., Deut. 6:4). But it is readily apparent in reading the fourth-century material that the subordinationists attempt to define oneness via Platonic categories ("Monad," and, later, "Unoriginate"), while the pro-Nicenes allow the Bible to define its own language.
8. Emerson, "The Role of Proverbs 8," 50. See, for instance, Basil of Caesarea, "The Third Theological Oration (Oration 29)," in *On God and Christ: The Five Theological Orations and Two Letters to Cledonius*, trans. Frederick Williams and Lionel Wickham, PPS 23 (Crestwood, NY: St Vladimir's Seminary Press, 2002), 69–92; Basil of Caesarea, *On the Holy Spirit*, trans. Stephen Hildebrand, PPS 42 (Crestwood, NY: St Vladimir's Seminary Press, 2011), 69–70, 87–88, 93–94; Augustine, *The Trinity*, 2nd ed., trans. Edmund Hill, ed. John Rotelle (Hyde Park, NY: New City, 2012), 72–73.
9. Particularly important in this regard is the fact that the Father and Son share divine names. See, for instance, Athanasius, *Discourse Against the Arians*, Books 1–4. On Proverbs 8 see especially 2.19 and following.

servant," à la Philippians 2:7–8. For instance, and as I (Matt) have noted elsewhere, "Athanasius uses this argument prolifically in his *Discourse Against the Arians*."[10] Finally, the pro-Nicenes were committed to a healthy understanding of the ineffability of God. Ultimately, human language cannot exhaust who God is in himself. Thus, we need to be careful when we use creaturely terms and analogies (like begottenness) to describe God's nature.

Pro-Nicenes interpreted texts that subordinationists claimed supported their position in light of these biblically rooted precommitments and with exegetical rigor. An example of this is seen in how they read Proverbs 8. A subordinationist might argue that Proverbs 8:22 clearly and plainly says that Wisdom is created by God and therefore that the Son—Wisdom—is less than the Father. The pro-Nicenes, however, took a variety of additional relevant factors into account as they read. First, they paid attention to the details of the text itself, details like genre and the original language. Regarding the former, Athanasius, for instance, notes that the content of Proverbs needs to be taken in light of the book's own writing style, and that, "what has been said in the book of Proverbs also has a proper sense (*orte dianoia*). The key to understanding it is the Greek title of the book of Proverbs, *paroimiai—paroimia* has two meanings: proverb, so *proverbium*, and likeness."[11] In other words, "To read Proverbs . . . means to take care not to take statements too concretely, when they are in fact using language that is metaphorical or figurative in some cases."[12] When we read Proverbs 8 and its description of Lady Wisdom, we have to be careful to do so in accordance with the genre at hand.

The pro-Nicenes were also careful to argue from the original languages. Although they mostly knew Greek, some, like Basil of Caesarea and Jerome, were also proficient in Hebrew. For instance, with respect to Proverbs 8,

> Athanasius . . . argues from the Greek text for a particular interpretation of the phrase ("he acquired me"), noting verbal parallels for [*ktizein*] (e.g., Prov. 9:1) that do not speak of "creating," and also employs what Matthew Bates has termed "prosopological exegesis."[13] This tactic identifies the speaker of particular verses; thus for Athanasius in Proverbs 8 the

10. Emerson, "The Role of Proverbs 8," 52. On Athanasius's reliance on partitive exegesis, see especially Book 2.
11. This is a quote from Athanasius cited by Luis Abramowski, "Das Theologische Hauptwerk Des Athanasius: Die Drei Bücher Gegen Die Arianer (Ctr. Arianos I–III), *Communio Viatorium* 42 (2000): 17 (author's translation).
12. Emerson, "The Role of Proverbs 8," 62.
13. Abramowski, "Das Theologische Hauptwerk Des Athanasius," 18. On the basic approach of prosopological exegesis, see Matthew Bates, *The Hermeneutics of Apostolic Proclamation: The Center of Paul's Method of Interpretation* (Waco, TX: Baylor University Press, 2012), 183–222.

> speaker in verse 22 is the incarnate Christ, while in verse 25 it is the eternal Logos.[14]

Basil disagrees, however. Using "both Hebrew and Greek to argue for his interpretation of the verse," he declares that "both the Hebrew *Vorlage* and the LXX translation are ambiguous." Additionally, according to Basil, "the phrase 'he created me from the beginning' is a *hapax* legomenon" and so should not be used to support any primary doctrine. Instead, we should understand it in the context of the rest of the biblical canon, and specifically "in light of other biblical teaching" about the Son.[15] All of these exegetical arguments, deployed in light of the biblically rooted precommitments above, lead the pro-Nicenes to reject subordinationist readings of texts like Proverbs 8:22–31.

Summary

What, then, is the contribution of the pro-Nicenes immediately after the first Council of Nicaea? It is to solidify and defend the hermeneutical rationale for the decisions made at the Council of Nicaea and in particular that the extrabiblical term *homoousios* renders an accurate judgment about the patterns of biblical language concerning the one and only God who exists in three persons: Father, Son, and Holy Spirit.[16] Primarily through the work of Athanasius in the east and Hilary in the west, Nicaea's judgments were shown to be entirely and thoroughly biblical. What remained was to iron out the terminology used to convey those judgments in addition to *homoousios* and to make similar defenses of the Spirit's full deity as Athanasius and Hilary had done with respect to the Son.[17]

---

14. Emerson, "The Role of Proverbs 8," 53.
15. Emerson, "The Role of Proverbs 8," 53. On this disagreement between Athanasius and Basil, see Mark DelCogliano, "Basil of Caesarea on Proverbs 8:22 and the Sources of Pro-Nicene Theology," *JTS* 59 (2008): 183–90. See also Eugen J. Pentiuc, "A Self-Offering God and His Begotten Wisdom (Proverbs 8:22–24)," *Greek Orthodox Theological Review* 46 (2001): 259–60.
16. See David S. Yeago, "The New Testament and the Nicene Dogma: A Contribution to the Recovery of Theological Exegesis," *Pro Ecclesia* 3 (1994): 152–64.
17. Athanasius and Hilary also defended the deity of the Spirit. See especially Athanasius's "Letters to Serapion on the Holy Spirit," in Athanasius and Didymus, *Works on the Spirit*, trans. Mark DelCogliano, Andrew Radde-Gallowitz, and Lewis Ayres, PPS 43 (Crestwood, NY: St Vladimir's Seminary Press, 2011), 51–138. Still, the focus in the first half of the fourth century was the deity of the Son, while in the latter half it was primarily the deity of the Holy Spirit.

REFLECTION QUESTIONS

1. What are ways that the pro-Nicenes' talk of the Trinity helps your prayer life?

2. How does the pro-Nicenes' teaching on the Trinity remind you of the Bible's teaching on the Trinity?

3. How do the questions asked and answers given by the pro-Nicenes remind you of questions you've asked about the Trinity while reading the Bible?

4. What is a passage in Scripture that has confused you but now seems clearer based on thinking through the pro-Nicenes' teaching on the Trinity?

5. What is one teaching strategy from the pro-Nicenes that could help you explain the Trinity to someone else?

QUESTION 16

What Was the Trinitarian Contribution of the Cappadocians?

In the last chapter we highlighted some of the hermeneutical and theological commitments of the pro-Nicene theologians in the decades after the Council of Nicaea. As we saw in chapter 14, the settlement achieved by the council was short-lived, with various figures offering their own interpretations to the creed's central doctrinal terms. We have drawn particular attention to the role of Athanasius, Alexander's successor in Alexandria, who persistently and courageously defended the doctrine of Nicaea against all heretical challengers. We also mentioned the similar contribution of Hilary of Poitiers, who is sometimes referred to as the Athanasius of the West. For his part, Athanasius suffered greatly during his long career in defense of the Nicene doctrine. Partly owing to his doctrinal recalcitrance in refusing to admit Arius back into the fellowship of the church and partly owing to his own rashness in handling certain heretical groups, Athanasius found himself on the losing side of imperial politics.[1] Despite being condemned to exile five different times for a total of seventeen years during the middle of the fourth century, Athanasius remained steadfast in his opposition to various imperial and ecclesiastical attempts at doctrinal compromise, insisting on the soundness of Nicaea's *homousion*. It is with good reason that he is often heralded as *Athanasius contra mundum*: "Athanasius against the world."

After Athanasius, the figures most responsible for defending Nicaea's legacy were the three theologians known as the Cappadocian Fathers, so named for their ministries as bishops in the region of Cappadocia in modern-day

1. For a helpful introduction to the historical developments during this period, see Henry Chadwick, *The Early Church*, rev. ed., Penguin History of the Church 1 (London: Penguin, 1993), 149–69.

Turkey. Basil of Caesarea (ca. 330–379), known to history as Basil the Great, was the eldest of the three. His younger brother Gregory of Nyssa (ca. 335/340–394) and their close friend Gregory of Nazianzus (ca. 330–390) rounded out the group. The sister of Basil and Gregory, Macrina, is also worth mentioning. She founded a monastic community in their family home and was revered by the brothers as an important theological influence in her own right.[2] The Cappadocians cast a long shadow in the theology and spirituality of the subsequent centuries, but nowhere is their influence felt more than in the church's Trinitarian doctrine. Gregory of Nazianzus would eventually become a rival pro-Nicene bishop in the capital city of Constantinople and would serve as the second president of the Council of Constantinople in 381 (for more on this history, see chapter 17). In this chapter we will explore the Trinitarian contribution of the Cappadocian Fathers under three main heads: their teaching on the eternal relations of origin, their co-option of the term *hypostasis* as a term for the divine persons, and their defense of the full deity of the Holy Spirit against the Macedonian heresy.

The Eternal Relations of Origin

It has sometimes been suggested that the Greek fathers "began" with the threeness of God and worked from there toward oneness while the Latin fathers "began" with the oneness of God and worked from there toward threeness. We will examine this so-called de Regnon thesis (named after the nineteenth-century French theologian Theodore de Regnon) in question 35 on social Trintitarianism.[3] But for now, we can note that this heuristic has been largely abandoned by more recent scholarship on the patristic era. In point of fact, there is a demonstrable unanimity among the Greek and Latin fathers after the fourth-century controversies when it comes to the main contours of Trinitarian doctrine (the *filioque* excepted; see question 28). We accept the judgment of Stephen Holmes when he writes, "The one who claims an East-West division, on any issue other than the narrow one of the filioque, is claiming something that the tradition never saw, and it is incumbent on him or her to specify the precise division, to demonstrate that it did in fact divide, and to account for the failure of generations of acute and holy theologians to perceive it."[4] Indeed, Holmes argues that Augustine was nothing other than a faithful interpreter of the Cappadocian doctrine. He goes on to state the mat-

2. See Gregory's panegyric on her life: Gregory of Nyssa, *The Life of Saint Macrina*, trans. Kevin Corrigan (Eugene, OR: Wipf & Stock, 2001). See also the role Macrina plays in Gregory of Nyssa in *On the Soul and the Resurrection*, trans. Catharine P. Roth, PPS (Yonkers, NY: St Vladimir's Seminary Press, 1993).
3. For an evaluation of de Régnon, see Michel Barnes, "De Régnon Reconsidered," *Augustinian Studies* 26.2 (1995): 51–79.
4. Stephen R. Holmes, *The Quest for the Trinity: The Doctrine of God in Scripture, History, and Modernity* (Downers Grove, IL: IVP Academic, 2012), 145.

ter more definitively: "There is no fundamental difference between East and West."[5] The Cappadocians, no less than Augustine, affirm the absolute unity of the persons in the one, simple divine essence and affirm the singular will, knowledge, and activity of God. Augustine, for his part, draws the same distinctions between the divine persons that the Cappadocians did: The divine persons differ only *relation-wise*, defined in terms of the eternal relations of origin and their corresponding temporal modes of action in the indivisible external operations of God (for more on Augustine, see question 18). In short, whatever the Cappadocian Fathers have to say about the personal distinctions between the divine persons, it does not detract from their affirmation that the incomprehensible God is one in essence, will, knowledge, and activity.

Still, clearly distinguishing the divine persons in terms of their eternal relations of origin appears to be one of the major contributions of the Cappadocians. Viewed from one perspective, Augustine and the subsequent Western tradition simply received and transmitted this Cappadocian doctrine. As the name "Father" indicates, the eternal First Person of the Godhead is unbegotten, unoriginated: He is from no one as the eternal Source of all. The idea that the Son is eternally begotten from the Father is rooted in the New Testament itself, and earlier strata of the Christian tradition already reflected on this theme. As the second-century father Justin Martyr asserted, God is never without his Word and Wisdom. Origen developed this eternal relation more precisely in terms of an *eternal generation* (for more on the second- and third-century fathers, see question 12). But it fell to the Cappadocians to defend more rigorously Nicaea's distinction that the Son is not created but rather eternally begotten of the Father before all worlds. The personal names for the divine persons given in the biblical revelation, Father and Son, mark out their eternal relations of origin. The Father is unbegotten, and the Son is eternally begotten of the Father. Against the Eunomians, a neo-Arian heretical group in the mid-fourth century, Gregory of Nazianzus asserts that the name Father "is not a name either of an essence or of an action, most clever sirs. But it is the name of the relation in which the Father stands to the Son, and the Son to the Father."[6] This relation marks out both sameness of essence (because the one begotten is of the same nature as the begetter), and distinction (the Son eternally has this selfsame essence *from* the Father). The important point for Gregory is that begetting is not creating (as the Nicene Creed made clear), but a precise definition of this eternal begetting is beyond the ken of mere mortals:

5. Holmes, *The Quest for the Trinity*, 146.
6. Gregory of Nazianzus, *The Theological Orations*, in *Christology of the Later Fathers*, ed. Edward R. Hardy (Louisville: Westminster John Knox, 1954), Oration 29.16. Note that the Five Theological Orations are Orations 27–31 in Gregory's corpus.

> First, cast away your notions of flow and divisions and sections, and your conceptions of immaterial as if it were material birth, and then you may perhaps worthily conceive of the Divine Generation. How was he begotten?—I repeat the question in indignation. The Begetting of God must be honored by silence. It is a great thing for you to learn that he was begotten. But the manner of His generation we will not admit that even angels can conceive, much less you. Shall I tell you how it was? It was in a manner known to the Father who begot, and to the Son who was begotten. Anything more than this is hidden by a cloud, and escapes your dim sight.[7]

The apophatic mode of theologizing expressed here is indicative of the Cappadocians' approach: The divine essence and the eternal relations of the divine persons are ultimately ineffable; they are a matter of belief and worship—the subject of contemplation, not comprehension.

As the Son is eternally *begotten* from the Father, so also the Spirit eternally *proceeds* from the Father. The language of procession comes from John 15:26: "But when the Helper comes, whom I will send to you from the Father, the Spirit of truth, who proceeds from the Father, he will bear witness about me." The Comforter is sent from the Father because he eternally proceeds from the Father, that is, he eternally *comes forth* from the Father. This relation of origin is distinguished from the eternal begetting of the Son, but it likewise marks out both sameness of essence and distinction of relation: The Holy Spirit "inasmuch as He proceeds from That Source [that is, the Father], is no Creature; and inasmuch as He is not Begotten is no Son; and inasmuch as He is between the Unbegotten and the Begotten is God."[8] The filioque controversy is still some ways off, but interestingly Gregory concludes that the Holy Spirit is "between" the Father and the Son in this eternal relation of procession. As with the mystery of eternal generation, the eternal procession of the Holy Spirit transcends our abilities to comprehend it:

> What then is procession? Do you tell me what is the unbegottenness of the Father, and I will explain to you the physiology of the generation of the Son and the procession of the Spirit, and we shall both of us be frenzy-stricken for prying into the mystery of God. And who are we to do these things, we who cannot even see what lies at our feet, or number the sand of the sea, or the drops of rain, or the days of eternity, much less

7. Gregory of Nazianzus, *The Theological Orations*, Oration 29.8.
8. Gregory of Nazianzus, *The Theological Orations*, Oration 31.8.

> enter into the Depths of God, and supply an account of that Nature which is so unspeakable and transcending all words?[9]

The procession of the Holy Spirit is distinct from the generation of the Son, but it too remains a mystery that is received, not an article that can be mastered. In sum, the divine persons share equally and eternally in the divine essence, which is simple and ineffable, and are only distinguished by their particular modes of being in that one divine essence, namely, the eternal relations of origin.

The Terminology of Person: Three *Hypostaseis*

Another major contribution of the Cappadocian Fathers concerns the term assigned to speak of the three divine persons. In Greek, the term *prosopon* (person) had already been employed for this purpose. The Latin *persona* had been similarly used all the way back to the influential writings of the North African lay theologian Tertullian. The term *hypostasis* (with its Latin equivalent *substantia*) had been used as a rough equivalent to the term *ousia*, which marked out the divine essence. Recall the crucial phrase of the Nicene Creed: *homoousia* (Latin, *consubstantialem*). The semantic overlap between *ousia* and *hypostasis* led the fathers of the first ecumenical council to expressly forbid the usage of the latter with reference to the distinctive divine persons:

> And those who say "there was once when he was not" or "he was not before he was begotten" or "he came into existence from nothing" or who afterward affirm that the Son of God is of another *hypostasis* or substance, or a creature, or mutable or subject to change, such ones the catholic and apostolic church pronounces accursed and separated from the church.[10]

If the persons are one *ousia*, so they must be one *hypostasis*, upon pains of Arianism.

But there was an older tradition that had employed the term *hypostasis* to refer to the three persons. Origen, who had formulated the notion of the eternal generation of the Son, had spoken of three hypostaseis.[11] Despite Origen's own Trinitarian peculiarities and his mixed reception in the fourth century, the option remained open that *hypostasis* might be a useful term to stand in for the three persons, provided it could be sufficiently distinguished from the

---

9. Gregory of Nazianzus, *The Theological Orations*, Oration 31.9.
10. "The Creed of the Synod of Nicaea (June 19, 325)," in *The Trinitarian Controversy*, trans. and ed. William G. Rusch (Philadelphia: Fortress, 1980), 49
11. See Origen, *On First Principles: A Readers Edition*, trans. John Behr (Oxford: Oxford University Press, 2019), 1.1.8, 36.

one *ousia* of the Godhead. A council convened by Athanasius at Alexandria in 362 allowed for either usage of *hypostasis*: either as a term of unity or a term of distinction.[12] It fell to the Cappadocians to take the decisive step of distinguishing *ousia* from *hypostasis* in order to use the latter as a term of distinction. Basil of Caesarea states the matter succinctly:

> It is not enough to count differences in the Persons (*prosōpa*). It is necessary also to confess that each Person (*prosōpon*) exists in a true *hypostasis*. The mirage of persons (*prosōpa*) without *hypostaseis* is not denied even by Sabellius, who said that the same God, though he is one subject, is transformed according the need of each occasion and is thus spoken of now as Father, now as Son, and now as Holy Spirit.[13]

Recall that the Sabellians taught a form of modalistic monarchianism (see question 13): Father, Son, and Holy Spirit do not mark out three eternally existing subsistences but are rather simply distinct modes of God's successive (not simultaneous) revelation of himself to humanity. Basil fiercely opposed the error of modalism, but he acknowledges here that even the Sabellians were comfortable using the language of three *hypostaseis*. How much more should the orthodox feel compelled to use it, precisely in order to forestall any interpretation of the three persons that reduced them to mere modes of revelation? *Prosōpon* was a fine enough term, and it had the advantage of having a rather straightforward parallel in the Latin *persona*, but it was insufficient to shut out the Sabellian error, which had interpreted it more in line with its classical usage in the ancient theater: distinct masks that a single character might wear. So, for Basil, it is "not enough" to affirm three *prosopa*. From now on, the orthodox must also affirm three distinct *hypostasesis*. The reception of this development in the West was initially negative, with theologians such as Jerome fearing that it would undermine the affirmation of one *substantia*, the Latin parallel of *hypostasis*. But *substantia* had its own complexities of usage, and eventually *hypostasis* would be accepted as the standard Greek term for the three divine persons, owing in large part to the influence of the Cappadocians.

The Holy Spirit: The Lord and Giver of Life

As we saw on question 13, one of the heresies that followed the various so-called Arian heresies of the mid-fourth century was the error of the Macedonians. Named after Macedonius (d. 360), bishop of Constantinople, this

12. Khaled Anatolios, *Retrieving Nicaea: The Development and Meaning of Trinitarian Doctrine* (Grand Rapids: Baker Academic, 2011), 23.
13. Basil of Caesarea, *Epistle* 210.5.36–41, as cited in Anatolios, *Retrieving Nicaea*, 23.

heresy denied the true divinity of the Holy Spirit. The heretics who held this position were also referred to as the *Pneumatomachi*, the "fighters against the Spirit." Athanasius, for his part, called them the *Tropici*, because of their use of "tropes," or interpretations of biblical texts, to defend their cause. Athanasius discerned in the Tropici error an alliance with Arianism itself: Just as the Arians had denied the deity of the Son, so also the Tropici denied the true deity of the Holy Spirit.[14] Both Basil of Caesarea and Gregory of Nyssa penned works titled *On the Holy Spirit* to combat this error. The fifth of Gregory of Nazianzus's *Five Theological Orations* (Orations 29–33), preached in Constantinople during the height of the controversies, likewise affirms the coequality and coeternality of the Holy Spirit with the Father and Son.

In Basil's *On the Holy Spirit*, he takes up the challenge that the distinct prepositional phrases (what he calls "syllables") assigned to the three divine persons indicate an order of being. If all things are "of" the Father but only "through" the Son and "in" the Spirit, does that then indicate a subordination of being? Basil answers forcefully in the negative. In any event, sometimes the Scriptures speak of all created things being "through" the Father as well (e.g., Rom. 11:36). All of these biblical prepositional phrases place all three divine persons on the Creator side of the Creator-creature distinction. Far from implying any kind of subordinationism, they teach instead the "indissoluble union" of the divine persons.[15] Basil marshals an impressive array of biblical texts and themes that demonstrate the full deity of the Spirit as the "Lord," the giver of both spiritual life and gifts, and the possessor of divine glory. Not least among these biblical texts is the baptismal formula, which is spoken over each Christian in their initiation to the Christian faith:

> If the Lord did not indeed conjoin the Spirit with the Father and Himself in baptism, do not let them lay the blame of conjunction upon us, for we neither hold nor say anything different. If on the contrary the Spirit is there conjoined with the Father and the Son, and no one is so shameless as to say anything else, then let them not lay blame on us for following the words of Scripture.[16]

Christian faith confesses one God in *three* distinct *hypostaseis*, and those who would deny this basic Christian tenet are, according to Basil, "blasphemers."

14. See Athanasius, *Letters to Serapion on the Holy Spirit*, in Athanasius the Great and Didymus the Blind, *Works on the Spirit*, trans. Mark DelCogliano, Andrew Radde-Gallwitz, and Lewis Ayres, PPS 43 (Yonkers, NY: St Vladimir's Seminary Press, 2011).
15. Basil of Caesarea, *On the Holy Spirit* 14.31, 32, 33 (*NPNF*[2] 8:20).
16. Basil of Caesarea, *On the Holy Spirit* 10.24 (16).

Gregory of Nyssa makes a similar argument in his *On the Holy Spirit*. Those who would deny the true divinity of the Spirit are committing "blasphemy." Like his elder brother, Gregory appeals to the Scriptures but also to the received tradition in defense of the deity of the Spirit, writing,

> If, then, the Holy Spirit is truly, and not in name only, called Divine both by Scripture and by our Fathers, what ground is left for those who oppose the glory of the Spirit? He is Divine, and absolutely good, and Omnipotent, and wise, and glorious, and eternal; He is everything of this kind that can be named to raise our thoughts to the grandeur of His being.[17]

The Holy Spirit thus possesses the attributes of God, performs the actions of God, and receives the adoration that is due only to God. He is called in Scripture both Lord and God, and he possesses by nature the very same honor and glory as the Father and Son. In another work, *On "Not Three Gods,"* Gregory explains that the distinct biblical prepositions used for the divine persons indicate order of indivisible action, not any subordination of being,

> Thus, since among men the action of each in the same pursuits is discriminated, they are properly called many, since each of them is separated from the others within his own environment, according to the special character of his operation. But in the case of the Divine nature we do not similarly learn that the Father does anything by Himself in which the Son does not work conjointly, or again that the Son has any special operation apart from the Holy Spirit; but every operation which extends from God to the Creation, and is named according to our variable conceptions of it, has its origin from the Father, and proceeds through the Son, and is perfected in the Holy Spirit.[18]

Since God is one, God acts as one. The doctrine of inseparable operations—that all of God's external actions are carried out indivisibly by all three divine persons—is often associated with Augustine, who gives it its classic formulation. But we find the very same teaching here in Gregory of Nyssa. There is only one action in creation, redemption, or any other divine operation, but each divine person participates in that indivisible action according to his personal mode of subsistence. God's actions proceed from the Father, through the Son, and in the Holy Spirit. But, crucial for both Basil and Gregory, the Spirit's inclusion in this indissoluble action clearly indicates his full deity.

---

17. Gregory of Nyssa, *On the Holy Spirit, Against the Macedonians* (*NPNF*[2] 5:315–25).
18. Gregory of Nyssa, *On "Not Three Gods"*(*NPNF*[2] 5:331–36).

Gregory of Nazianzus concurs with his Cappadocian compatriots on the deity and glory of the Holy Spirit. In his Fifth Theological Oration (Oration 31), Gregory argues that God is a single source of light but in a threefold manner:

> The Father was "the true light, which lightens every man coming into the world." The Son was "the true light, which lightens every man coming into the world." The other Comforter was "the true light, which lightens every man coming into the world." Was and was and was, but was one thing. Light thrice repeated; but one light and one God. This was what David represented to himself long before when he said, "In your light shall we see light." And now we have both seen and proclaim concisely and simply the doctrine of God the Trinity, comprehending out of Light [the Father], Light [the Son], in Light [the Holy Ghost].[19]

As eternal light, the Holy Spirit is coequal with the Father and the Son. Macedonianism, for Gregory, amounts to a kind of Arianism of the Holy Spirit: "If ever there was a time when the Father was not, then there was a time when the Son was not. If ever there was a time when the Son was not, then there was a time when the Spirit was not. If the one was from the beginning, then the three were so too."[20] We have already seen how Nazianzen exposits the person of the Holy Spirit in terms of his incomprehensible eternal procession from the Father. As such, the Spirit possesses the very same essence as the one from whom he eternally proceeds. The Spirit is of the same substance as the Father and Son. As with the other two Cappadocians, Gregory understands this doctrine not as a mere academic puzzle but as an earnest matter of salvation and worship. At the conclusion of his oration, he reiterates his aim: "to persuade all others also to the best of my power to worship Father, Son, and Holy Ghost, the one Godhead and power. To him belongs all glory and honor and might for ever and ever. Amen."[21]

Conclusion

The Cappadocian Fathers represent the culmination of a long century of efforts to defend the Nicene doctrine against its heretical detractors. Their major contributions on this front are threefold: They distinguished the divine persons with respect to their eternal relations of origin; they co-opted (as it were) the term *hypostasis*, making it stand in for the three persons as truly

---

19. Gregory of Nazianzus, *The Theological Orations*, Oration 31.3.
20. Gregory of Nazianzus, *The Theological Orations*, Oration 31.4.
21. Gregory of Nazianzus, *The Theological Orations*, Oration 31.33.

distinct modes of being in God; and they defended the full deity, honor, and glory of the Holy Spirit against the Macedonian heresy. As we will see in the next chapter, these contributions map onto the historical events that led to the Council of Constantinople in 381 (at which Gregory of Nazianzus presided for a time), which would eventually be received as the Second Ecumenical Council after the "Great Synod" of Nicaea.

REFLECTION QUESTIONS

1. The Cappadocians were concerned with what we would consider technical questions. Why do these technical questions matter pastorally and spiritually?
2. What are ways that the Cappadocians' talk of the Trinity helps your prayer life?
3. How does the Cappadocians' teaching on the Trinity remind you of the Bible's teaching on the Trinity?
4. What is a passage in Scripture that has confused you but now seems clearer based on thinking through the Cappadocians' teaching on the Trinity?
5. What is one teaching strategy from the Cappadocians that could help you explain the Trinity to someone else?

QUESTION 17

What Happened at the Council of Constantinople?

Nicaea sparked decades of ecclesiastical and imperial debates on its authority and meaning. Constantinople, on the other hand, finally settled many of the theological issues among the orthodox, though its authority as an ecumenical council took time to be discerned (and Arians and other heretical groups persisted outside the church's domain for centuries to follow). Our treatment of the Council of Constantinople will proceed in three steps: the council's historical and theological background, its proceedings and rulings, and its theological legacy and contribution.

Historical and Theological Background

As our discussion of Athanasius (question 15) and the Cappadocians (question 16) indicated, the decisions of the council of Nicaea did not produce a lasting peace in the ensuing decades. It took courageous and dogged determination for these pro-Nicene theologians to defend Nicaea's key terms and insights. The many political twists and turns of the fourth century lie beyond the scope of this chapter. It is sufficient to note that at various points throughout the mid-fourth century, Arian, semi-Arian, and other mediating positions held sway among the imperial powers. This was especially true during the 350s when the emperor Constantius achieved sole power and persecuted the pro-Nicenes. We have already noted how Athanasius was frequently exiled for his pro-Nicene views. Hilary was also exiled. Other pro-Nicenes were forced to acquiesce and recant their views (such as the aging Ossius of Cordoba).[1]

1. We noted in question 14 (note 3) some of the resources on the history and theology of the fourth-century debates. Once again, we would point readers to the helpful summaries in Leo Donald Davis, *The First Seven Ecumenical Councils (325–787): Their History*

Theologically, several alternatives to Nicaea's *homoousion* emerged. Some theologians, such as Aetius and Eunomius, doubled down on the Arian position: The Son is a creature with a different nature than the Father. The Father shares certain divine prerogatives with the Son, but the Son remains a created being, distinct from the ingenerate and immutable God. The Son is unlike (*anomia*) the Father and of a different substance (*heteroousia*). The Arians were willing to accept a unity or harmony of *will* between the Father and Son, but they could not embrace a unity of *nature*.[2] Athanasius and others acknowledged that the divine unity was *according to* the Father's will, but it was not brought about *by* the Father's will. The unity of the divine persons is natural and substantial, not merely a matter of consent.

Some theologians of the fourth century sought a mediating position between the heteroousians and the homoousians. A statement known as the Fourth Creed of Antioch was presented several times throughout the century as a possible compromise. It clearly distanced itself from Arian views but stopped short of using Nicaea's *homoousion*. Many were content with describing the Son as *like unto* the Father. These so-called *homoian* proposals were often presented as a kind of compromise position. Other theologians, especially Basil of Ancyra, espoused the alternative term *homoiousion*: like unto essence, or of a similar substance. This formulation was stronger than a mere affirmation of likeness or similarity, but it still stopped short of the *homoousion*. In the middle of the century, Arian and *homoian* bishops reigned in many Eastern sees. In the west, Milan became a hotbed for the Arian position. But after several imperial successions and due to the unflagging work of pro-Nicenes like Athanasius, Hilary, Basil and his younger brother Gregory, the tide began to turn toward the Nicene position. By the late 370s, the eastern emperor Theodosius had been won to the Nicene cause, and the new bishop of Milan, Ambrose—one of the great Latin "doctors" of the patristic era—was a committed pro-Nicene.

As we noted in question 13 on the early Trinitarian heresies, the years between Nicaea and Constantinople I also witnessed a growing attention being given to the person and nature of Holy Spirit. Some groups, even those who affirmed the Son's divinity, subordinated the Spirit to the Father and the Son. Athanasius clashed with one such group he called the *Tropici*, because of the "tropes," or interpretative maneuvers, they made to deny the deity of the Holy Spirit. A related and more widespread group known as the Macedonians (named after their leader, Macedonius) flatly denied the deity of the Spirit, arguing that the Spirit was created by the Father and Son. Pro-Nicene

---

and Theology (Collegeville, MN: Liturgical, 1990). See 81–133 for Davis's treatment of Constantinople I. We follow his concise summary in much of what follows.

2. See Khaled Anatolios, *Retrieving Nicaea: The Development and Meaning of Trinitarian Doctrine* (Grand Rapids: Baker Academic, 2011), esp. 33–98 for this particular contrast.

theologians like Athanasius (*Letters to Serapion*) and Basil (*On the Holy Spirit*) opposed the Macedonians, referring to them as Pneumatomachians: "fighters against the Spirit." Still, many theologians were hesitant to refer to the Holy Spirit as "God" or to affirm that he is *homoousios* with the Father and Son.[3]

In the lead-up to the Council of Constantinople, few figures were as clear or as courageous in defending the doctrine of the Trinity, including the full deity of the Holy Spirit, as Gregory of Nazianzus. Assigned to the eastern capital of Constantinople, though there was a rival Arian who also claimed the bishopric, Gregory preached a series of sermons sometime during AD 379–380 that would come to be known as his *Five Theological Orations*.[4] In these masterful defenses of orthodoxy, Gregory affirmed the essential sameness and personal distinctions of the three divine persons. The three are one in all things except for their eternal relations of origin: the Father is unbegotten, the Son is eternally begotten of the Father, and the Spirit eternally proceeds from the Father. Gregory did not shy away from affirming that the Spirit is indeed *homoousios* with the Father and Son. In 380 Theodosius condemned and deposed the Arian bishops, and Gregory was affirmed as the sole bishop of Constantinople.

The Council Convenes

In 381, Theodosius convened a council of Eastern bishops in the capital city. At its convening, the council could hardly be considered truly ecumenical. Only one western bishop was present, and that by accident. The bishop of Rome was not even invited; the bishop of Thessalonika acted as his representative. The council's ecumenical status was only officially affirmed at the Council of Chalcedon in 451. Some scholars even question whether the creed associated with the council—what we know today as the Nicene, or Niceno-Constantinopolitan, Creed—was actually produced during the council. The canons of the council would only be embraced by the Western church hundreds of years later.[5] Despite this apparent "unecumenical" context, the council and its creed definitively settled the theological debates that had plagued the church throughout the fourth century. In the end, there is good reason to embrace the authenticity of the council's creed as it was investigated and affirmed by council fathers of Chalcedon in 451.

3. See Athanasius, Letters to Serapion on the Holy Spirit and Didymus, On the Holy Spirit, in Works on the Spirit, trans. Mark DelCogliano, Andrew Radde-Gallwitz, and Lewis Ayres (Yonkers, NY: St Vladimir's Seminary Press, 2011) and Basil the Great, *On the Holy Spirit*, trans. Stephen Hildebrand (Yonkers, NY: St Vladimir's Seminary Press, 2011).
4. Gregory of Nazianzus, *On God and Christ: The Five Theological Orations and Two Letters to Cledonius*, trans. Frederick Williams and Lionel Wickham (Yonkers, NY. St Vladimir's Seminary Press, 2002).
5. For a summary of the debate over these issues, see Davis, *The First Seven Ecumenical Councils*, 119–29.

But the Council of Constantinople was not convened without controversy. Three different bishops presided over the months-long council. The second of these, Gregory of Nazianzus himself, eventually resigned under western pressure that he had illegitimately assumed the bishopric of Constantinople. Some overtures of compromise were made to the Macedonians (the creed does not apply the *homoousion* to the Holy Spirit and it does not refer to him as *theos*, God). But the Macedonian bishops were unsatisfied and eventually left the council. The council condemned a number of heresies: the Arians and Eunomians, the Pneumatomachians, the Sabellians and Marcellians. It also previewed the Christological debates of the coming century by condemning the heresy of Apollinaris, who had denied the full humanity of Christ, arguing that the Son only assumed a human body in the incarnation with the person of the Word taking the place of the human soul in Christ. Against this heresy, Gregory of Nazianzus had argued if there is a part of our humanity that the Son did not assume, then that part remains outside the scope of his saving work. "The unassumed is unhealed," was his axiom.[6] At the council, Gregory's position was upheld and the Apollinarian position condemned.

The Council's Theological Legacy

The council produced a creed that is most often referred to as the Nicene Creed because of its shared language with the creed of Nicaea in 325. Historically, Constantinople's Creed is a separate document; it both omits and expands upon the language of Nicaea. Still, there is good reason to view these two councils and these two creeds as parts of the same theological trajectory and agenda. The text of the so-called Niceno-Constantinopolitan Creed is as follows:

> We believe in one God, the Father All Governing, creator of heaven and earth, of all things visible and invisible.
>
> And in one Lord Jesus Christ, the only-begotten Son of God, begotten from the Father before all time, Light from Light, true God from true God, begotten not created, of the same essence as the Father, through Whom all things came into being; Who for us men and because of our salvation came down from heaven, and was incarnate by the Holy Spirit and the Virgin Mary and became human. He was crucified for us under Pontius Pilate, and suffered and was buried and rose on the third day, according to the Scriptures; and ascended to heaven, and sits on the right hand of the Father, and will come again with glory to judge the living and the dead. His kingdom shall have no end.

---

6. Gregory of Nazianzus, Epistle 101, in *Christology of the Later Fathers*, ed. Edward R. Hardy (Louisville: Westminster John Knox, 1954), 216.

> And in the Holy Spirit, the Lord and life-giver, Who proceeds from the Father, Who is worshiped and glorified together with the Father and Son, Who spoke through the prophets;
>
> And in one, holy, catholic, and apostolic Church. We confess one baptism for the remission of sins. We look forward to the resurrection of the dead and the life of the world to come. Amen.[7]

The creed takes the same threefold division as Nicaea. It likewise takes aim at a number of heresies. Arianism in all of its forms (including Eunominanism) is excluded by the *homoousion* and the distinction between begetting and creating: The Son is begotten but not made. The semi-Arianism of the Macedonians is also excluded. Though the *homoousion* is not applied to the Holy Spirit, the substance of its affirmation is there: The Spirit is the Lord (a divine title) and Giver of life (a divine operation). He is no mere creature but is placed on the divine side of the ledger and is worshiped and glorified along with the Father and Son. His personhood is distinguished not by creation but by procession, an eternal and immanent relation in God's own inner life. The Apollinarians may also be targeted by the creed's insistence that the Son takes his humanity from the Virgin Mary (rather than bringing his flesh from heaven). The Sabellian, or Modalist, error is also excluded because the divine persons are eternally distinct; the reign of the incarnate Son will even last forever ("whose kingdom shall have no end").

Summary

The primary theological contribution of Constantinople lies in its ability to hold together both the essential sameness of and the relational distinctions between the three divine persons. The Father and Son are of the same substance (*homoousion*). The Spirit likewise is the Lord who is to be worshiped and glorified jointly with the Father and Son. The three are distinguished not by substance, by will, or by role. They are distinguished only by relation. The Son is begotten from and the Holy Spirit proceeds from the unbegotten Father. The scriptural names for the persons faithfully communicate who they are. The Son is from the Father. The Spirit comes forth from the Father. These relations of origin secure at once the substantial equality of and the personal distinction of the three persons. How generation and procession differ is left unstated. Gregory had argued that no mere mortal can fully understand this distinction. As we will see in a later chapter, the western church would develop a distinction between these two eternal emanations in terms of the *filioque*: The Spirit proceeds from the

---

7. John H. Leith, ed., *Creeds of the Churches: A Reader in Christian Doctrine from the Bible to the Present*, 3rd ed. (Louisville: Westminster John Knox, 1982), 33.

Father *and the Son*. But at Constantinople, the basic affirmations of orthodoxy were set: Father, Son, and Holy Spirit are one God, and yet they are really and eternally distinguished by their relations of origin.

REFLECTION QUESTIONS

1. What are ways that the Council of Constantinople's talk of the Trinity helps your prayer life?

2. How does Constantinople's teaching on the Trinity remind you of the Bible's teaching on the Trinity?

3. How do the questions asked and answers given by the Council of Constantinople remind you of questions you've asked about the Trinity while reading the Bible?

4. What is a passage in Scripture that has confused you but now seems clearer based on thinking through Constantinople's teaching on the Trinity?

5. What is one teaching strategy from Constantinople that could help you explain the Trinity to someone else?

QUESTION 18

What Was the Trinitarian Contribution of Augustine?

Augustine of Hippo is perhaps the most influential theologian in the history of the church after the time of the apostles. The famous quip about Plato's significance in the history of Western philosophy has often been adapted to Augustine in the discipline of theology: The whole history of Western theology is, in a sense, simply the footnotes to Augustine. Augustine continues to exert influence among both Roman Catholics and Protestants on the whole range of theological topics: biblical interpretation, Christian doctrine, political philosophy, sacramentalism, ethics, and more. B. B. Warfield once described the Reformation itself as Augustine's doctrine of grace triumphing over Augustine's doctrine of the church.[1] Among this incredible output, Augustine also wrote extensively on the central dogma of the Christian faith: the Holy Trinity.[2]

While many important theologians of the late fourth and fifth centuries are worthy of consideration (including Ambrose, Jerome, and Cyril of Alexandria), no other theologian exerted the kind of influence that Augustine of Hippo did on the church's Trinitarian thought. His monumental *De Trinitate* provides his most sustained reflection on the Trinity,[3] but Trinitarian themes can be found throughout his corpus. *De Trinitate* is perhaps most well-known for the psychological analogies Augustine employs as a way of understanding how three divine persons can be one God. But the work as a whole is much

1. B. B. Warfield, *Calvin and Augustine* (Philadelphia: P&R, 1956), 322.
2. Much of the material in this chapter originally appeared in R. Lucas Stamps, "The Trinity," in *Historical Theology for the Church*, ed. Jason G. Duesing and Nathan A. Finn (Nashville: B&H Academic, 2021), 47–70.
3. Augustine, *The Trinity*, 2nd ed., trans. Edmund Hill, ed. John Rotelle, The Works of Saint Augustine 5 (Hyde Park, NY: New City, 2012).

more concerned with the kind of biblical exegesis that undergirds the doctrine of the Trinity.

Missions and Processions

For instance, one of the orienting principles of *De Trinitate* is the dynamic between the temporal missions of the Son and Spirit and the eternal processions that they reveal. According to Augustine, a Trinitarian mission is a visible manifestation of either the Son or Spirit, sent from the Father (and from the Son, in the case of the mission of the Holy Spirit). Augustine grounds this conversation exegetically in a number of ways. One such instance occurs when, in the earlier parts of the work, Augustine considers whether or not the theophanies of the Old Testament constitute missions of one or another divine person. For example, is the angel of the Lord, the man who wrestled with Jacob, or the fourth man in Daniel's fiery furnace a mission of the Son? After a careful consideration of several OT texts, Augustine concludes that it is not always possible to determine whether any of the OT theophanies are meant to terminate upon a particular divine person or whether it is the whole Godhead who is manifested in them. Instead, we are to look to the NT for the definitive divine missions: The Son is revealed in his being sent from the Father in the incarnation and the Holy Spirit is revealed in his being sent from the Father as a dove at Jesus's baptism and as cloven tongues of fire on the day of Pentecost.

These missions unveil the triune nature of the one true God. The missions, in turn, reveal the divine persons' eternal relations to one another. The Son is *sent from* the Father because he *is from* the Father in his eternal generation. The Spirit is *sent from* the Father and Son because he *is from* the Father and Son in his eternal procession. Thus, the temporal missions reveal and correspond to the eternal processions. Again, we see the principle that God is as he reveals himself to be. To be clear, not everything that obtains in the temporal missions can be read back into the eternal processions, as it were. For example, the Son is subordinate to the Father in virtue of his taking the form of a servant in his humanity: "The Father is greater than I" (John 14:28). But in virtue of his consubstantiality with the Father, the eternal generation of the Son does not imply any subordination in the being of God: "I and the Father are one" (John 10:30). And, as we noted in an earlier chapter, Augustine (like his pro-Nicene predecessors) grounds this distinction between speaking of the Son "in the form of God" and speaking of the Son "in the form of a servant" by referencing Philippians 2:6–7, in which Paul makes precisely the same distinction.[4]

Inseparable Operations

Another important insight that emerges from *De Trinitate* and Augustine's other writings on the Trinity is the emphasis on the Trinity's inseparable oper-

4. See, e.g., Augustine, *The Trinity*, 1.15, 20, 28.

ations. Augustine did not invent this doctrine (the Cappadocians emphasized it as well), but he provides one of the classic expressions of it:

> For according to the Catholic faith, the Trinity is proposed to our belief and believed—and even understood by a few saints and holy persons—as so inseparable that whatever action is performed by it must be thought to be performed at the same time by the Father and by the Son and by the Holy Spirit.[5]

The doctrine is sometimes summarized in the Latin phrase *opera trinitatis ad extra indivisa sunt*: The external works of the Trinity are indivisible, or inseparable. All that God does outside of himself (*ad extra*) in creation, providence, redemption, and judgment, he performs as Father, Son, and Holy Spirit. Certain divine works may be appropriated (the language of appropriation would become important in medieval reflections on the Trinity) to certain divine persons. We may say that the Father creates, the Son redeems, and the Spirit sanctifies. But this manner of speaking should not be taken to imply that the works of the Trinity constitute a kind of division of labor in which one divine person carries out an act separate from the others. No, it is the triune God who creates, redeems, and sanctifies. Because God is one, he acts as one. Each of the divine persons is to be identified, essence-wise, with the one, simple divine being, and, therefore, all of the Trinity's external works are inseparable. Still, each divine person's involvement, so to speak, in the inseparable works of the Trinity is marked by his own distinct personal property. Gregory of Nyssa had already given expression to this same truth in his *On "Not Three Gods"*:

> If, then, every good thing and every good name, depending on that power and purpose which is without beginning, is brought to perfection in the power of the Spirit through the Only-begotten God, without mark of time or distinction (since there is no delay, existent or conceived, in the motion of the Divine will from the Father, through the Son, to the Spirit): and if Godhead also is one of the good names and concepts, it would not be proper to divide the name into a plurality, since the unity existing in the action prevents plural enumeration.[6]

---

5. Augustine, *Epistle* 11.2. Cited in Stephen R. Holmes, *The Quest for the Trinity: The Doctrine of God in Scripture, History, and Modernity* (Downers Grove, IL: IVP Academic, 2012), 132.
6. Gregory of Nyssa, "On Not Three Gods," in (NPNF^2 5:335).

So, for Gregory and for Augustine after him, there is an inseparable unity in the divine operations. But there is also an order (Greek, *taxis*) to the Trinity's work, marked here by Gregory's use of differing prepositions: The motion is from the Father, through the Son, and to the Spirit.

Psychological Analogies

As mentioned above, Augustine's *De Trinitate* is often associated with his use of psychological analogies in book 9 of the work. Only after giving a lengthy exegetical defense of the orthodox doctrine of the Trinity does Augustine turn to reflections of a more speculative sort. Augustine suggests that the best candidate for an analogy of God lies in the creature who bears the image of God: humanity. Can we see a picture of the tripersonal God in a lover, a beloved, and the love between them? Is there an analogy of the Trinity in the mind, its understanding, and its will to love? Augustine believed that triads like these (mind-understanding-love or mind-memory-will) have the potential to cast light on both the unity and the distinctions of the divine persons. These speculations, it should be noted, have their limitations, but they are not entirely without scriptural support. The NT does speak of the Son as the Logos (Word, Reason) of the Father. And the Holy Spirit is often associated with the themes of love and gift and is said to be the Spirit of the Father and the Spirit of Christ—in other words, the shared Spirit of both. Later in the medieval era, Thomas Aquinas would take up these themes in his exposition of the Trinity.

One final note on Augustine is worth mentioning: the relationship of his so-called Latin approach to the Trinity to the Greek-speaking eastern approach of, say, the Cappadocians. It has sometimes been argued, going back to Theodore de Régnon in the late nineteenth century, that Latin Trinitarianism "begins" from the unity of the divine persons and asks how they can be three, while eastern Trinitarianism "begins" from the distinction of the divine persons and asks how they can be one.[7] The assumption of the so-called de Régnon thesis is that there is a sharp wedge between the two traditions on the priority of unity versus distinction. But more recent scholarship has called into question this dichotomy and has demonstrated that the two theological traditions, while distinct in some ways, exhibit much more family resemblance than any fundamental difference in orientation. The quotations from Augustine and Gregory of Nyssa cited above show at least part of this convergence: Gregory is as eager to guard the unity and inseparability of the triune works as Augustine is. Likewise, Augustine is as concerned with affirming the real distinctions between the divine persons as Gregory is. The Trinitarian

---

7. Theodore de Régnon, *Études de Théologie Positive Sur La Sainte Trinité*, 3 vols. (Paris: 1892–1898). For an evaluation of de Régnon, see Michel Barnes, "De Régnon Reconsidered," *Augustinian Studies* 26 (1995): 51–79.

missions reveal not a unipersonal, modalistic God but real relations of origin that distinguish the divine persons from all eternity.

Summary

Augustine of Hippo was perhaps the most influential theologian in church history after the time of the apostles. So, it is no surprise that he made important contributions to the church's foundational doctrine: the doctrine of the Trinity. He embraces the Trinitarian orthodoxy of the fourth century and develops it in important ways. Three contributions are especially noteworthy: his articulation of the missions and processions of the Son and Spirit (that the sendings of the Son and Spirit reveal who they are in their eternal processions from the Father); his insistence upon the doctrine of inseparable operations (that all of God's external works are carried out indivisibly by all three divine persons); and his exploration of "psychological analogies" for the Trinity (that mind, understanding, and will can point to the doctrine of the Trinity). In these are other ways Augustine becomes a standard authority for Western articulations of this most crucial Christian doctrine.

REFLECTION QUESTIONS

1. How would you evaluate Augustine's psychological analogies for the Trinity? How does the Trinity relate to the image of God in human beings?

2. What are ways that Augustine's talk of the Trinity helps your prayer life?

3. How does Augustine's teaching on the Trinity remind you of the Bible's teaching on the Trinity?

4. What is a passage in Scripture that has confused you but now seems clearer based on thinking through Augustine's teaching on the Trinity?

5. What is one teaching strategy from Augustine that could help you explain the Trinity to someone else?

QUESTION 19

What Was the Trinitarian Contribution of Thomas Aquinas?

Thomas Aquinas (ca. 1225–1274) was an Italian Dominican who is widely considered one of the greatest theologians in Christian history. He is one of the foremost representatives of the scholastic method that arose in the newly formed Western universities. He is perhaps best known for his massive *Summa Theologiae*, which treats virtually every topic and question in theology, philosophy, and ethics. But he also penned a shorter work aimed at defending Christian theology against unbelieving objections (*Summa contra Gentiles*), as well as commentaries on Scripture, Aristotle, and Peter Lombard's *Sentences* and a number of disputations on various theological topics. Though there are certainly other medieval scholastics worthy of careful study, Thomas's influence is difficult to overstate—not only on the Roman Catholic tradition but also among the later Protestant scholastics as well. His theology represents well the scholasticism of the high medieval period, synthesizing the biblical and patristic sources and integrating them within an Aristotelian metaphysic (that is, an understanding of being and reality shaped by the Greek philosopher Aristotle). At the risk of being cheeky, we can summarize Thomas's Trinitarian contribution by counting to five: one essence, two processions, three persons, four relations, five notions.[1]

One Essence

For Thomas, like Augustine before him, there is an absolute unity and equality when it comes to the essence of Father, Son, and Holy Spirit. After considering

1. For an academic treatment of Thomas's doctrine of the Trinity, see Gilles Emery, *The Trinitarian Theology of Saint Thomas Aquinas*, trans. Francesca Aran Murphy (Oxford: Oxford University Press, 2007). See also the introduction to Thomas's Trinitarian theology by Joseph Wawrykow in his "Bonaventure and Aquinas," in *The Oxford Handbook on the Trinity*, ed. Gilles Emery and Matthew Levering (Oxford: Oxford University Press, 2011), esp. 190–94. See also the select bibliography in that work on 194–96.

ways to demonstrate the existence of God (*ST* 1.2), Thomas begins his theology proper by treating the essence of God (1.3–13). For Thomas, God is simple, that is, non-composite (1.3). God is one in the strictest sense: He is supremely one and supremely undivided. He is not one of a kind or a genus, as if there could in theory be more than one god though only one happens to exist. No, for God, his existence is his essence; he is being itself subsisting. The doctrine of the Trinity does not in any way undermine this essential simplicity and unity. In God, essence is the same as person. Each of the divine persons is identical with the divine essence. The divine essence is not some fourth thing in addition to the three persons. Each divine person *just is* the divine essence (though they subsist as that essence in distinct modes; more on this below). Put simply, each of the three persons is truly and fully God. Therefore, all of the divine attributes are predicable of all three divine persons. They only differ in their relations to one another.

The essential sameness of the three persons points to another pair of doctrines in Thomas's Trinitarian theology: the doctrine of appropriation and the doctrine of inseparable operations. Sometimes a divine attribute can be appropriated to (Latin, *appropriare*, "to take as one's own") a particular divine person, but this is only a manner of speaking. The appropriation serves to highlight the unique personhood of that divine person. For example, wisdom can be appropriated to the Son; the Son is the Word and Wisdom of the Father. But this appropriation in no way suggests that the Father or the Holy Spirit is any less the possessor of the divine attribute of wisdom. It simply underscores that the Son is the eternal Word of the Father. Likewise, goodness can be appropriated to the Holy Spirit as the gift and love of the Father and Son, even though goodness is a divine attribute equally shared by the three persons. And because God is one, God always acts as one. Like Augustine before him, Thomas asserts that all of God's operations, or acts, outside of himself (*ad extra*) are inseparably and indivisibly carried out by all three divine persons. There is no division of labor in the Trinity. Father, Son, and Holy Spirit act inseparably in creation, redemption, and sanctification—but each in his own mode or manner of acting. As we will see below, the persons are distinguished by eternal processions in God's own inner life (*ad intra*). These distinct modes of being, in turn, yield distinct modes of operation when God acts in creation and providence. So, while the action is singular and unified, each person participates, so to speak, in that single action in a manner fitting to his own personhood. The works of God are carried out from the Father, through the Son, and in or by the Holy Spirit. In short, the distinct modes of being and action (and Scripture's appropriated language highlighting those distinctions) do not in any sense undermine the essential sameness of the three divine persons. There is only one God, and each divine person is that God. And because God is one, he acts as one in inseparable unity.[2]

2. For an academic treatment of the doctrine of inseparable operations, see Adonis Vidu, *The Same God Who Works All Things: Inseparable Operations in Trinitarian Theology* (Grand

Two Processions

What then distinguishes Father, Son, and Holy Spirit, in Thomas's view? The remaining terms we will discuss spell out the answer to this question. Most fundamentally, the distinctions between the persons are grounded in two eternal emanations, or processions, in the life of God: the eternal generation of the Son and the eternal procession (or spiration) of the Holy Spirit. In the *ST*, this is actually where Thomas begins his discussion of the Trinity proper (at question 27 in the *Prima Pars*). These processions are distinguished from creation in that they are both eternal and intrinsic to the life of God: They never had a beginning, and they do not produce a second and a third god but the same God in a threefold manner. The eternal generation of the Son from the being of the Father is indicated by the very names given to these two persons in Scripture: Father and Son. Son indicates both *fromness* and *likeness*. The Son has his origin in the Father, and he is of the same substance as the Father with regards to his essence.

There is a second procession in God: the eternal procession of the Holy Spirit as the love and gift of the Father and Son. This procession is truly distinct from the generation of the Son. Like Augustine, Thomas employs an analogy to human psychology to explain the distinction: An act of the intellect is distinguishable from an act of the will (1.27.3). So, as word is distinct from love, so the Son is distinct from the Holy Spirit. Thomas also distinguishes generation from procession in that word is sourced in the Father alone while love has its origin in both the Father and the Son. Thus, Thomas sides with his own western tradition on the question of the filioque: The Sprit proceeds not from the Father alone but from the "joint spiration" of the Father and the Son. The third person is said in Scripture to be the Spirit of both the Father and the Son. He is sent by both Father and Son in his temporal mission. And because the missions are grounded in and follow upon the processions, the Spirit eternally proceeds from both Father and Son.

Three Persons

The two processions correspond to two persons, in addition to the person of the Father. Therefore, there are exactly three persons in the Godhead: Father, Son, and Holy Spirit. Thomas conceives of a person in Boethian terms: A person is an individual substance of a rational nature.[3] This definition holds true, by way of analogy, even for God. Substance language when applied to God can be tricky. Sometimes substance can be synonymous with the essence of

---

Rapids: Eerdmans, 2021). For an accessible introduction to the topic, see Matthew Y. Emerson and Brandon D. Smith, *Beholding the Triune God: The Inseparable Work of Father, Son, and Spirit* (Wheaton, IL: Crossway, 2024).

3. This influential definition of personhood comes from the sixth-century Roman philosopher Boethius in his work *Liber de Persona et Duabus Naturis.*

God, in which case God is a singular substance. But substance (Latin, *substantia*) is also parallel to the Greek term *hypostasis*, which signifies the three persons. Thus, substance can be used to refer to the three individual persons who subsist in the singular divine nature. And since the divine nature is rational, Boethius's definition holds true for the divine persons. Still, Thomas seems to prefer the term subsistence (*subsistentia*) to refer to the persons (1.29.2, reply obj. 2). Thomas carefully parses several terms in this regard: substance, subsistence, suppositum, hypostasis, and person. For our purposes, it is sufficient to note that there are many different kinds of individually existing things; what distinguishes a person is that it possesses reason.

When interpreting Thomas, we must be careful not to import modern or colloquial meanings to the term *person*. The divine persons are not "people," that is, (super)human beings. Neither are the divine persons distinct centers of consciousness, with differing minds and wills. No, the divine persons are one in mind and will because they are one in being and essence. For Thomas, the divine persons are constituted only in virtue of their relations to one another (more on the four "relations" in the next section). They are "subsistent relations." Person is, therefore, predicated of God and humans analogically, not univocally. Human persons are not distinguished in virtue of relations, which are accidental in creatures. But in God, relations are substantial, not merely accidental. Again, the persons are constituted precisely by their relations to one another. Because of their essential sameness, no other distinctions are permissible. Each of the divine persons is fully and eternally God. They only differ in virtue of their eternal relations of origin.

Four Relations

So, the two processions yield three persons. Among these three persons there are precisely four relations: one on each pole, so to speak, of the two processions. In the eternal generation of the Son from the Father are two relations: the paternity (fatherhood) of the Father and the filiation (sonship) of the Son. Similarly, in the eternal procession of the Holy Spirit are two relations: the joint spiration of Father and Son and the procession of the Holy Spirit. Thomas grounds these divine relations in the names given to the persons in Scripture: "The Father is denominated only from paternity; and the Son only from filiation. Therefore, if no real paternity or filiation existed in God, it would follow that God is not really Father or Son, but only in our manner of understanding; and this is the Sabellian heresy" (1.28.1). Thomas is here making a thoroughly Athanasian point: Father names who God is essentially and eternally. He is not Father merely in virtue of being the Creator. He is the eternal Father of the eternal Son. To deny real relations in God is to commit the error of Sabellius, who held that Father, Son, and Holy Spirit were simply distinct modes of successive revelation, not really and eternally persons. The relations adjoined to the eternal procession of the Holy Spirit also take their cues from scriptural divine naming. The very name "Spirit" indicates a kind "breathing out," or spiration (note how Jesus breathes on the apostles in John 20:22). "Procession" too is taken from Scripture (e.g., John 15:26). For Thomas, these biblical names indicate not only what God does in the economy of salvation but who God is in his own immanent life.

These relations are intrinsic to who God is. They are not accidental but essential. In other words, they are not optional add-ons to God but are essential to his very being as God. Recall that for Thomas, God is simple: All that is in God is God. So, the relations, like the persons, are identical with the divine essence. Nevertheless, they are really distinct from one another. They are, indeed, relations of "opposition" (from *oppositus*, "set against"); that is, they are distinct from each in reality, not just in our understanding. They are essentially identical but still logically distinct. There is and can only be four relations in God because there are only two processions. Again, there is a relation on either side of each procession: the person(s) who is the principle and the person who proceeds from that principle. Thus, in the case of eternal generation, the Father is the principle and the Son is the person proceeding from it. And in the case of eternal procession, the Father and Son together are the joint principle, and the Spirit is the person proceeding from it.

Five Notions

To retrace our steps, God is one in essence and yet there is a plurality in this one God. There are two eternal processions: the eternal generation of the Son from the Father and the eternal procession of the Spirit from the Father and Son. These processions yield three distinct persons: Father, Son, and Holy Spirit, whose personhood is constituted precisely by their relations to one another. There are, then, a total of four divine relations between them: paternity, filiation, spiration, and procession. The final category that we consider from Thomas is perhaps less well-known to modern readers: There are five *notions* in God. Thomas, like other medieval theologians, makes a distinction between *essential terms* that are shared equally by all three persons, and *notional terms* that distinguish the three persons.[4] A Trinitarian notion (*notitio*), as Thomas defines it, is "the proper idea (*propria ratio*) whereby we know a divine person" (1.32.3). Since the persons are distinguished only by relation, one might expect that there are only four notions, since there are precisely four relations between the three persons. But a fifth notion obtains with respect to the Father: Since he proceeds from no other person, we can attribute to him not only paternity (the notion already conceived in his relation to the Son) and spiration (the notion conceived in his relation to the Spirit) but also

4. Thomas Joseph White, *The Trinity: On the Nature and Mystery of the One God*, Thomistic Ressourcement Series 19 (Washington, DC: The Catholic University of America Press, 2022), 434.

innascibility, or unbegottenness. The other four notions correspond to the four relations. The total comes to five notions: innascibility and paternity (by which we know the Father), filiation (by which we know the Son), spiration (by which we know the Father and Son jointly), and procession (by which we know the Holy Spirit).[5]

Thomas also speaks of *notional acts*, which are the internal (*ad intra*) acts of the persons in relation to one another.[6] Again, all of God's external acts (*ad extra*) are carried out indivisibly by all three persons. These essential acts are common to the three persons. But notional acts are those internal operations that are founded in the eternal relations of origin. "It is a property of the Father to beget the Son," as Thomas quotes Augustine (1.41.1). The processions of understanding and love constitute the persons as such. In knowing himself eternally, the Father begets the Son. In their shared love, the Father and Son spirate the Spirit. These notional acts are not freely chosen by the Father (which was the Arian error) but are true of God eternally and naturally.

Summary

There is more to Thomas's rich Trinitarian theology than these five steps, but they summarize well the content and form of his approach to this crucial doctrine. In his scholastic treatment of the doctrine, there is one essence (the shared divine nature), two processions (eternal generation and eternal spiration), three persons (Father, Son, and Spirit), four relations (paternity, filiation, joint spiration, and procession), and five notions (innascibility, paternity, filiation, joint spiration, and procession). Some have accused Thomas of being coldly rationalistic in his Trinity doctrine. Others have suggested that he does not sufficiently integrate the doctrine into his entire theological program. In fact, Thomas argues that human knowledge of creation and redemption is grounded in the revelation of two foundational doctrines: the doctrine of Christ and the doctrine of the triune God. Further, though he uses extrabiblical terminology, Thomas develops his Trinitarian doctrine explicitly from the divine names revealed in Holy Scripture. In this perspective, Thomas's technical Trinitarian distinctions are simply the distillation of the biblical revelation of the one God who is eternally Father, Son, and Holy Spirit.

---

5. Bonaventure, a contemporary of Thomas who would merit his own extensive treatment, adds to the Father's personal property the notion of "fecundity," or "fruitfulness": The Father possesses a fullness by which he is the "fountain-head" of the other persons. See, for example, Bonaventure, *Journey of the Mind to God*, ed. Stephen F. Brown, trans. Philotheus Boehner (Indianapolis: Hackett, 1956), 14. See also Bonaventure, *The Soul's Journey to God, The Tree of Life, The Life of Saint Francis*, trans. Ewert Cousins (Mahwah, NJ: Paulist, 1978), 24–27.
6. White, *The Trinity*, 435–38.

REFLECTION QUESTIONS:

1. What are the advantages and disadvantages of the scholastic distinctions we see in a theologian like Thomas Aquinas?

2. What are ways that Aquinas's talk of the Trinity helps your prayer life?

3. How does Aquinas's teaching on the Trinity remind you of the Bible's teaching on the Trinity?

4. What is a passage in Scripture that has confused you but now seems clearer based on thinking through Aquinas's teaching on the Trinity?

5. What is one teaching strategy from Aquinas that could help you explain the Trinity to someone else?

SECTION B

The Trinity in the Reformation and Modern Periods

QUESTION 20

What Were the Major Trinitarian Developments of the Reformation Era?

The Protestant Reformation of the sixteenth century created lasting divisions in Western Christianity over several key doctrines: Scripture and tradition, the sacraments, the nature of the church, the Marian dogmas, and more. But the Reformation did not seek to overthrow the church's creedal foundations on the core doctrines of the Trinity and the incarnation. The major Protestant Reformers explicitly affirmed the essential elements of the Trinitarian orthodoxy. Sometimes the Reformers could express ambivalence about using extrabiblical terms when articulating the doctrine, but, once we account for certain developments that took place in their thinking on the issues, their mature Trinitarian theology is undeniably orthodox. This chapter will explore the major Trinitarian developments of the Reformation era under three headings: Trinitarian orthodoxy, theological exegesis, and doctrinal clarity.

Trinitarian Orthodoxy

The Reformers were committed to the broad outlines of the doctrine of the Trinity as it was formulated in the patristic era and received and developed in the medieval era. In the early tumult of the Reformation, it is possible to detect a reaction against postbiblical tradition that could seem, at first glance, to undermine the authority of the creedal and conciliar pronouncements of previous eras. As Scott Swain notes, quoting Francois Wendel, "When Caroli [a professor of theology at the University of Paris, who interacted with Calvin] demanded that Calvin subscribe to the ancient creeds, the Genevan Reformer displayed a 'somewhat curious attitude' . . . and refused to do so."[1] In an early edition of his *Loci Communes*, Philip Melanchthon argued that the Trinity

1. Scott Swain, "The Trinity in the Reformers," in *The Oxford Handbook on the Trinity*, ed. Gilles Emery and Matthew Levering (Oxford: Oxford University Press, 2011), 228.

does not belong to "the essence of theology."[2] Luther famously proclaimed at the Diet of Worms that his conscience was bound to Scripture and right reason alone, not to popes and councils. As we will see, one of the distinctives of the Protestant approach to the Trinity lies in its insistence that the doctrine can and should be borne out by faithful exegesis of Holy Scripture, which is the sole *principium* of Christian doctrine.

Despite this apparent diminution of traditional formulae, the Reformers were nonetheless remarkably conservative and orthodox in their Trinitarian conclusions. In theory, Calvin preferred the use of biblical language to affirm the doctrine but acknowledged that heretical teachings demand extrabiblical formulations in order to safeguard and defend what the Scriptures themselves teach about the doctrine.[3] He was comfortable affirming the traditional language of a divine person as a "hypostasis" or "subsistence" in the one shared essence of the Godhead. The three are each "distinguished by a special quality," that is, an "incommunicable" property of personhood.[4] The three act in unity but also in a particular order: "To the Father is attributed the beginning of activity, and the fountain and wellspring of all things; to the Son, wisdom, counsel, and the ordered disposition of all things; but the Spirit is assigned the power and efficacy of that activity."[5] Thus, Calvin affirms the doctrine of inseparable operations as well as the doctrine of *taxis*: There is an order of personal modes in the indivisible action of God. Calvin defends the essential equality and relational distinctions of the persons against heresies both ancient and contemporary, not only the ancient Arians but also modern heretics like Michael Servetus. The three persons are coequal and coeternal. The Son and the Spirit are no less divine than the Father. The Son is, indeed, *autotheos*, God in himself (more on this below).[6] The Son's incarnational obedience is no evidence against his eternal equality with the Father because the Son's self-emptying (that is, the veiling but not the divestiture of his glory) must be accounted for.[7] Thus, Calvin utilizes the ancient practice of partitive exegesis, carefully discerning where Holy Scripture speaks of the Son of God as such and where it speaks of him in his role as the incarnate Mediator. Throughout his treatment of the doctrine, Calvin is explicitly indebted not only to the Scriptures but also to the church fathers, including Gregory of Nazianzus, Augustine, and others.

Similarly, Martin Luther's mature thought makes space for reflection not only on the economic activity of the divine persons but also of their

2. Quoted in Swain, "The Trinity in the Reformers," 228.
3. John Calvin, *Institutes of the Christian Religion*, ed. John T. McNeill, trans. Ford Lewis Battles (Louisville: Westminster John Knox, 1960), 1.13.5.
4. Calvin, *Institutes*, 1.13.6.
5. Calvin, *Institutes*, 1.13.7.
6. Calvin, *Institutes*, 1.13.23.
7. Calvin, *Institutes*, 1.13.26.

"immanent" relations: the "immanent birth" of the Son and the "immanent procession" of the Holy Spirit. Luther explicitly affirms the traditional doctrine of the eternal generation of the Son as the true image of the Father:

> And although all human beings and angels are also made in the image of God, they are not, however, the image or substance of his nature, nor have they been made or arisen out of his divine nature. But Christ arose out of the Father's divine nature from eternity and is his substantial image . . . which has the Father's divine nature wholly and completely in itself, and of which nature is itself, not made or created out of something else, just as the divine substance is not made or created out of something else.[8]

The Son is born eternally from the Father's nature and therefore possesses that very same nature. The Father and Son are "distinct according to the Person but one and undivided according to the substance."[9] Likewise, the Holy Spirit proceeds with "an immanent proceeding, which does not depart from the Godhead." The Spirit, therefore, shares in the very same nature as the first two persons. The three are only distinguished by the eternal relations of origin: "The Father is of no one; the Son is of the Father, but born; the Holy Spirit is of the Father, but proceeding."[10]

The divine persons "keep the very same terms of differentiation when they reveal themselves to us, outside of the Godhead, in the creatures." It is fitting that the Son is physically born of Mary because he is eternally born of the Father. It is fitting that the Spirit is sent from the Father and Son because he eternally proceeds from the Father and Son. The economic missions of the Son and Spirit are the "external likeness or image" of the divine persons' "internal essence."[11] Thus, the Augustinian Luther echoes the familiar formulations of Western Trinitarianism: The temporal missions reveal and communicate the eternal processions.

Theological Exegesis

Thus far, we have seen that the Reformers were well within the parameters of historic Trinitarian orthodoxy. They affirmed the essential sameness and personal distinctions of Father, Son, and Holy Spirit. They affirmed the coequality and coeternity of the divine persons. They affirmed the eternal relations

---

8. Martin Luther, *Career of the Reformer IV*, vol. 34 of *Luther's Works*, ed. Lewis W. Spitz (Philadelphia: Muhlenberg, 1960), 221.
9. Luther, *Career of the Reformer*, 222.
10. Luther, *Career of the Reformer*, 218.
11. Luther, *Career of the Reformer*, 218

of origin. They affirmed the inseparability of divine action toward creation, even as they affirmed the distinct personal modes of action within it. And they did all of this in direct dependence upon the church fathers and the ancient ecumenical creeds. While the Reformers reached orthodox conclusions regarding the Trinity, their distinctive commitment to the doctrine of *sola Scriptura* demanded a robust biblical defense of the Trinity. As we noted in question 3 on theological method, the Reformers were dependent upon a distinct understanding of the relationship between Scripture and tradition. Reformation historian Heiko Obermann's categories are once again worth noting. The Roman Catholic Church operated with a "Tradition II" understanding of tradition, which received the magisterial tradition of the church as a second source of revelation alongside Scripture: that is, as a kind of dogmatic supplement to the Bible. The Reformers, on the other hand, operated with a "Tradition I" understanding of tradition: The tradition is a derivatively authoritative but second-order reflection on the definitive revelation of God in Holy Scripture. The tradition, in this sense, serves as an exegetical guide but not a source of divine revelation.[12] So, while the fathers and the ancient creeds function as a consensus of historic biblical interpretation, it cannot replace a close reading of the Bible itself, which is the sole inspired and infallible written revelation of God. Thus, if there is a distinctive Trinitarian contribution of the Reformation, it lies in the theological exegesis that undergirds the orthodox doctrine.

Operating from a focus on the literal/historical sense of Scripture, Calvin sometimes rejected certain proof texts that had traditionally been marshaled in defense of the doctrine of the Trinity.[13] For example, Calvin understood the citation of Psalm 2 in Hebrews 1:5 ("You are my Son; today, I have begotten you") not as a reference to the Son's immanent generation from the Father but as a reference to the Son's *ad extra* work as the Mediator, the definitive revelation of God in salvation history.

> As to his being begotten, we must briefly observe, that it is to be understood relatively here: for the subtle reasoning of Augustine is frivolous, when he imagines that to-day means perpetuity or eternity. Christ doubtless is the eternal Son of God, for he is wisdom, born before time; but this has no connection with this passage, in which respect is had to men, by whom Christ is acknowledged to be the Son of God after the

---

12. Heiko Obermann, *Forerunners of the Reformation: The Shape of Late Medieval Thought* (Cambridge: James Clarke & Co., 1966), 58. See also Heiko Obermann, *Harvest of Medieval Theology: Gabriel Biel and Late Medieval Nominalism* (Grand Rapids: Baker Academic, 2000), 361–412. Swain, in his summary of the Reformation's Trinitarian theology, notes these distinctions as well ("The Trinity in the Reformers," 229).
13. Swain, "The Trinity in the Reformers," 230.

> Father had manifested him. Hence that declaration or manifestation which Paul mentions in Rom. 1:4, was, so to speak a sort of external begetting; for the hidden and internal which had preceded, was unknown to men; nor could there have been any account taken of it, had not the Father given proof of it by a visible manifestation.[14]

Augustine and many others in the history of interpretation had taken the psalm and its quotation in Hebrews to refer to the eternal "today" of the Son's generation. But Calvin demurs, opting for a "relative" and "external" understanding of begetting in Hebrews 1:5 (and Rom. 1:4). To be sure, Calvin affirms the doctrine of eternal generation (in his own distinctive way); the Son is, indeed, eternally "born," an "internal" begetting that precedes and grounds its external manifestation in the economy of redemption. But Calvin sees the traditional exegesis of Hebrews 1:5 as an instance of what we might call "the right doctrine from the wrong text."[15] We might critique Calvin's hermeneutical strictures here, but it is sufficient for our present purposes to highlight his commitment to the integrity of the historical sense of Scripture, which made him more circumspect when interpreting traditional Trinitarian prooftexts.

This passage from Calvin's commentaries highlights another key feature of Reformation Trinitarian theology: the priority placed upon the history of salvation. At the risk of oversimplification, we might say that Calvin moves from the order of knowing to the order of being, whereas certain medieval approaches tended to work in the opposite direction (for example, Thomas Aquinas's *ST*). As Calvin puts it in the above quotation, the eternal begetting of the Son was "hidden and internal" and "unknown to men." The external manifestation of the Son, however, reveals who he is as the one eternally born of the Father. This circumspection with regard to the immanent Trinity is consistent with Calvin's overarching emphasis on Christ as the Mediator: We first come to know the incarnate God-Man, with all of his saving benefits, and only then can we speak of who he is eternally. Likewise, Calvin was often reticent to speak of those things that lie beyond our comprehension. Elsewhere, Calvin warned against an "audacious inquisitiveness" that attempts to search into God's essence, "which is rather to be adored than curiously investigated."[16] Calvin and Luther, as we have seen, did affirm the traditional doctrines related to God's immanent relations, but they did so in response to God's self-giving revelation in the economy of redemption.

---

14. John Calvin, *Commentaries on the Epistle of Paul the Apostle to the Hebrews*, trans. John Owen (Grand Rapids: Baker, 1999), 42.
15. We borrow this phrase from G. K. Beale, ed., *The Right Doctrine from the Wrong Texts? Essays on the Use of the Old Testament in the New* (Grand Rapids: Baker, 1994).
16. Calvin, *Institutes*, 1.5.9.

So, where did Calvin find exegetical support for the doctrine of the Trinity? While he did reject some traditional proof texts, by no means did he reject all. The divine names—Father, Son/Word/Wisdom, Spirit of God, and so on—indicate who the persons are. Even before the apostles, the Old Testament had taught in fainter tones the deity of the Son and Spirit (Calvin interprets Psalm 110 and the angel of the Lord as indications).[17] Calvin even appeals to the traditional understanding of Proverbs 8 and the wisdom "begotten of God before all time," who presides "over the creation of things and all God's works."[18]

Indeed, Calvin marshals an impressive array of texts to demonstrate the deity of the Son and of the Holy Spirit. They bear the names, possess the attributes, perform the works, and receive the worship of God himself. And yet they, with the Father, are the very same God. They share all things in common as regards the divine essence but are distinguished as persons. The Son is the "stamp of the Father's hypostasis" (Heb. 1:3), which Calvin interprets as the person (not the essence) of the Father.[19] So, Calvin believes there is good exegetical basis for speaking of three hypostases in the Godhead. In short, Calvin (as representative of the Reformers), sometimes limits himself to the historical meaning of certain Trinitarian proof texts but follows the tradition on many more. The Scriptures plainly teach that there is one God; that Father, Son, and Holy Spirit are equally and eternally God; and that they differ from one another personally, not essentially.

Doctrinal Clarity: The *Autotheos*

One final matter is worthy of attention as we conclude our brief discussion of Reformation Trinitarianism: Calvin's controversial doctrine of the Son's self-existence: the so-called *autotheos* ("God of himself"). In developing this doctrine, Calvin rejects the notion that the divine essence of the Father is infused into the other divine persons in their eternal processions. He even denies a formulation that would seem to be fairly well-attested in the patristic tradition (especially among the Greek fathers), namely, that the Father is "the fountainhead and beginning of deity."[20] In denying these ideas, Calvin is concerned to affirm the absolute equality and consubstantiality of the three divine persons. The divine attribute of aseity (self-existence) describes the common divine essence and is, therefore, shared by all three persons. Because the Son bears the divine name (YHWH: "I Am"), the Son must be accounted as self-existent: "With respect to his deity his being is from himself."[21] Calvin

17. Calvin, *Institutes*, 2.15.3; 1.13.10.
18. Calvin, *Institutes*, 1.13.7.
19. Calvin, *Institutes*, 1.13.7.
20. Calvin, *Institutes*, 1.13.23.
21. Calvin, *Institutes*, 1.13.23.

also grounds his argument in a defense of the filioque. If the Father alone is the "essence-giver," as Calvin's opponents claimed, then the Father alone must grant deity to the Holy Spirit as well.[22] But in concert with Western Trinitarianism, Calvin wants to affirm that the Third Person is the shared Spirit of both Father and Son. Calvin seems to think that if the Father is seen as the sole fountain of deity, from whom the other persons derive their deity, then the Father alone would be God himself.

Calvin does not, however, deny the eternal relations of origin. He simply believes that these relations must be understood in terms of personhood, not in terms of the divine essence being infused or transferred. All three divine persons are self-existent and eternally so. Thus, the eternal processions must be understood in terms of personhood, not the bestowal of deity:

> Therefore we say that deity in an absolute sense exists of itself; whence likewise we confess that the Son since he is God, exists of himself, but not in respect of his Person; indeed, since he is the Son, we say that he exists from the Father. Thus his essence is without beginning; while the beginning of his person is God himself.[23]

One might object that the Son's generation is likewise eternal, such that if nothing can be both bestowed and eternal, then neither can the Son's personhood. Furthermore, Calvin's rejection of the Father's communication of the divine essence to the Son seems to counter the Nicene Creed itself, which affirms that the Son is "God of God." Biblically, we might also point to John 5:26, which seems to affirm both the Son's self-existence ("life in himself," ESV) and the fact that he received this divine attribute in his eternal generation ("granted the Son," ESV). Critics of the *autotheos* thus accuse Calvin of a dangerous innovation here. On the other hand, many Reformed theologians have seen the *autotheos* as an important clarification that is entirely consistent with Nicene Trinitarianism. Eternal generation, say these defenders, is about the Son's personhood, not about the derivation of deity, which would undermine the Son's aseity.[24] In any event, the *autotheos* remains an important contribution to Trinitarian doctrine from the period of the Reformation.

Summary

Accounting for diversity and development in and among the Reformers, we can nevertheless discern the broad outlines of orthodox Trinitarianism in

22. Calvin, *Institutes*, 1.13.23.
23. Calvin, *Institutes*, 1.13.25.
24. For a survey of the literature on these debates, see Swain, "The Trinity in the Reformers," 235.

their writings. The classical terms were defended and utilized, the ancient creeds confessed, and the ancient heresies rejected. Still, the Reformers' focus on the economic revelation of the Trinity in the literal sense of Scripture caused them to reconsider some of the traditional proof texts for the eternal processions, even as they retained others and continued to affirm the traditional doctrine itself. Finally, Calvin's *autotheos* represents an important test case for this doctrinal and interpretive approach: The traditional doctrine of eternal generation was retained but clarified, given Calvin's biblical and theological concerns.

REFLECTION QUESTIONS

1. What is the relationship between Scripture and subsequent church tradition, including the ecumenical creeds and councils?
2. Why might it be important to affirm that the Son is *autotheos* (God in himself)?
3. What are ways that the Reformers' talk of the Trinity helps your prayer life?
4. How does the Reformers' teaching on the Trinity remind you of the Bible's teaching on the Trinity?
5. What is one teaching strategy from the Reformers that could help you explain the Trinity to someone else?

QUESTION 21

What Were the Major Trinitarian Developments of the Post-Reformation Era?

In this chapter we will survey some of the most important articulations of the doctrine of the Trinity from the era just after the Reformation to the eve of the so-called revival of the doctrine in the twentieth century. This is admittedly a large portion of time to cover, and we must be highly selective. We will discuss three main historical developments during this time period: the scholastic treatment of the doctrine of the Trinity in the period of Protestant Orthodoxy, the rise of anti-Trinitarianism (of both the biblicist and the rationalist varieties), and the development of the doctrine in an American context (looking specifically at Jonathan Edwards and then the Princetonians).

Post-Reformation Orthodoxy

The "post-Reformation" era, like all attempts at historical periodization, is a fluid time marker. Any attempt to carve up historical eras is inescapably subjective, value laden, and in many ways arbitrary. Still, it is helpful, even as heuristic, to consider the post-Reformation period as a distinct historical moment. "Protestant Orthodoxy," as it is often called, was marked by a confessional consolidation and systematic articulation of Protestant theology. Richard Muller's influential work on the Reformed orthodox tracks the era from roughly 1565 to 1725. He divides the era into three main phases (early, high, and late) with further subphases within them.[1] The era is complex, and

1. Richard A. Muller, *Post-Reformation Reformed Dogmatics: The Rise and Development of Reformed Orthodoxy, ca. 1520 to ca. 1725*, 4 vols., 2nd ed. (Grand Rapids: Baker Academic, 2003), 1:27–32.

any attempt at summary necessarily overlooks important nuances. But we can make some broad generalizations and point readers to the thorough work of Muller and others.

In earlier historiography about this era, it was sometimes fashionable to draw a sharp distinction between the theology of the Reformers and those who came after them. "Calvin versus the Calvinists" and "Luther versus the Lutherans" were common motifs in this approach. The story that was often told on this front pits the biblically grounded, tradition-wary, and philosophically suspicious approach of the Reformers themselves against the philosophically rigid and overly rational systemization of theology among the Protestant orthodox. This caricature has come in for severe criticism in recent decades. Muller's work stands out in this regard, as does the work of Paul Helm and many others.[2] What we can say is that the *substance* of the Reformers' confessional beliefs and those of their heirs were largely the same, while the *style* in which those beliefs were articulated and the *scope* of their broader doctrinal context were sometimes noticeably different. Luther wrote no systematic theology (unless you count his catechisms). His doctrinal beliefs are spread across a wider generic landscape: pamphlets, sermons, commentaries, the "table talk" sayings, and so on. The Lutheran orthodox, who consolidated Luther's views, on the other hand, were highly systematic in their theological articulations. To pick some examples, consider the impressive work of Martin Chemnitz (1522–86) or Johann Gerhard (1582–1637). Among the Reformed, we do have Calvin's *Institutes of the Christian Religion*, but it is mainly a handbook on Bible doctrine and does not employ the same kinds of systematic argumentation that can be found among the medieval scholastics. But the Reformed orthodox, such as Francis Turretin (1623–86) or Wilhelmus à Brakel (1635–1711), did set out to write in a more scholastic mode and with reference to the broader catholic tradition that came before the Reformation.

Regarding the doctrine of the Trinity, we have seen that the Reformers did in fact affirm the substance of the historic doctrine, despite their sometimes-pointed polemic against tradition and the medieval scholastics. Both Luther and Calvin affirm the essential unity of the Godhead and the personal distinctions within the Godhead, defined in terms of the eternal relations of origin. The early Reformation confessions already set this orthodox standard. But as we move toward the post-Reformation era, an era of consolidation and conveyance, again, there are noticeable differences in style and scope. The period is characterized by a kind of *scholasticism*: that is, a method of theological investigation done in the *schools* or universities. This method was influenced not only by medieval scholasticism (with its penchant for philosophical, especially Aristotelian, engagement and for careful

2. Paul Helm, *Calvin and the Calvinists* (Edinburgh: Banner of Truth Trust, 1982).

logical distinctions) but also by the intellectual trends of Renaissance humanism (including a careful study of texts in their original languages and historical contexts).[3] As Muller notes, the Protestant orthodox/scholastics were keen both to codify the confessional beliefs of the Reformers and also to set those beliefs in the context of entire systems of Christian doctrine. This latter task meant that they were more apt to develop the doctrine of the Trinity in terms that reach back to the medieval and patristic eras than the Reformers sometimes were.

Turretin, the seventeenth-century heir to Calvin's Genevan Academy, stands out as both a representative and an excellent exemplar of this approach.[4] Turretin engages in a more sustained interaction with the patristic and medieval sources of the doctrine. He leans more heavily upon technical vocabulary employed by the fathers and the medieval scholastics: essence, substance, *suppositum*, person/hypostasis, *emperichoresis*, and so on. Still, the resonances with Calvin remain. Turretin still places primary emphasis on the biblical revelation; a "newness of words" is useful to the degree that it does not introduce a "newness of things."[5] Once again, the methodological differences between the Reformers and the Protestant Orthodox should not obscure their substantial agreement concerning the doctrine itself.

Unitarianism

Another movement that ran parallel to the Protestant scholastics was the rise of various forms of anti-Trinitarianism or unitarianism. Stephen Holmes identifies two main versions: biblical (we might say "biblicist") anti-Trinitarianism and rational anti-Trinitarianism.[6] Already during the Reformation era itself, Michael Servetus had developed a version of the biblicist variety, with deadly consequences for himself in Calvin's Geneva. In the post-Reformation period, the work of Faustus Socinus was especially influential—and infamous. An Italian theologian and minister in the Minor Reformed Church of Poland, Socinus denied the deity of Christ and affirmed instead a kind of adoptionist Christology in which God was active in and through Jesus. Socinus did affirm the virgin birth, the resurrection, the ascension, and the second coming of Jesus. But for Socinus Jesus is only "divine" in a qualified sense. The Father alone is God.

Socinus's teachings spread across Europe, including on the British Isles,

3. Muller, *Post-Reformation Reformed Dogmatics*, 1:34–37.
4. For his defense of the Trinity, see Francis Turretin, *Institutes of Elenctic Theology*, 3 vols., trans. George Musgrave Giger, ed. James T. Dennison Jr. (Phillipsburg, NJ: P&R, 1992), 1:253–310.
5. Turretin, *Institutes*, 1:260
6. This section follows Holmes's helpful summary: Stephen R. Holmes, *The Quest for the Trinity: The Doctrine of God in Scripture, History, and Modernity* (Downers Grove, IL: IVP Academic, 2012), 170–81.

where John Biddle became the "Father of English Unitarianism."[7] These biblicist anti-Trinitarians wanted to stick with the language of the Bible and lampooned extrabiblical concepts like modes of subsistence. Unitarianism became especially prominent among certain dissenters, including among the General Baptists. Even among the orthodox, there arose a certain suspicion of extrabiblical terms and a preference for the plain language of the Bible. The rejection of clearer Trinitarian formulae by the majority in the Salters' Hall controversy represents this reticence.[8] Confessions of faith in the eighteenth century and beyond (especially in the North America) became less dependent upon older creedal and conciliar language, favoring phrases taken directly from Scripture. These trends left some Protestant groups vulnerable to the subtle undermining of Trinitarian orthodoxy.

Holmes also points to several "rational" anti-Trinitarians who were working not from a naïve biblicism but from an embrace of Enlightenment philosophy. Deists such as John Toland and Lord Herbert of Cherbury sought to develop a pared-down faith based on reason and universal religious experience. Kant's *Religion with the Boundaries of Mere Reason* represents this philosophical approach well.[9] For Kant, the truths of morality are discernable by reason alone. Religious texts, like the gospel accounts of Jesus's life, are useful only insofar as they provide illustrative support to those universally accessible truths. In Kant's reckoning, Jesus is not the Second Person of the Trinity but rather the supreme exemplar of morality. Friedrich Schleiermacher, the father of Protestant liberalism, frames his own views in more noticeably historical terms but was still influenced by this Kantian approach. For Schleiermacher, contrary to the orthodox view, Jesus does not have two "natures," as if nature were a term that could be predicated of both God and humans. Instead, for Schleiermacher, Jesus is the supreme example of the God-consciousness—the "feeling of absolute dependence"—that is present to some degree in every religion and every human being.[10] Thus, it is no accident that the doctrine of the Trinity is relegated to the "conclusion" of Schleiermacher's *The Christian Faith*, a place that many have remarked feels more like an appendix. Schleiermacher believes that the traditional formula of the doctrine is open to criticism and sympathizes with those who reject it entirely, though he wants to leave space for a rearticulation of the doctrine on his own theological terms: "the union of the Divine Essence with human nature both in the personality of Christ and in the common

7. Holmes, *The Quest for the Trinity*, 172.
8. See Jesse Owens, "The Salters' Hall Controversy of 1719" (PhD diss., Southern Baptist Theological Seminary, 2021).
9. Immanuel Kant, *Religion within the Boundaries of Mere Reason, and Other Writings*, ed. Allen Wood and George di Giovanni (Cambridge: Cambridge University Press, 1998).
10. Friedrich Schleiermacher, *The Christian Faith*, ed. H. R. Mackintosh and J. S. Stewart (Edinburgh: T&T Clark, 1928), 12–18.

Spirit of the Church."[11] In any event, he sees the doctrine as having only an indirect bearing on his central theme of God-consciousness.

American Trinitarianism

In this final section we turn our attention to Trinitarian theology on the American continent in the eighteenth and nineteenth centuries. For our purposes, we will highlight the Trinitarian contribution of just two major theologians: Jonathan Edwards (1703–58) and Charles Hodge (1797–1878). Edwards is an intriguing theologian for a number of reasons. He was an enormously influential figure during the colonial era both in terms of the revivals we refer to as the Great Awakening and in terms of his theological contributions. His adaptations of Calvinist theology influenced the Baptist founders of the modern missions movement, William Carey and Andrew Fuller. His theology also represents an interesting triangulation of Reformed orthodoxy, the religious experience of the revivals, and interaction with Enlightenment philosophy.

Edwards's Trinitarian contribution rests largely on his development and extension of the doctrine of appropriations.[12] According to this traditional doctrine, while all the divine attributes are shared equally by all three divine persons, it is nonetheless appropriate to speak about certain divine attributes with reference to a particular divine person in order to highlight that person's distinctive personal property. So, for example, while all three persons share in the divine attribute of wisdom, Scripture often appropriates this attribute to the Son because the Son is the eternal Word and Wisdom of the Father. Likewise, while all three persons share in the divine attribute of love, love (along with the related theme of gift) is often associated with the Holy Spirit. Especially influenced by Augustine and later medieval theologians, the Western tradition came to speak about the Holy Spirit as the mutual love of the Father and the Son. Edwards begins from this basic conceptual framework but extends it in some fairly idiosyncratic ways. Edwards maintains that God's excellency requires that there be a plurality in the Godhead: God as the most excellent being must know himself and love himself.[13] The Father is the prime mode of the Godhead, while the Son is identified with the wisdom of the Father and the Spirit with the mutual love between the Father and the Son. Edwards explains in a summative passage:

---

11. Schleiermacher, *The Christian Faith*, 738.
12. For Edwards's development of these themes, see Jonathan Edwards, *Discourse on the Trinity*, vol. 21 of *The Works of Jonathan Edwards*, ed. Sang Hyun Lee (New Haven, CT: Yale University Press, 2002).
13. For an evaluation of Edwards's Trinitarianism, which makes note of the influence of philosophical idealism upon it, see Ralph Cunnington, "A Critical Examination of Jonathan Edwards's Doctrine of the Trinity," *Themelios* 39 (2014): 224–40.

> And this I suppose to be that blessed Trinity that we read of in the holy Scriptures. The Father is the Deity subsisting in the prime, unoriginated and most absolute manner, or the Deity in its direct existence. The Son is the Deity generated by God's understanding, or having an idea of himself, and subsisting in that idea. The Holy Ghost is the Deity subsisting in act or the divine essence flowing out and breathed forth, in God's infinite love to and delight in himself. And I believe the whole divine essence does truly and distinctly subsist both in the divine idea and divine love, and that therefore each of them are properly distinct persons.[14]

Much of his treatment here and elsewhere sounds similar to the traditional Augustinian view, but upon closer inspection it appears that Edwards is developing that view in novel ways. Unlike the Augustinian/Thomistic view, which understands appropriation simply as a manner of speaking (all of the attributes, including wisdom and love, are actually shared equally by all three divine persons), Edwards seems to be actually identifying these attributes with the Second and Third Persons, respectively. What undergirds their unity, then, is not so much the shared divine essence but a kind of perichoretic unity: the persons' interpenetration of one another. On Edwards's view, it seems that the attributes of wisdom and love are distinct subsistences.[15] The implications of this view would, therefore, be puzzling and rather disturbing, threatening to undermine the essential sameness of the divine persons as well as the doctrine of divine simplicity. In any event, Edwards's view represents an imaginative, if problematic, development of the doctrine of the Trinity.

Charles Hodge develops his Trinitarian theology in a more traditional and less adventuresome vein. In his *Systematic Theology*, Hodge first treats the doctrine's biblical foundation, then its historic articulation, and finally its philosophical form. Much of his treatment is simply a restatement of the received doctrine. He affirms one divine essence, three distinct persons (defined in terms of relations of origin), inseparable operations, and so on.[16] He defends the doctrine against the various heresies that have arisen against it, both ancient and modern. Still, Hodge does make a distinction between the Nicene faith itself and certain Nicene fathers, the latter of which, to Hodge's

14. Edwards, *Discourse on the Trinity*, 131.
15. For a detailed account and evaluation of these matters, see Kyle C. Strobel, *Jonathan Edwards's Theology: A Reinterpretation*, T&T Clark Studies in Systematic Theology (London: Bloomsbury, 2013).
16. Though Holmes does note that Hodge seems to redefine the term "person" to mean an individual subject, he does affirm one mind and will in the Godhead (*The Quest for the Trinity*, 191).

mind, speculated needlessly as the meaning of doctrine's central tenets (e.g., eternal generation).[17] Interestingly, a later Princeton theologian, B. B. Warfield, would come to question the doctrine of eternal generation altogether, arguing that the personal names (Father, Son, and Holy Spirit) connote only likeness and not origin.[18] For Hodge's part, he does affirm the eternal relations of origin but leaves them relatively undefined. He does believe that they imply a kind of "subordination" but only in terms of "the mode of subsistence and operation." Hodge expressly denies that this "subordination" concerns the divine "being and perfection."[19] But neither should his teaching be confused with contemporary models that argue for a subordination of "function" or "role." Hodge grounds his view in historical precedent (Augustine, the Athanasian Creed, etc.) and, again, understands the subordination in terms of the order implied in the relations of origin and the external modes of action.

Summary

We have been obviously selective in covering the roughly four hundred years between the Reformation era and the twentieth century. But these broad trends are instructive: the scholastic codification of Protestant Trinitarianism in the post-Reformation era, the rise of biblicist and rationalist anti-Trinitarianism, and the peculiarities of American Trinitarianism. In the next chapter, we will explore the so-called Trinitarian revival of the twentieth century and evaluate how closely it aligns with the consensus doctrine that we find from the late fourth century through the period of Protestant Orthodoxy.

REFLECTION QUESTIONS

1. In your experience, are evangelical Protestants well-versed in the texts of their own tradition (the Reformation and post-Reformation theologians)? How can we better retrieve these foundational authors for our own time?

2. How would you respond to someone who claims to believe in the complete trustworthiness of the Bible but does not believe in the doctrine of the Trinity?

---

17. Charles Hodge, *Systematic Theology*, 3 vols. (New York: Charles Scribner's Sons, 1871), 1:462
18. B. B. Warfield, "Trinity," in *International Standard Bible Encyclopedia*, ed. James Orr, 5 vols. (Chicago: Howard-Severance, 1915), 5:3012–22. Fred Sanders has formatted a helpful annotated version of Warfield's essay here: http://scriptoriumdaily.com/wp-content/uploads/2015/10/Warfield-Trinity-Study-Edition.pdf. See also Scott R. Swain, "B. B. Warfield and the Biblical Doctrine of the Trinity," *Themelios* 43 (2018): 10–24.
19. Hodge, *Systematic Theology*, 1:464.

3. What are ways that the post-Reformation theologians' talk of the Trinity helps your prayer life?

4. How do the post-Reformation theologians' teaching on the Trinity remind you of the Bible's teaching on the Trinity?

5. What is one Trinitarian principle from the post-Reformation theologians that could help you explain the Trinity to someone else?

QUESTION 22

What Is the "Trinitarian Revival" of the Twentieth Century?

"Its roots are hard to isolate, and the styles within it vary widely, but the current Trinitarian revival itself is unmistakable."[1] So wrote Ronald Feenstra and Cornelius Plantinga in 1989. According to these evangelical theologians, "virtually every serious theological movement of recent years has sought on its own terms to state and shape Trinitarian doctrine."[2] Similarly, in 1995 the German Lutheran theologian Christoph Schwöbel wrote of the late "renaissance of Trinitarian theology."[3] These comments are indicative of a prominent story that has often been told about Christian theology in the twentieth century. Whereas the previous century or two had relegated the doctrine of the Trinity to an afterthought or else found difficulty integrating the doctrine into the whole system of Christian belief, the twentieth century witnessed a revival of the doctrine and its centrality. Theologians such as Karl Barth, Karl Rahner, John Zizioulas, Wolfhart Pannenburg, Jürgen Moltmann, Robert Jenson, and Colin Gunton are cited in defense of this revival thesis.

But some have questioned whether this renewed interest actually constitutes a true *revival* of the doctrine as it was historically developed. Stephen Holmes has written perhaps the most forceful critique in this vein. In his 2012 *The Quest for the Trinity*, Holmes explains his thesis: "In brief, I argue that the explosion of theological work claiming to recapture the doctrine of the Trinity that we have witnessed in recent decades in fact misunderstands

1. Ronald Feenstra and Cornelius Plantinga Jr., eds., *Trinity, Incarnation, and Atonement: Philosophical and Theological Essays* (Notre Dame, IN: University of Notre Dame Press, 1989), 3.
2. Feenstra and Plantinga, *Trinity, Incarnation, and Atonement*, 3.
3. Christoph Schwöbel, ed., *Trinitarian Theology Today: Essays on Divine Being and Act* (Edinburgh: T&T Clark, 1995), 1.

and distorts the traditional doctrine so badly that it is unrecognizable."[4] His claim is more historical than biblical or theological: There is indeed a discernable consensus doctrine of the Trinity, and the twentieth-century revival departs from it in some decisive ways. Holmes defends his thesis by carefully exegeting the patristic doctrine and its reception in the medieval and Reformation eras. In our estimation, Holmes's case is persuasive. Some twentieth-century theologians hewed closer to the traditional doctrine than others, but the "revival" as a whole was more about reconstrual than retrieval. Still, these trends are worthy of careful study and consideration on their own right. In this chapter we will survey and evaluate some of the most important Trinitarian developments in the twentieth century. We will focus particular attention on four main figures. We will examine the seminal influence of Karl Barth and then look at a representative from each of the three branches of Christianity: Karl Rahner (Roman Catholic), John Zizioulas (Orthodox), and Jürgen Moltmann (Protestant).[5]

Karl Barth

"Prior to Karl Barth the doctrine of the Trinity had played a minor role in modern Protestant theology," writes George Hunsinger.[6] Whereas Schleiermacher had relegated the doctrine to an appendix, Barth "front-load[ed]" the doctrine and thus "sparked a major revival of interest in the ancient doctrine itself, one that surged in the second half of the twentieth century and that shows no signs of abating to this day."[7] Like claims about the Trinitarian revival as a whole, aspects of this assessment can surely be disputed. But what cannot be disputed is the significance and influence of Barth's monumental theological achievement in *Church Dogmatics*, and especially its systemically Trinitarian framework.

In terms of his articulation of the doctrine of the Trinity itself, Barth is noticeably orthodox and even traditional. Barth maintains that we must hold in dialectical tension a twofold affirmation: unity in trinity, and trinity in unity.[8] In regard to the divine oneness, Barth happily utilizes the traditional formulae of essence and substance; the triune God is, indeed, one

4. Stephen R. Holmes, *The Quest for the Trinity: The Doctrine of God in Scripture, History, and Modernity* (Downers Grove, IL: IVP Academic, 2012), xv.
5. Some of these themes and figures appear elsewhere in this volume. We invite the reader to consult especially question 25 (on the immanent and economic Trinity) and question 29 (on the doctrine of perichoresis).
6. George Hunsinger, "Karl Barth's Doctrine of the Trinity, and Some Protestant Doctrines after Barth," in *The Oxford Handbook of the Trinity*, ed. Gilles Emery and Matthew Levering (Oxford: Oxford University Press, 2011), 294.
7. Hunsinger, "Karl Barth's Doctrine of the Trinity," 294.
8. Karl Barth, *Church Dogmatics: Volume 1—The Doctrine of the Word of God, Part 1*, 2nd ed., trans. G. W. Bromiley, ed. G. W. Bromiley and T. F. Torrance (London: T&T Clark, 2008), 368.

Subject and one Lord. But in regard to the divine threeness, Barth is much more reticent to use the traditional term "person." Instead, he prefers the language of distinct "modes of being" in the one divine essence, which, as we have seen elsewhere, has important historical precedents. Barth's concern is that modern usage tends to conflate "person" with "personality." Thus, to speak of three personalities in the Godhead would lead to "the worst and most extreme expression of tritheism." If we are thinking of "personality," then there is only one in the Godhead, "which belongs to the one unique essence of God." In any event, Barth recognizes, this was not the traditional usage of the term "person." The divine "persons" were, in the traditional formulation, precisely "modes of being subsisting in their mutual relations."[9] Thus, Barth seems to believe that in order to preserve the content of the traditional doctrine, we must be willing to adapt and clarify its terminology. As Holmes puts it, "[I]t is clear that Barth's motive for this departure is only to preserve with complete clarity the doctrine of the Trinity that he had discovered in the tradition."[10] Barth's formal articulation of the Trinity turns out to be a faithful rendering of the Western doctrine: one essence, three modes of being distinguished by relations of origin, the filioque, perichoresis (understood as a function of essential unity), appropriations, inseparable operations, and so on.

The more controversial aspects of Barth's Trinitarianism cluster around his understanding of the relationship between God's triune being and God's acts in the world, especially his works of revelation and reconciliation. Barth is insistent that God's revelation is the "root" of the doctrine of the Trinity, not just in the sense that the revelation of God in Christ (as attested in Scripture) is the source of our knowledge of the Trinity but also in the sense that revelation itself logically grounds the doctrine.[11] Revelation presupposes both an "unimpaired unity" and an "unimpaired distinction" in God as "Revealer, Revelation, and Revealedness."[12] The subject, predicate, and object of God's revelation can only ever be the one triune God in his concrete revelation, as witnessed in the Bible. This God is revealed nowhere else.[13] Furthermore, Barth also insists that the Son of God can never be conceived of apart from his reconciling work as the incarnate Christ. The incarnation is not, as Holmes summarizes, a "second moment" in the life of the Son.[14] There is no *Logos asarkos*, no Word without flesh, but only the Son as he has determined to be for us in his incarnate ministry. As one of

9. Barth, *Church Dogmatics*, I/1:348.
10. Holmes, *The Quest for the Trinity*, 8.
11. See Hunsinger's commentary on *Church Dogmatics*, I/1: 304–33 in Hunsinger, "Karl Barth and Some Protestant Theologians," 296–97.
12. Barth, *Church Dogmatics*, I/1:295.
13. This is related to Barth's rejection of natural revelation.
14. Holmes, *The Quest for the Trinity*, 6.

Barth's students, Thomas F. Torrance, often put it, "There is no God behind the back of Jesus."[15]

So, does all of this mean that God's acts—creation, revelation, reconciliation, redemption—somehow constitute God's own being? Is God's revelation, for instance, identical with God's own being? Or, as Holmes baldly states, "Does this mean that God chooses to be Trinity?"[16] This is a hotly disputed question among Barth scholars, and we lack the space and, frankly, the expertise to adjudicate all of these matters of Barthian interpretation. Suffice it to say, there are some who interpret Barth in more traditional ways (such as Hunsinger and Paul Molnar) while others (most notably, Bruce McCormack) see Barth's views as more radical and seek to press their implications even further.[17] The former interpreters highlight places in Barth where he underscores the contingency of creation and the ontological priority of God's being as antecedent to any of his freely chosen acts. The latter interpreters, on the other hand, see the seeds of something quite revolutionary in Barth, namely, the notion that God's act constitutes his very being or even that God's act has ontological priority over his being (in McCormack's interpretation).[18] In any event, Barth certainly draws a tight connection between God's act and God's being and at least leaves the door open to the more radical interpretation. Even if he himself did not walk through that door, other theologians of the "Trinitarian revival" would.

Karl Rahner

We will discuss the Trinitarian theology of the Roman Catholic theologian Karl Rahner in more detail in question 25 (on the immanent Trinity and economic Trinity). For now, we simply introduce Rahner's most important and contested contribution to the doctrine: Rahner's Rule. Rahner states his fundamental axiom in straightforward terms: "The 'economic' Trinity is the 'immanent' Trinity and the 'immanent' Trinity is the 'economic' Trinity."[19] The distinction between the immanent Trinity and the economic Trinity is roughly the difference between what the Greek fathers called *theologia* and *oikonomia*, respectively: God in himself, absolutely considered, and God in

15. Thomas F. Torrance, *The Christian Doctrine of God: One Being Three Persons*, Cornerstones (London: Bloomsbury, 2016), 5.
16. Holmes, *The Quest for the Trinity*, 7.
17. See George Hunsinger, "Election and the Trinity: Twenty-Five Theses on the Theology of Karl Barth," *Modern Theology* 24, no. 2 (2008): 172–98; Paul Molnar, *Divine Freedom and the Doctrine of the Immanent Trinity: In Dialogue with Karl Barth and Contemporary Theology* (London: T&T Clark, 2002); and Bruce McCormack, "Election and the Trinity: Theses in Response to George Hunsinger," *Scottish Journal of Theology* 63, no. 2 (2010): 203–24.
18. See the survey of the debate, including the most relevant literature, in Holmes, *The Quest for the Trinity*, 7 n. 20.
19. Karl Rahner, *The Trinity*, trans. Joseph Donceel, Milestones in Catholic Theology (New York: Herder & Herder, 1970), 22.

his saving acts, relatively considered. Rahner's claim is that there are not, in fact, two trinities but only one. God is in himself as he reveals himself to be in his acts. Like Barth, Rahner seems concerned to avoid the notion that the incarnation is a "second moment" in the Son's life, that somehow we can conceive of the Son apart from his incarnate mission. Rahner even seems to have a problem with the received doctrine of inseparable operations, in which the divine persons are said to operate indivisibly in every external act of the Trinity. For Rahner, though the unified triune God is the efficient cause in all of God's external acts, each divine person has his own unique relatedness to the created order. The incarnation is just one particular "instance" of the more general category of distinct economic relations.[20]

Interpretations of Rahner's Rule have been varied. Similar to the reception of Barth's Trinitarian theology, Rahner has been interpreted in more conservative ways and in more radical ways. Rahner, also like Barth, articulated the technical details of the doctrine of the Trinity in explicitly orthodox terms. Also like Barth, Rahner expressed a certain reticence with regard to the use of the term "person," but unlike Barth, he preferred to define the word properly rather than replace it.[21] If Rahner's Rule simply means that God is as he reveals himself to be, then it is consistent with more traditional approaches. But if the rule means that God's activity determines God's being or that the economy can be conflated with God's own eternal life, then the worries that attend a Barthian actualistic ontology (that God's being *is* his act) would pertain here as well. God's being is necessary, while his acts in creation and redemption are freely chosen and therefore contingent. But despite the ambiguity and potentially problematic implications of Rahner's Rule, it nevertheless serves as a helpful reminder that God's redemptive revelation reveals God as he actually is in himself. It also rightly grounds our reflection on the Trinity in the concrete acts of the Son and Spirit as recorded in the New Testament.

John Zizioulas

The Greek Orthodox bishop and theologian John Zizioulas is another exemplar of the twentieth-century Trinitarian revival. Zizioulas's main contribution lies in his interpretation of the Cappadocian Fathers and their understanding of personhood. As we discussed in a previous chapter, one of the important theological maneuvers made by the Cappadocians was their co-option of the term *hypostasis*, a term of being that had previously been used as roughly synonymous with *ousia*, and their implementation of that term as a designator for Father, Son, and Holy Spirit. Zizioulas sees this terminological shift as an

20. Rahner, *The Trinity*, 27. For a discussion of Rahner's revisions of the doctrine of inseparable operations, see Adonis Vidu, *The Divine Missions: An Introduction* (Eugene, OR: Cascade, 2021), 45–46.
21. Rahner, *The Trinity*, 42–45, 56–57.

ontological advance as well: being and communion, relationality, are correlative. As Holmes summarizes Zizioulas's interpretation of the Cappadocians, "The basic nature of reality was no longer substance, but relationship."[22]

One important part of Zizioulas's argument relies upon the Eastern Orthodox notion of God the Father as the "cause" of the other two persons. For Zizioulas, the being of God, then, is not simply an ontological given but a freely willed decision. The Father "confirms through 'being' His *free* will to exist. And it is precisely His Trinitarian existence that constitutes this confirmation: the Father out of love—that is, freely—begets the Son and brings forth the Spirit."[23] This takes us very close to the more radical interpretation of Barth's actualistic ontology: For Zizioulas, in a very real sense, God freely wills to be Trinity. This view of the Trinity naturally implies a brand of social Trinitarianism, in which the three persons are conceived of as distinct centers of consciousness and will. Like other versions of social Trinitarianism, Zizioulas grounds this view in a particular interpretation of the Greek fathers in distinction from the Latin fathers and sees it as programmatic for human relationality as well. In Zizioulas's case, the application is ecclesiological: The Trinity underwrites episcopal church polity. But as we argue in the chapter on social Trinitarianism (question 35), these developments misread the patristic sources and come dangerously close to a kind of tritheism. In the fourth-century controversy, it was actually the Arians and the Eunomians who connected the begetting of the Son (and the procession of the Spirit) to the will of the Father. The orthodox took pains to ground the Trinitarian relations not in a unity of will but in a unity of being.[24]

Jürgen Moltmann

The German Lutheran theologian Jürgen Moltmann represents an important manifestation of the "revival" among Protestants in the latter part of the twentieth century. Moltmann exemplifies a fairly radical form of the social Trinitarian tendencies that characterize much of the "revival." Moltmann explicitly critiques Rahner's reticence to speak of the divine persons as distinct "subjects" ore "centres of activity."[25] Moltmann maintains that we must conceive of persons, including the divine persons, in relational terms. The divine persons do not constitute "one substance" or "one identical subject." Instead, similar to Zizioulas, Moltmann grounds their oneness in terms of their "unitedness."[26]

---

22. Holmes, *The Quest for the Trinity*, 13.
23. John Zizioulas, *Being as Communion: Studies in Personhood and the Church*, Contemporary Greek Theologians 4 (Crestwood, NY: St Vladimir's Seminary Press, 2007), 41.
24. Khaled Anatalios, *Retrieving Nicaea: The Development and Meaning of Trinitarian Doctrine* (Grand Rapids: Baker Academic, 2011), 41.
25. Jürgen Moltmann, *The Trinity and the Kingdom: The Doctrine of God*, trans. Margaret Kohl (Minneapolis: Fortress, 1993), 145.
26. Moltmann, *The Trinity and the Kingdom*, 150.

Oneness is preserved not by appeal to the traditional categories of being and substance but only in terms of perichoresis, the mutual indwelling of the three persons. We discuss the weaknesses both of social Trinitarianism (question 35) and of this misuse of the doctrine of perichoresis (question 29) in the chapters devoted to those subjects. Here we simply restate the worries that many others have noted regarding Moltmann's Trinitarianism: It is difficult to see how he can avoid the error of tritheism (that there are three gods). The ways that he cashes out his view in relation to the atonement only worsens this fear. Moltmann sees the death of Christ as quite literally the suffering of God as such—not merely the suffering of a divine person in and through his human nature, mind you (the traditional position; see question 34), but the suffering of God in such a way that it "determines the inner life of God from eternity to eternity."[27] It will come as no surprise that we find this rejection of the traditional categories highly problematic. Preserving those categories—a God one in being/substance/will and distinct in mode of being/relation of origin and a Christ who has two natures, one impassible and one passible—allows us to account for all that Scripture says about God and Christ. The traditional categories do not replace or supplement the Bible, but they developed and received consensus support precisely because of their fit to the biblical text.

Summary and Concluding Evaluation

There are other important thinkers and developments in the so-called Trinitarian revival that we could mention: Hans Urs von Balthasar's Roman Catholic incorporation of Barth, Wolfhart Pannenberg's theology of history, Eberhard Jüngel's understanding God's "becoming," Robert Jenson's harvesting of these various developments, and interesting debates among analytic philosophers of religion. But these soundings in the twentieth century suffice to show that many of the developments were a step away from traditional formulations rather than a return to them. Some of the theologians we have mentioned hewed closer to the tradition (Barth and Rahner), while others strayed further from it (Zizioulas and Moltmann). As we survey this material, two central themes emerge. First, the revival was concerned to connect God's being as Trinity to his acts in redemption. There is much to appreciate in this emphasis. It is true that God is as he reveals himself to be and that we must repeatedly return to the biblical revelation of God in Christ as the starting point for all Trinitarian departures. But it is a mistake to collapse the distinction between God's being and act altogether. We must insist that God is Trinity antecedently and independently of any of his acts of creation, reconciliation, or redemption. Though God's decision to become incarnate in Jesus Christ is eternally willed, the effects of that eternal decision are freely and contingently

27. Moltmann, *The Trinity and the Kingdom*, 161.

chosen and must be distinguished from the Son's necessary existence as the only begotten Son from the Father.

A second theme that emerges for some in the Trinitarian revival is a tendency toward social Trinitarianism: toward seeing the divine persons as distinct centers of consciousness and will and even as distinct subjects or agents. Barth and Rahner rightly highlight this misconception of the key term "person." Though we wish to retain this venerable term (which goes all the way back to Tertullian in the second century), we appreciate the emphasis of Barth and Rahner in providing a definition of the term that will avoid seeing the divine threeness in social or psychological terms. The divine persons are not distinct psycho-volitional subjects but are instead distinct modes of being in the one being of God. They are distinguished not by mind or will, subjectivity or personality, but by their eternal relations of origin. Each divine person is the one divine essence in a distinct mode.

In some quarters a Trinitarian revival is still needed but one true to the name, that is, one grounded in Scripture and the consensual tradition. Such a revival will want to avoid the errors of the first so-called revival: of conflating the being and acts of God and of transmuting the divine persons into distinct gods.

REFLECTION QUESTIONS

1. Why is it important to distinguish God's acts in creation and redemption from his antecedent being?

2. What is the danger in conceiving of the divine persons as distinct centers of consciousness and will?

3. How can we promote a genuine revival of the creedal doctrine of the Trinity?

4. How do the questions asked and answers given by modern theologians remind you of questions you've asked about the Trinity while reading the Bible?

5. What is one principle from the modern theologians that could help you explain the Trinity to someone else?

PART 4

The Trinity and Christian Doctrine

SECTION A

The Classical Doctrine of the Trinity

QUESTION 23

What Does It Mean That God Is One in Essence?

As we begin Part 4, we want to review what we have covered thus far. To this point, we have introduced the basic contours of the doctrine of the Trinity, its significance, and a methodology for studying it (Part 1). We have also explored the biblical teaching on the Trinity in each major section of Scripture (Part 2) and surveyed some of the most significant developments in the history of the doctrine (Part 3). We now turn our attention to theological consolidation, that is, to harvesting this biblical and historical material for the properly *theological* articulation of the doctrine. Recall that theology concerns itself with God and with all things in relation to God. For the most part, these chapters will deal the former, namely, with God himself, or theology proper. But even here, theology speaks of God in a twofold sense: absolutely and relatively.[1] To speak about God absolutely is to consider who God is in the eternal beatitude of his own inner life (*ad intra*): the one God in his threefold mode of existence as Father, Son, and Holy Spirit. To speak about God relatively is to consider who God is in relation to his external works (*ad extra*): creation, providence, redemption, and judgment. These chapters will treat God under both aspects. For example, we will discuss the divine missions, or sendings, of the Son and Spirit (*ad extra*) that reveal the eternal processions of the Son and Spirit (*ad intra*). There is, further, a twofold way of ordering the two considerations. God's inner life has priority in the order of being, but God's external acts have priority in the order of knowing. To put it simply: God acts as he acts because he is who he is, but we know who he is because he acts as he acts.

The first several chapters in this section set out to define some of the key

1. For more on these categories, see John Webster, "What Makes Theology Theological?," *Journal of Analytic Theology* 3 (2015): 17–28.

terms and concepts in the articulation of the doctrine of the Trinity. Some terms speak about God in his oneness and others in his threeness. This chapter considers what it means to say that God is one in *essence*.

Extrabiblical Terminology

We might wonder at the outset why we need terms that lie outside the Bible. Isn't the language of Scripture sufficient? Doesn't extrabiblical, technical vocabulary suggest that we need to improve upon the Bible? Aren't debates about Trinitarian terms in danger of the "quarrels about words" that the apostle warns against (1 Tim. 6:4)? To be sure, some have seen the historical doctrine of the Trinity as an aberration or deviation from Scripture. The early modern Socinians had an aversion to creedal Christianity that led them to deny the deity of Christ and the doctrine of the Trinity. Protestant liberalism likewise tended to pit the Bible against subsequent Christian orthodoxy. Adolf von Harnack famously suggested that early Christian dogma was more influenced by Hellenistic (Greek) thought than the simple, moral message of Jesus. But even among evangelicals, there has sometimes been an aversion to the language of the creeds and councils in favor of a kind of biblicism. Especially since the nineteenth century and perhaps especially in a North American context, many evangelicals have adopted a "no creed but the Bible" approach to the faith. To highlight this tendency among one evangelical tradition, Baptist confessions of faith evince a noticeable shift away from creedal language as we move from the seventeenth-century English context (the era of Baptist origins among the English Separatists) to an eighteenth- and nineteenth-century American context.[2]

So why utilize extrabiblical language? In one sense, we might simply admit that we should not have to. The Bible speaks plainly enough; it is only because of the distortions of false teachers that explanation is needed. As we saw in question 20, this was the response of John Calvin to this question: "Indeed, I could wish they [that is, extrabiblical theological terms] were buried, if only among all men this faith were agreed on: that the Father and Son and Spirit are one God, yet the Son is not the Father, nor the Spirit the Son, but that they are differentiated by a peculiar quality."[3] Centuries before Calvin, Athanasius had also expressed a preference for explicitly biblical language (*engraphōn*), but conceded that "unwritten" (*agraphōn*) terms can still render the proper

2. See, for instance, Rhyne Putman, "Baptists, *Sola Scriptura*, and the Place of the Christian Tradition," in *Baptists and the Christian Tradition: Towards an Evangelical Baptist Catholicity*, ed. Matthew Y. Emerson, Christopher W. Morgan, and R. Lucas Stamps (Nashville: B&H Academic, 2020), 27–54.
3. John Calvin, *Institutes of the Christian Religion*, ed. John T. McNeill, trans. Ford Lewis Battles (Louisville: Westminster John Knox, 1960), 1.8.5.

"judgment" (*dianoia*) of Scripture.[4] The later Genevan theologian, Francis Turretin, drew on this same distinction between words that were "in-written" (*engraphos autolexei*) and terms that are not "altogether un-written" (*agraphos*): "Although it is not lawful to form any doctrines not in Scripture, yet it is lawful sometimes to use words which are not found there if they are such as will enable us either to explain divine things or to avoid errors."[5] A term can be formally "un-written" in Scripture but still express faithfully what the Scripture teaches.

But there is a more positive way to explain the need for extrabiblical language. The very fact that the church has been commissioned to preach and teach the word of God necessitates and sanctions the use of human words. The seventeenth-century Baptist John Gill gives several reasons why this extrabiblical language is indispensable. To demand that we simply limit ourselves to repeating the words of Scripture would, in Gill's mind, "destroy all exposition and interpretation of Scripture," would make preaching "in a great measure useless," would "cramp all religious conversation about divine things, if not destroy it," would hamper any expression of biblical faith, and would leave the church unable to distinguish between true and false interpretations of Scripture.[6] So, to the degree that the preaching and teaching of Scripture is sanctioned by the Scriptures themselves, so too is theologizing from the Scriptures. We have also already referenced the distinction that David Yeago draws between "concepts" and "judgments." Even though later Christian doctrine utilizes *concepts* that are not explicitly found in Scripture (like *homoousios*) or are not found in Scripture with the same kind of technical specificity (like *hypostasis* in Heb. 1:3), they might still, nevertheless, render the same judgment as the New Testament (as when, for example, Paul speaks about the Son as being in the "form of God" and possessing "equality with God" [Phil. 2:6]).[7] In sum, extrabiblical terminology need not be seen as an imposition nor as an improvement upon the biblical language; it can be seen as a faithful distillation of biblical truth in its comprehensive scope and in response to various doctrinal errors.

The Essential Unity of the Divine Persons

Several terms emerged in the patristic-era Trinitarian debates that expressed the orthodox understanding of God's oneness. The central term in the Nicene

4. See Steven J. Duby, *Jesus and the God of Classical Theism: Biblical Christology in Light of the Doctrine of God* (Grand Rapids: Baker Academic, 2022), 41. Duby cites Athanasius, *De decretis* 31–32 (pp. 27–28).
5. Francis Turretin, *Institutes of Elenctic Theology*, 3 vols., trans. George Musgrave Giger, ed. James T. Dennison Jr. (Phillipsburg, NJ: P&R, 1992), 1:1.
6. John Gill, *A Complete Body of Doctrinal and Practical Divinity*, 2 vols. (Grand Rapids: Baker, 1978; repr., London: Tegg & Co., 1839), 1:xii–xvi.
7. David S. Yeago, "The New Testament and the Nicene Dogma: A Contribution to the Recovery of Theological Exegesis," *Pro Ecclesia* 3 (1994): 152–64.

creed, *homoousios*, contains one of them: Father and Son (and Holy Spirit) are one *ousios*—one being. Other Greek terms also named God according to his unity (for example, *physis*, "nature," and *theotēs*, "deity"). In Latin, there were likewise several terms that highlighted God's oneness or unity: *natura* ("nature"), *substantia* ("substance"), and *essentia* ("essence").[8] To speak about God as one in essence or nature (and three in persons) goes all the back to Tertullian, who also coined the term *trinitas* ("Trinity").[9] The three divine persons are not simply three coequal and coeternal divine essences. They are the numerically same divine essence. It is also important to note that the divine essence is not some fourth thing alongside the three persons. Each divine person simply is the divine essence in his own proper mode (we will address these distinctions more in the next chapter).

To say that there is only one divine essence is to say that there is only one God. This commitment to monotheism is the universal testimony of the biblical witness. To be sure, Old Testament Israel did not always live up to this monotheistic commitment and its corresponding monolatrous demand (that is, the demand of exclusive worship), but the teaching of both the Old and New Testaments is consistent on this point: There is and can only be one living and true God.[10] Consider, for example, several pivotal texts from the OT. Let us begin with the Shema of Deuteronomy 6:4–6: "Hear, O Israel: The Lord our God, the Lord is one. You shall love the Lord your God with all your heart and with all your soul and with all your might. And these words that I command you today shall be on your heart." There may be several ways to render the Hebrew text of verse 4, but each of them underscores the same point: God—YHWH, Israel's covenant Lord—is one; he is unified; he is exclusively God. Note again that monotheism entails monolatry: God's exclusively oneness demands an exclusive love on the part of his covenant people.

Another key OT text that emphasizes the oneness of God can be found in the Ten Commandments, or Ten Words, of Exodus 20: "And God spoke all these words, saying, 'I am the Lord your God, who brought you out of the land of Egypt, out of the house of slavery. You shall have no other gods before me.'" The first commandment might even be translated, "You shall have no

8. There are mixed reviews in the Christian tradition when it comes to applying "substance" to the oneness of the divine persons, owing to the fact that the term had two meanings in Aristotelean metaphysics. For a discussion of substance language and the Trinity, see Duby, *Jesus and the God of Classical Theism*, 72–76.
9. Tertullian, *Against Praxeus*, trans. Ernest Evans (London: SPCK, 1948).
10. We take the language of "monolatry" from Bauckham's *Jesus and the God of Israel*. Bauckham defines the term on page 5, and then discusses it further throughout the book (e.g., 11, 18, 63, 82–83, 97, 109). A common assumption in much contemporary scholarship of the Hebrew Bible/Old Testament is that Israel's religious perspective is better classified as henotheistic rather than monotheistic: that YHWH is supreme over many rival gods. While it is true that the Old Testament envisages rival spiritual entities, these created spiritual powers are in no way on the same metaphysical plane as the one true Creator God.

other gods in my presence." The point is not that Israel is free to worship many gods provided YHWH comes first on a list of rankings. The point is that no other gods may even be entertained in Israel's mind and heart. Again, monotheism and monolatry go together.

The prophecy of Isaiah provides another important OT witness to the oneness of Israel's God. In one sense, the book is one long polemic in favor of the exclusive deity of YHWH over against the false gods of the nations. To pick just one text, consider Isaiah 45:5–6:

> I am the LORD, and there is no other,
> besides me there is no God;
> I equip you, though you do not know me,
> that people may know, from the rising of the sun
> and from the west, that there is none besides me;
> I am the LORD, and there is no other.
> I form light and create darkness;
> I make well-being and create calamity;
> I am the LORD, who does all these things.

The negations are most forceful here: There is no other God; there is none besides me; there is no other. The Lord alone is God; the gods of the nations are mute idols. No other god controls the fate of the world—both the light and the darkness, both well-being and calamity. No other god can declare the end from the beginning. No other god can establish its immutable counsel and purpose (45:10).

The New Testament, no less than the Old, affirms this fundamental Jewish commitment to monotheism. Jesus repeats the Shema with its teaching on the oneness of God and the response of exclusive love that it demands (Mark 12:29–30). In a number of places the apostle Paul echoes this teaching:

> Therefore, as to the eating of food offered to idols, we know that "an idol has no real existence," and that "there is no God but one." (1 Cor. 8:4)

> Yet for us there is one God, the Father, from whom are all things and for whom we exist, and one Lord, Jesus Christ, through whom are all things and through whom we exist. (1 Cor. 8:6)

> For there is one God, and there is one mediator between God and men, the man Christ Jesus. (1 Tim. 2:5)

The last two texts highlight an important development in the NT teaching: There is only one God, but Jesus himself is somehow identified with him as the "Lord" (*kurios*, the Greek translation of the divine name in the Septuagint) alongside the Father. Elsewhere Paul includes the Spirit as well: "There is one body and one Spirit—just as you were called to the one hope that belongs to your call—one Lord, one faith, one baptism, one God and Father of all, who is over all and through all and in all" (Eph. 4:4–6). As we demonstrated in the biblical chapters, each of the three divine persons is identified with Israel's one God. The deity of the Father is assumed throughout the NT (with the Greek word *theos* most often, though not exclusively, appropriated to him). As we have seen, the Son and Spirit are identified as God in a variety of ways: The attributes, actions, appellations, and adoration reserved only for Israel's God is applied to them as well. Jesus puts the matter simply: "I and the Father are one" (John 10:30). Similarly, Paul identifies the Lord Jesus with the Holy Spirit: "The Lord is the Spirit" (2 Cor. 3:17). So, how do we account for both sides of this biblical teaching? How do we reconcile the fact that the NT identifies three distinct persons with Israel's one God while at the same time unflinchingly affirming that there is only one God? Either there are three gods or else the life of the one God entails some kind of multiplicity.

This "problem" that emerges from the biblical text prompted the Trinitarian terminology in the first place. The biblical teaching exerted a kind of "exegetical pressure," to use Kavin Rowe's phrase,[11] on the church to account for the oneness and the threeness of the one true God. As we have seen, the church came to speak about this dynamic in these terms: one essence, three persons. So, to say that God is one in essence is to say this: Each of the divine persons is the very same God in terms of his being or nature. The three share in the numerically singular being of God. They share all of the same divine attributes: aseity, simplicity, immutability, impassibility, eternity, omnipresence, omnipotence, omniscience, holiness, justice, righteousness, goodness, truth, and so on. They are identical in every way except in their personal relations to one another (see next question). To put it in Saint Augustine's terms, there exists an absolute equality and sameness in the Holy Trinity: "According to the Scriptures, Father and Son and Holy Spirit in the inseparable equality of one substance present a divine unity."[12] Everything that we say about the three essence-wise, we would have to say fully and equally of all three. The only distinctions we can draw between them must be said relations-wise, not essence-wise. As Pseudo-Dinonysius puts it, there is a twofold divine naming at work in the Scriptures. There are unified names that are common to all three (holy, good, love, etc.), and there are differentiated names that are proper to each (Father, Son, Spirit, begotten, proceeding, etc.). This "redoublement" follows

11. C. Kavin Rowe, "Biblical Pressure and Trinitarian Hermeneutics," *Pro Ecclesia* 11 (2002): 295–312.
12. Augustine, *The Trinity*, 2nd ed., trans. Edmund Hill, ed. John Rotelle, The Works of Saint Augustine 5, (Hyde Park, NY: New City, 2012), 1.7.

the pattern of Scripture itself, which speaks about God in terms that are common/essential and in terms that are proper/personal.[13]

Summary

The biblical teaching on the essential sameness of the divine persons has several important entailments. We mention just a few here. First, because God is one in essence, the three persons can only properly be distinguished by their relations. The three are not distinguished by mind, intellect, will, or power. These are essential attributes or perfections that are inherent to the divine essence and thus are shared equally by the three divine persons. Again, the persons are not distinguished essence-wise but only relation-wise. As we will see in the next chapter, the three divine persons are distinguished only by their eternal modes of subsistence (i.e., their eternal relations of origin) and by their corresponding modes of action (the ordering within the indivisible action of God). Second, because God is one in essence, God acts as one. All of God's external acts are carried out indivisibly and inseparably by all three divine persons. There is not a division of labor in the Holy Trinity. There is a unity—not merely a harmony—of action. The ordering within this one act (Greek *taxis*) does not undermine this fundamental unity. Third, because God is one in essence, each of the divine persons is equally, fully, and eternally God and therefore is the proper object of worship, devotion, obedience, and adoration. There is no hierarchy of divinity between the three. The Father is not "more God" than the Son, and the Son is not "more God" than the Spirit. The three are "together worshiped and glorified," as the Nicene Creed affirms. It seems fitting, then, to end this chapter with one of the church's oldest hymns, the *Gloria Patri*:

> Glory be to the Father, and to the Son:
> and to the Holy Ghost;
> As it was in the beginning, is now, and ever shall be:
> world without end. Amen.

REFLECTION QUESTIONS

1. What are the benefits (and potential costs) of using extrabiblical terminology to explain the doctrine of the Trinity?
2. Why is it important to affirm that there is only one divine essence?

---

13. Jamieson and Wittman, *Biblical Reasoning*, 99–100.

3. How do Christians sometimes inadvertently undermine the essential unity of the divine persons?

4. What are ways that the Bible's teaching on the essential unity of the Trinity helps your prayer life?

5. What is a passage in Scripture that has confused you but now seems clearer based on thinking through the Bible's teaching on the essential unity of the Trinity?

QUESTION 24

What Does It Mean That God Is Three in Persons?

We ended the previous chapter by noting how the Bible names God in a twofold, or "redoubled" way. There are unified names common to the Godhead, and there are differentiated names proper to each divine person. The simple way to summarize the teaching of Scripture, as it has been received in Christian orthodoxy from the earliest centuries, is to speak about God as one in essence and three in persons. So, just what does it mean to say that God is three in *persons*?

Answering this question requires addressing the more fundamental question: What is a person? Answers vary in the history of philosophy and of theology, not to mention the variety of answers one might hear in contemporary discourse. What we mean by a *divine* person may or may not overlap with definitions of personhood in other contexts. We must bear in mind the analogical nature of divine predication. Our language about God is neither univocal (meaning precisely the same thing as when it is applied to creatures), nor is it equivocal (meaning something completely different than when it is applied to creatures). Rather, our language about God is always analogical. There is a sufficient *similarity* but not a precise univocity. Our divine predication is always analogical because the Creator is qualitatively distinct from (not merely quantitively greater than) the creature. God is not on the same metaphysical plane as his creatures. So when we say, for example, that God is good and that a particular created thing is good, we cannot mean that the two things participate in goodness in the same way, with God simply getting the greater share. God is not just another being in the world, albeit the greatest. Instead, he is the source and cause of existence in everyone and everything else. God is, as scholastic theologians have put it, "being itself subsisting." Every created thing derives its existence by participating or sharing in God's existence.

We must bear in mind this principle of analogy when we apply the term "person" to God. Still, it would be a mistake to *deny* personhood of God.[1] God is personal in that he is a "someone" rather than a "something."[2] He is not an impersonal force or concept; he is the living and true God who is full of knowledge, wisdom, and power and who acts mightily to create, sustain, and govern the world. God is more than personal; he is, indeed, tripersonal—a trinity of persons in eternal relation to one another. As with his other perfections, God's personhood is the source and cause of creaturely personhood. The relations of the divine persons are the ontological ground of all other relations. But, again, we must bear in mind the analogical mode of our language about God's personhood.

What the Divine Persons Are Not

Given the analogical nature of divine personhood, we must say a bit more about what the divine persons are *not*. If analogy involves both a similarity and a dissimilarity, let us consider first the dissimilarity. For starters, we must simply restate the fundamental Trinitarian distinction: The three divine persons are not three distinct beings or essences. Gregory of Nyssa, a fourth-century father, wrote an important treatise to a certain Ablabius, the familiar title of which summarizes this point succinctly: *On "Not Three Gods."*[3] In the case of God, three persons do not equal three natures or essences. Unlike human nature, the divine nature is not a genus or kind that can exist in discrete specifications. The three persons share—or, more precisely, simply *are*—the numerically singular divine essence. To put it colloquially, the three divine persons are not three *people*. The divine persons are not human persons.

One entailment of this distinction between human and divine persons is a rejection of the idea that the divine persons constitute distinct centers of consciousness and will. Certain versions of modern social Trinitarianism have distinguished the persons in precisely this way, but it must be forcefully asserted that this way of distinguishing the persons is out of step with the mainstream Christian tradition. We should not import a modern psychological definition of personhood back into the historic doctrine of the Trinity.

---

1. According to Brian Davies, "classical theism" is to be distinguished from the revisionist views he labels "theistic personalism" precisely in that the latter has God as a person. While we are sympathetic to his critique of these revisionist views, we still think both Scripture and tradition compel us to speak of God in personal (tripersonal) terms, provided we recognize the analogical nature of this language. See Brian Davies, *An Introduction to the Philosophy of Religion*, 3rd ed. (Oxford: Oxford University Press, 2004).
2. We borrow this memorable distinction from Robert Spaemann, *Persons: The Difference between "Someone" and "Something,"* trans. Oliver O'Donovan (Oxford: Oxford University Press, 2006).
3. Gregory of Nyssa, *On "Not Three Gods"* (NPNF[2] 5:333–36).

Person does not equal *personality*. If the three persons each possessed his own distinct mind and will, then it would be very difficult to avoid the conclusion that they are three distinct beings or gods. To be sure, the three persons do possess mind and will, but it is the shared mind and will of the one divine essence. Each person has (or *is*) the one divine mind and will in his own distinct mode, but the three are not distinguished as three discrete minds. God is not like Cerberus, the three-headed dog of ancient mythology.

It should also be noted that the three persons are not to be distinguished by differing levels of authority. We address the contemporary notion of "eternal relations of authority and submission" in another chapter (question 33), but we simply note the entailment here: Since the persons are not distinguished by will, they cannot be distinguished by distinct hierarchically ordered expressions of will. The three persons share the identically same divine power/authority, which is an attribute of the shared divine essence. Relatedly, neither should we distinguish the divine persons according to distinct roles or functions in the created order. According to the doctrine of inseparable operations, everything God does *ad extra* he does indivisibly as Father, Son, and Holy Spirit: one action performed by the one God. The persons are not carrying out three different, even if harmonious, actions in creation, providence, and redemption. There is only one action/operation, even though there are three distinct modes of personal action: from the Father, through the Son, by the Holy Spirit.

What the Divine Persons Are

So what, then, is a divine person? Christian philosopher Boethius offered a standard, more general definition of a person: A person is an individual substance of a rational nature.[4] Thomas Aquinas and others have applied this definition to the Trinitarian persons as well. On the Boethian definition, a person is one particular kind of *substance* (in Aristotle's first sense of that term): a discrete existing thing. But a person is unique among substances in that it is *of a rational nature*, that is, it is possessed of reason and intellect. Humans and angels qualify as persons, but rocks or dogs do not. Because persons possess reason, they represent, according to Thomas, "what is most perfect in nature." As such, it is "fittingly applied to God," though once again in an analogous and "more excellent way."

Several Greek and Latin words have emerged in the history of Christian doctrine to mark the three persons. As we saw in the chapters on the patristic era, *prosōpon* (Greek) and *persona* (Latin) were borrowed from the ancient theater to name particular actors in the drama. *Hypostasis* became the favored

4. Boethius, *Contra Eutychen et Nestorium*, 3.5. For a translation and discussion of the relevant passage, see Phillip A. Rolknick, *Person, Grace, and God* (Grand Rapids: Eerdmans, 2019), 39–40.

Greek term for the three persons after the Council of Chalcedon and signified the three in their eternal relations of origin.

In Latin, the picture was a bit more complicated. Etymologically, *hypostasis* and *substantia* are parallel. Both mean "something that stands under or grounds things."[5] But *substantia* had its own distinct and technical senses in Aristotelian metaphysics, which has complicated its applicability to the divine persons. In one sense, substance is parallel to the Greek term *ousia*, and thus to the divine essence. In another sense, substance is parallel to the post-Constantinopolitan usage of *hypostasis*, and thus to the divine persons. Provided that one can apply the term substance in this latter sense to the three persons, the Boethian definition of person is apt: A divine person is an individual substance—distinct in relation from the other two—who subsists in the singular, rational nature of God.

Additional Latin terms include *subsistentia* and *suppositum*. A *subsistence* is a particular mode of being proper to substances (not merely the kind of being that would be true of accidental properties). And a *suppositum* is a particular kind of subsistence, namely, one that exists as a singular entity and not as a part of another.[6] A person/hypostasis, then, is rational subsistence or suppositum.

All of these technical distinctions are meant to serve the fundamental Trinitarian distinction between essence and relation. The three are identical in all respects except for their eternal relations of origin (see question 26) and in how those relations are expressed in the economy of redemption. The persons are one in being but distinct in modes of being. They are one in their economic action but distinct in modes of action. To speak about the persons as distinct modes of being and action is emphatically not to say that they are merely distinct modes of consecutive manifestation or revelation, which is the Sabellian or modalistic heresy. The three are distinct in reality, not just in our understanding. But their distinctions are relational, not essential.

But it would be a mistake to conceive of the divine persons as *mere* relations. The persons are, rather, identical with the divine essence and differ only by the mode or manner in which each is the one identically same essence. The Father is the divine essence in an unbegotten and paternal mode. The Son is the divine essence in a begotten/filial mode. The Holy Spirit is the divine essence in a proceeding/spirated mode (that is, he comes forth from or is breathed out by the Father and Son). We will have more to say about these eternal relations of origin in subsequent chapters, but for now it is crucial to note that this notion of person-as-relation occupies a kind of middle space

---

5. Howard Robinson and Ralph Weir, "Substance," *The Stanford Encyclopedia of Philosophy* https://plato.stanford.edu/ARCHIVES/SPR2013/ENTRIES/substance/.
6. See Francis Turretin, *Institutes of Elenctic Theology*, 3 vols., trans. George Musgrave Giger, ed. James T. Dennison Jr. (Phillipsburg, NJ: P&R, 1992), 1:254.

between the classical, Aristotelian categories of substance and accidents. Relation, in this sense, becomes a crucially important Christian contribution to the very definition of personhood, as Joseph Ratzinger has pointed out—a contribution was prompted by the divine revelation of the Holy Trinity and the incarnation of the Word.[7] Personhood can no longer be defined merely in terms of substance and accidents (the latter of which is inapplicable to God in any event) but must expand to include the category of relation. With the divine persons as the exemplar, a person is best understood as a substance existing in mutual relations of self-giving love. Angelic and human personhood are patterned after and imperfectly mirror these fundamental relations of love: The Father begets the Son, and the Father and Son jointly breathe forth their shared Spirit.

Summary

The basic grammar of the Trinity should be familiar by now: God is one in essence and three in persons. But just what is a person (*prosopon*, *hypostasis*, *persona*)? In a Trinitarian context, three persons does not mean three "people," three distinct centers of consciousness and will, or three levels of authority. No, the three divine persons are one in essence, mind, will, and authority. What then is a divine person? Boethius's definition can serve as a starting point: A person is an individual substance of a rational nature. But in the case of the Trinity, there is only one rational nature: the shared divine essence or being. The three persons, then, are three modes of being and action in the one being of God, distinguished only by their eternal relations of origin: The Father is from no one, the Son is eternally begotten of the Father, and the Spirit eternally proceeds from the Father and Son. These three persons act in accordance with these distinct personal properties: The indivisible action of God is from the Father, through the Son, and by the Spirit.

REFLECTION QUESTIONS

1. What is the meaning of "person"? Can this term be applied both to divine persons and human (and angelic) persons?

2. How is our usage when applied to God both similar and different?

3. Why is it important not to define the divine persons in modern psychological terms?

---

7. Pope Benedict XVI, *Joseph Ratzinger in* Communio, *Volume 2: Anthropology and Culture* (Grand Rapids: Eerdmans, 2013), 103–18.

4. What are ways that studying the Bible's teaching on the three persons of God helps your prayer life?

5. What is a passage in Scripture that has confused you but now seems clearer based on thinking through the Bible's teaching on the three persons of God?

QUESTION 25

What Is the Difference Between the Immanent and the Economic Trinity?

Among the Greek fathers of the church, a distinction emerged early on between what we may say about God absolutely considered (*theologia*) and what we may say about God relative to his saving plan as it unfolds on the stage of human history (*oikonomia*). This distinction has developed in contemporary theology in terms of the immanent (or ontological) Trinity and the economic Trinity. Famously, twentieth-century Roman Catholic theologian Karl Rahner insisted on the absolute identity of these two concepts: The economic Trinity is the immanent Trinity, and the immanent Trinity is the economic Trinity (see question 25). The precise meaning and truth of this claim has been disputed. Some have even questioned whether the distinction is useful. This chapter explores the difference and relationship between these two modes of theologizing about God's Trinitarian being and action.

Defining the Terms

Applying the term *immanent* to the Trinity highlights God's life in himself. The word derives from the Latin *immanere* (*in* + *manere*): "to remain within." The concept is also referred to as the ontological Trinity, that is, the being of God as such (from the Greek *ontos*, "being"). The immanent Trinity is the strictest meaning of *theology*: discourse about God himself, or theology proper. Here theologians consider the existence of God, the divine attributes, and the eternal processions that constitute God's triune life. In this connection, theologian John Webster spoke about *theological theology*, that is, theology truly suited to the name: what we say about God in himself.[1] To be sure, our creaturely knowledge of God remains limited, analogical, and *ectypal* (a copy), in contrast

1. See, e.g., John Webster, "What Makes Theology Theological?" *Journal of Analytical Theology* 3 (2015): 17–28.

to God's perfect self-knowledge, his *archetypal* theological knowledge (the pattern). God remains incomprehensible to finite creatures. We may apprehend what God has revealed of himself, but we cannot circumscribe God and pin him down, so to speak, as the subject of our analysis. Further, what we know of God comes to us precisely through God's redemptive revelation. Still, there is utility, as we will see, in making the conceptual distinction between God's notional acts *ad intra* (the real distinctions that obtain between the persons in virtue of their eternal relations of origin) and God's creative and redemptive act *ad extra* (the indivisible but modally Trinitarian works of God outside of himself).

The term *economic* Trinity picks up the Pauline language of God's saving economy in human history. In Ephesians 1:10 Paul speaks about God's "plan" (*oikonomia*) for the fullness of time to unite all things in Christ. The word is related to the Greek term *oikos* ("house" or "household"), which, along with its derivatives, Paul uses liberally in his letters. The church is the household of God. The apostles are the stewards, or household managers, of the mysteries of God. The *oikonomia* is, as it were, the home economics of the triune God: the manner in which the Father orders his affairs in the saving acts of the Son and Spirit. The second-century theologian Irenaeus made particular use of this term to describe the Trinitarian shape of the *kanon*, or rule, of truth that is disclosed in the biblical revelation.[2] As we will see, the distinction between the immanent relations within God and the triune saving acts outside of God is necessary in order to safeguard the freedom and independence of God, lest we presume that God is constituted as Trinity precisely by the contingently willed affairs of human history.

Rahner's Rule

Karl Rahner was one of the most prolific and influential Roman Catholic theologians of the post-Vatican II twentieth century. His constructive theological program was especially concerned with the central doctrines of the Trinity and the incarnation. Our focus here will be upon his famous axiom that has generated rich reflection on the revelation of the Trinity to humanity. His 1967 book, *The Trinity*, summarizes succinctly what has come to be known as "Rahner's Rule": "The 'economic' Trinity is the 'immanent' Trinity and the 'immanent' Trinity is the 'economic' Trinity."[3] The quotation marks around the terms "economic" and "immanent" are significant for Rahner. His main burden is to express the conviction that there are not, in point of fact, *two* trinities with whom we have to do; there is only one Trinity whose revelation of himself in the economy of redemption discloses God as he is in himself. Rahner's concern is with versions of theology (such as that of Thomas Aquinas, but especially

2. Irenaeus of Lyons, *On the Apostolic Preaching*, trans. John Behr, PPS, 17 (Yonkers, NY: St Vladimir's Seminary Press, 2003).
3. Karl Rahner, *The Trinity*, trans. Joseph Donceel, Milestones in Catholic Theology (New York: Herder & Herder, 1970), 22.

those of modern Neo-Scholastic theologians) that treat the one God (*de Deo Uno*) as a discrete theological locus from God's self-revelation as a trinity of persons (*de Deo Trino*). Rahner believes it is a mistake to treat first the existence and attributes of the divine essence and only then append a doctrine of the eternal relations among the three divine persons. To do so disconnects the doctrine of the Trinity from the whole fabric of Christian theology and risks turning the Trinity into an obscure and ultimately dispensable theological curiosity. Rahner worries that Christians can become in practice "almost mere 'monotheists.'"[4] As he pointedly states, "We must be willing to admit that, should the doctrine of the Trinity have to be dropped as false, a major part of religious literature could well remain virtually unchanged."[5]

Rahner is also concerned with the scholastic speculation that any of the three divine persons could have become incarnate. Thomas Aquinas argues as much in his *ST* as do others in the history of doctrine.[6] For Rahner, if one admits even in theory that any divine person could become incarnate, then the incarnation ceases to be a reliable disclosure of the person of the Son as such. For Rahner, only the Logos could become visibly expressed in the incarnation because only the Logos is the eternal expression of the Father. The Son's temporal mission faithfully discloses his eternal procession from the Father. Indeed, his mission simply is his generation expressed in the economy of redemption. Central for Rahner is the idea that the self-revelation of God is not merely the manifestation of the undifferentiated divine essence but of each divine person in a "non-appropriated" manner. In other words, in the incarnation we are not dealing simply with a divine appropriation (that is, a manner of speaking about a particular divine person who is nevertheless accompanied equally by the other two divine persons in inseparable action) but with a revelation that is *proper to* the Son (that belongs to him distinctly).

Rahner extends this instance to the other persons as well: Each person is disclosed *properly* (not merely essentially) in the economy. Rahner critiques certain aspects of the Western doctrine of the Trinity, dating back to Augustine, and chooses instead to follow the logic of Scripture, the Nicene Creed, and the Greek fathers (as he interprets those sources), which grounded the unity of the Trinity not in a common divine essence but in the person Father, who is the font of the Son and Spirit. Rahner applies his thesis to God's self-communication in the economy of salvation by suggesting that God's work of grace in the redeemed is not merely an efficient cause (in the Aristotelian sense that medieval theologians

---

4. Rahner, *The Trinity*, 10.
5. Rahner, *The Trinity*, 10–11.
6. Thomas treats these issues in *ST*. Bonaventure argues that while the incarnation was brought about by all three persons indivisibly, it is especially fitting for the Word, the second person, to be the incarnate mediator, since "he is the intermediate one of the three [divine] persons." Bonaventure, *Breviloquium*, trans. Dominic V. Monti, Works of Bonaventure, vol. 9 (Saint Bonaventure, NY: Franciscan Institute, 2005), 138.

employed) but a kind of "quasi-formal" cause. It cannot be a strictly formal cause or else the Creator-creature distinction would be erased. But a merely essential cause would not do justice to the ways in which the divine persons communicate their very selves in union with the human being. In sum, Rahner maintains that the God we encounter in the economy is precisely the same God, without remainder, that we contemplate when considering the immanent Trinity.

There is more that could be said of Rahner's learned and sophisticated thesis, but this brief synopsis serves our purposes. What are we to make of his axiom? Critiques of Rahner's Rule worry that a strict identity between the immanent Trinity and economic Trinity without remainder could suggest that the persons are constituted precisely by their self-communication to the creature. This identity would thus threaten the divine freedom in the economy. Rahner attempts to head off this criticism by affirming that the divine missions are indeed the free and sovereign expression of the processions in the economy. But he also critiques the medieval notion that God bears no "real" relation to the redeemed. The denial of "real" relations in God was not meant to suggest that God is aloof and unrelatable but rather that God's being is not constituted as such by its relation to creation, whereas the creature's relation to God is "real" in this sense: Our relation to God is self-constituting, but God's relation to us is not. Rahner, on the other hand, maintains that the mediation of himself in the economy involves a "real mediation in God's inner life." If it did not involve a real "difference" in God, then we would risk a kind of "economic Sabellianism" or modalism.[7] So, the worry remains: Does God need the economy, as it were, to be who he is?

We might also critique Rahner's interpretation of the Augustinian/Thomistic tradition that he rejects. It is true that the medieval theologians speculated, as a matter of reflection on the shared omnipotence that the divine persons share in common, that any of the persons is capable of incarnation. But the medievals also explicitly affirmed that there is a *fittingness* to the incarnation of the Second Person; as the Logos of the Father, it is fitting that he is expressed as the incarnate Logos. Rahner's alleged disconnect between the missions and the processions need not apply. As Augustine forcefully maintained, the mission of the incarnate Son truly expresses who he is as the eternally generated Son, even if not everything that obtains in the economy can be read back into, so to speak, the eternal processions. In other words, what Rahner wants can be had in the traditions that he critiques.

Still, there is much to commend in Rahner's approach if one interprets it in ways more sympathetic to traditional formulations. The Trinity we encounter in the economy is indeed the only Trinity there is. The missions are the economic expression of the immanent processions. The Son who is *sent from* the Father in his generation from Mary is the same Son who *is from* the Father in his eternal generation. The Spirit who is *sent from* the Father and Son in his visible mission

7. Rahner, *The Trinity*, 38.

is the same Spirit who *is from* the Father and Son in his eternal procession. These are truths that the Western tradition have happily affirmed, even if the category of fittingness stops short of a strict necessity that prohibits the theoretical possibility of other incarnations (a point that did not figure prominently in the medieval formulations in any event; affirming the possibility of other incarnations was meant to underscore the omnipotence of all three divine persons). In point of fact, only the Son has become incarnate, and thus the incarnation takes on a kind of contingent necessity, which fittingly reveals who the Son is in his eternal personhood.

Other theologians have taken a similar tack as Rahner and pressed it even further. On Bruce McCormack's interpretation of Karl Barth, for example, God's being as Trinity is constituted precisely by his electing act to be God for us in the man Christ Jesus.[8] Similarly, the Orthodox theologian John Zizioulas argues that God's being is determined by his action (see question 22). These various attempts to draw a strict identity between *theologia* and *oikonomia* are even more open to the charge that God loses his sovereign freedom in the economy, collapsing the distinction of God's *ad intra* divine processions and his *ad extra* works of grace.

The Relationship Between *Theologia* and *Oikonomia*

What, then, is the relationship between the immanent Trinity and the economic Trinity? In assessing and clarifying Rahner's axiom, Thomistic theologian Gilles Emery helpfully underscores the most relevant points. "First, it is necessary not to conflate the eternity of God and the time of the economy."[9] While the economy reveals the Trinity as it truly is, it does not make the Trinity what it is. Second, and related, the immanent Trinity is necessary, while the economy of salvation is contingently willed by the Trinity. God might not have created a world at all, and his decision to redeem the world through the missions of the Son and Spirit is freely and graciously willed. It is important here to affirm that the processions of the Son and Spirit are not voluntarily willed by the Father. Contrary to the ancient Arian heresy, the Father is Father by nature, not by will. Third, we must not conflate God's life *ad intra* with what may be known about him by creatures through his *ad extra* works. "The economy does not exhaust the mystery of the Trinity."[10] God is incomprehensible; there is more (but never less) than what he has revealed about himself truly in the economy. Finally, Emery notes, the human participation enabled by the economy does not exhaust what we will know of him only in glory, in the beatific vision.[11] God is truly known in the economy in a threefold manner

8. Bruce McCormack, "Election and the Trinity: Theses in Response to George Hunsinger," *Scottish Journal of Theology* 63, no. 2 (2010): 203–24.
9. Gilles Emery, *The Trinity: An Introduction to Catholic Doctrine on the Triune God*, trans. Matthew Levering (Washington, DC: The Catholic University of America Press, 2011), 177..
10. Emery, *The Trinity*, 177.
11. Emery, *The Trinity*, 177.

that is a faithful revelation of who he is in his own immanent life, but, again, the economy can never exhaust the mystery of the blessed Trinity.

Summary

We might add to Emery's helpful clarifications that not everything that obtains in the economy can be, so to speak, read back into the inner life of God. For example, the economy involves the Second Person in a hypostatic union with a human nature. Thus, the man Christ Jesus states that "the Father is greater" than he (John 14:28). The human obedience of Christ is, to be sure, *fitted to* his personal property as the one generated from the Father, the one who has his origin in the unbegotten Father. But it would be a mistake to read a relationship of authority and submission, which obtains in the economy according to the Son's human nature, back into the inner life of God, where the Son's generation signals origin and not inferiority or subordination. In the end, Emery wonders whether it is beneficial even to frame the doctrine in terms of two trinities: one immanent and the other economic. This is a point that Rahner himself seems to be making with his axiom, but Rahner seems to be unable to avoid the lack of clarity by succumbing to this very framing. Emery suggests that a better path is laid by speaking of the missions and the processions. The missions truly reveal and communicate but do not constitute the processions.[12] Or, to return where we began this chapter, *oikonomia* discloses *theologia*, but the former does not exhaust the latter.

REFLECTION QUESTIONS

1. What is the difference between the immanent Trinity and the economic Trinity? Is it useful to make this distinction?

2. What are the costs of collapsing the distinction between the immanent Trinity and economic Trinity?

3. What are ways that understanding the distinctions between the immanent and economic Trinity helps your prayer life?

4. What is a passage in Scripture that has confused you but now seems clearer based on thinking through the distinctions between the immanent and economic Trinity?

5. How can understanding the distinctions between the immanent and economic Trinity help you explain the Trinity to someone else?

---

12. Emery, *The Trinity*, 178.

QUESTION 26

How Can God Be One in Nature but Three in Persons?

To say that God is one God in three persons means that we affirm two things at once. First, there is only one God, who is without rival from other gods or demigods or any other creature. There is, in other words, an unbridgeable gulf between this Creator God and every other thing in existence; on one side is God and God alone, and on the other side is every creature, every single thing that exists apart from God.[1] The second affirmation is that this one God exists in three distinct persons. As we have seen, this confession is based on the biblical data that describes Father, Son, and Holy Spirit each with appellations (names), attributes, actions, and adoration that are reserved for God. So, to state it again, the Christian confession is that God is one God who exists in three persons: Father, Son, and Holy Spirit. Each of the three persons is equally God, and eternally so.

Trinitarian Math

Of course, the very next question—asked by every five-year-old with basic math skills in every Sunday school class—is how God can be both *one* and *three* at the same time. Church history is full of wrong answers to this conundrum—from subordinationism, which makes the Son and the Spirit somehow "less God" than the Father; to Sabellianism, which makes God wear what we might call "person masks" at different points in salvation history, so that at times he's the Father, at other times the Son, and at still other times the Holy Spirit. Both of these errors, along with other heresies throughout church history, are something less than the full affirmation of the oneness of God and of his existence as three distinct but equal persons. Subordination-

1. On this "Creator/creature distinction," see Tyler Wittman, *God and Creation in the Theology of Thomas Aquinas and Karl Barth* (Cambridge: Cambridge University Press, 2019).

ism and other related errors reject the notion that each person of the Trinity is equally God. Instead, one person—almost always the Father—has some kind of ontological priority over the others. Sabellianism and related errors make the opposite mistake—they reject the notion that God is one God who exists in three persons *at the same time*, or *eternally*. Yes, Father, Son, and Spirit are equally God, but they do not each exist at once or for eternity. Instead, God is only one of them at any given time.

The early church combatted both of these errors by formulating a doctrine of the Trinity that rested on a teaching called the eternal relations of origin.[2] The fundamental question that led to this doctrine is this: How can God be one God who exists in three persons, each of whom is equally and eternally God? Early Christian theologians like Athanasius, Gregory of Nazianzus, Basil of Caesarea, Gregory of Nyssa, and Hilary of Poitiers recognized that this question could not be answered by making distinctions that were rooted in God's attributes, appellations, actions, or deserved adoration. If, say, the Father alone should receive ultimate glory, then this means the Father is somehow *more* God than the Son or Spirit. Or, if the Son has a different will from the Father, then they do not share the same will and so have different natures. Or again, if the Spirit has different attributes than the Father or Son that are not shared by the latter two persons, then their natures and their essences are distinct and not one. On the other hand, the Bible affirms that each person is distinct from the others. The theologians of the early church thus recognized that, in order to describe God accurately, they had to do so in such a way that maintained the distinction between the persons while also maintaining their essential oneness.

The doctrine of the eternal relations of origin does just that. This linchpin of Nicene orthodoxy says that the persons of God are distinguished by how each of them subsist in the divine essence, *and only by that fact*. They are not distinguished by any attribute or set of attributes, any action or set of actions, any name or set of names other than their personal names, or by gradations in how much they should be worshiped or glorified. Instead, they are *only* distinguished by how they relate to one another, a set of relations that has existed eternally and is only concerned with the communication of the divine essence.

Before we proceed, we need to be clear about two things. First, the divine essence is not some separate "thing" apart from the three persons of God, as if

2. On the development of the doctrine of the Trinity in the early church, see, for instance, Khaled Anatolios, *Retrieving Nicaea: The Development and Meaning of Trinitarian Doctrine* (Grand Rapids: Baker Academic, 2011); Lewis Ayres, *Nicaea and Its Legacy: An Approach to Fourth-Century Trinitarian Theology* (Oxford: Oxford University Press, 2006); Matthew Bates, *The Birth of the Trinity: Jesus, God, and Spirit in New Testament and Early Christian Interpretations of the Old Testament* (Oxford: Oxford University Press, 2016); and John Behr, *The Way to Nicaea*, Formation of Christian Theology 1 (Crestwood, NY: St Vladimir's Seminary Press, 2001).

there is really a "quadrinity"—Father, Son, Spirit, and Essence. No, the divine essence simply is Father, Son, and Spirit in relation to one another. So when we say that the eternal relations of origin are how the persons subsist in the divine essence, or that this doctrine is related to the communication of the divine essence, we do not mean that the essence is separate from the persons. They aren't lobbing the divine essence to one another in an eternal game of hot potato. Rather, the persons in relation just are the essence, and vice versa. So, the eternal relations of origin are not passing around some separate substance or essence between the persons but instead are just how the persons relate to one another as the three persons of the one God.

A second caveat is that terms like "begottenness" and "procession" are revealed to us by Scripture and tell us accurately who God is but that cannot exhaustively describe him. They are, to use the terminology of the Christian tradition, analogical terms. That is, they tell us the truth about God but not in an exhaustive or univocal way. Because they are analogical, they tell us the truth—they are not equivocal, saying one thing but meaning another. But because they are analogical, they are also not one-to-one correspondence with reality—like any analogy, these terms only take us so far. With respect to the eternal relations of origin, when we say that the Father *begets* the Son, we are *not* saying that this happens in a creaturely mode. The Father does not beget the Son in a creaturely mode because (1) this does not happen in time (it is an *eternal* relation) and (2) this does not happen via procreation or any other creaturely act involved in begetting. Rather, the term "begotten" is analogical. It tells us the truth about the Son; namely, that he is the same essence as the Father precisely because he receives that same essence from the Father. But the analogy also only takes us so far, since this begottenness, unlike creaturely begetting, does not happen in time and it does not happen via creaturely means of procreation. We have to bear this analogical nature of human language about God as we discuss the eternal begottenness of the Son and the eternal procession of the Spirit.[3]

A (Brief) Biblical Case for the Eternal Relations of Origin

While thus far we have focused on technical terminology, or what the church has called "theological grammar," this is a thoroughly biblical doctrine. Although we will discuss many of these exegetical arguments and others in subsequent chapters on the Son's begottenness and the Spirit's procession, here we summarize the biblical basis for the doctrine of the eternal relations of

3. See on the analogical nature of theological reflection, and particularly with respect to the eternal generation of the Son, Gregory of Nazianzus, "Oration 28" and "Oration 29," in *On God and Christ: The Five Theological Orations and Two Letters to Cledonius*, PPS 23 (Crestwood, NY: St Vladimir's Seminary Press, 2002), 37–92.

origin as a whole. The church has historically argued for its exegetical rationale in the following ways.[4]

One God in Three Persons

The twin biblical affirmations that there is one God (Deut. 6:4) and that the Father, Son, and Spirit are each equally God because they share titles (Lord, God, Almighty, etc.), attributes (power, wisdom, etc.), and actions (creation, salvation) have to be reconciled. When we couple this with the radical distinction we see in Scripture between Creator and creature, there is no "mediatorial" or semidivine option for Son and Spirit. Because they equally share in divine titles, actions, and attributes, and because there is no such category as a mediatorial being in the biblical worldview, the Bible demands acknowledging that these three are equally God while also acknowledging that there is only one God.

John 5:26 and "Life in Himself"

Exactly how these three persons are distinct persons while also being one God is addressed biblically in a few different ways. The testimony of Scripture is that they share equally in the essence of God—what makes God is his essence, which is his authority, power, will, goodness, mercy, holiness, etc. So, for instance, Father and Son share equally in the creation and therefore in their authority over that creation (e.g., Col. 1:15–18). How, then, are they distinguished? Texts like John 5:26 give us a good start. The Father has life in itself and gives the Son life in himself.

The context of John 5 indicates that the Son is clearly speaking of his equality with the Father in his divinity (namely in the actions of judging and raising the dead). Even if, though, we want to say that he is expressing how these characteristics work themselves out in his incarnate state, John 5:26 is set within the larger context of comparing the Father and the Son's divinity. Further, it is difficult to read the phrase "life in itself" as a reference to the incarnation. If this were referring to the incarnation, the text would be saying that the same kind of life the Father has is now given to the Son in his becoming incarnate. How is that so? What exactly would it mean for the Father's divine life to be the same as the Son's incarnate life? It would make more sense, especially given the context, to say that the Father has life in himself—a characteristic that is only true of God—and has given the Son life in himself. The Father here communicates what it means to be God to the Son.

4. The following originally appeared as Matt Emerson, "A Summarized Biblical Case for Eternal Generation," *Biblical Reasoning*, June 29, 2016, https://secundumscripturas.com/2016/06/29/a-summarized-biblical-case-for-eternal-generation/.

Proverbs 8 and the Father's Begotten Wisdom
Proverbs 8:22–31 is notoriously difficult, especially for modern readers. But when we think canonically, it becomes a bit clearer. Christ is clearly identified as the Wisdom of God (1 Cor. 1:24) and, synonymously, the Word or Logos of God (John 1:1–13). He is the one through whom the Father creates (Col. 1:15–18). For Proverbs 8:22–31 to be speaking of anyone but the Son, therefore, would make little sense of these New Testament references to the Son as God's Wisdom. Further, for the Father in Proverbs 8 to have some wisdom other than the Son would make little sense. We thus have to deal with Proverbs 8:22–31 in a way that makes sense of how God can "birth" his Wisdom before time began and therefore before he actually creates anything.[5] Now, with John 5 and Proverbs 8, we have two texts that give us "generating" language to speak of the relationship between Father and Son.[6]

Names: Father, Son, and Spirit
Perhaps even more important than individual texts is the pattern of texts we see throughout Scripture, a pattern that consistently names these three as Father, Son, and Spirit. This points not only to their triunity but to the way that triunity exists, namely through a Father-Son-Spirit relation.[7] Now here we have to make a choice. What does it mean for there to be a Father-Son relation? And this really is the rub. Does it mean, as the tradition has consistently argued, that the Father begets, or generates, the Son? Certainly this is true of the analogy the language is using: human fatherhood and sonship. A son is typically a son through receiving his human essence via the father's generation. But, on the other hand, authority and submission is another characteristic of many father/son relationships. So, how do we choose between the two? While I could give you the historical logic here, I'll stick with my biblical guns and go to a particular text.

Philippians 2:5–11 and the "Form of God"/"Form of a Servant" Pattern
This passage begins by noting that Jesus, prior to his incarnation, was "in the form of God." This is not saying the Son was some sort of demigod, or lesser

5. On the hermeneutical rationale, particularly as found among early church theologians, for seeing eternal generation of the Son in Proverbs 8:22–31, see Matthew Y. Emerson, "The Role of Proverbs 8: Eternal Generation and Hermeneutics Ancient and Modern," in *Retrieving Eternal Generation*, ed. Fred Sanders and Scott Swain (Grand Rapids: Zondervan Academic, 2017), 44–66.
6. For further discussion on Proverbs 8, see my essay cited in the footnote above, as well as the next chapter in this book. The point here is simply to give a brief overview of the doctrine of the eternal relations of origin.
7. On the biblical data, particularly in the Pauline corpus, that speaks of this Father-Son-Spirit relation, see Wesley Hill, *Paul and the Trinity: Persons, Relations, and the Pauline Letters* (Grand Rapids: Eerdmans, 2015).

than God, but that he was in his essence, his form, truly God. Prior to his economic work of salvation as most fully seen in his incarnation, we speak of the Son as taking the "form of God." But when he becomes incarnate, he takes on the "form of a servant." Notice here that the point at which the Son becomes a servant—becomes submissive—to the Father, is at the incarnation.

It is clear, then, that the submission of the Son belongs to God's life in the economy of salvation, his action of redemption, and not prior to it. There is no submission of the Son prior to his work of redemption. Therefore when we see texts (e.g., 1 Cor. 11:3) that talk of the submission of "Jesus" or "Christ" or "Jesus Christ" (or, as in the unique case of 1 Cor. 15:28, "the Son"), we should look to Paul's words in Philippians 2:5–11 for the exegetical key. These passages are not, according to the "form of God"/"form of a servant" pattern in Philippians 2:5–11, speaking of the Son's eternal life with the Father but of his submission to the Father in the economy of salvation. The point here is that the Son and Father are not distinguished in eternity by a relation of authority and submission but by (and only by) their eternal relations of origin.

To sum up, the Bible affirms the oneness of God and his threeness as Father, Son, and Holy Spirit. While the persons are distinct from each other, their distinction in the Bible does not lie in differences, either by quality or quantity, in attributes, appellations, actions, or adoration. Rather, the one and only way that the persons are distinguished from one another in the Bible is through the language of *eternal relations of origin*.

The One God's Threeness in Relation

Given these theological and biblical foundations, what then are the eternal relations of origin? There are four relations in the classic doctrine of the Trinity: paternity, sonship, common spiration, and procession.[8] First, paternity is the relation the Father has to the Son, because the Father *eternally begets the Son*. This, of course, brings into play the second relation: that of sonship, which belongs to God the Son. He is *the eternally begotten Son* of the Father from eternity. Third, *common spiration* belongs to the Father and Son. That is, the Father and Son eternally spirate the Spirit, where the term "spirate" is a reference to biblical language about the Spirit being "breathed out" by the Father and the Son. Finally, *the Spirit proceeds* from the Father and, according to the Western tradition, from the Son (see the next two chapters for more on these concepts and their biblical support).

8. On the classic view of these four relations, as well as the five "notions" of the Trinity, see Gilles Emery, *The Trinitarian Theology of Saint Thomas Aquinas*, trans. Francesca Aran Murphy (Oxford: Oxford University Press, 2007), esp. 51–102. For a contemporary articulation of the doctrine of the eternal relations of origin, see Fred Sanders, *The Triune God*, New Studies in Dogmatics (Grand Rapids: Zondervan Academic, 2016), 121–54.

Modes of Subsistence

What does all this mean? First, it means that the Father's mode of subsistence in the divine essence is *unbegotten* (known as *innascibility* in the Christian tradition). He does not receive the divine essence from anyone but rather "has life in himself" (John 5:26). Second, it means that the Son subsists in the divine essence as the *only begotten*, because the Father "has given it [to the Son] to have life in himself" (John 5:26). In other words, the Son subsists in the divine essence through being eternally begotten of the Father. And third, it means that the Spirit subsists in the divine essence as the *one who proceeds* from the Father and the Son, the love and gift of the first two persons of the Trinity. The Holy Spirit subsists in the divine essence through being eternally spirated by the Father and the Son.

Personal Distinction in Relation, Perfect Unity in Nature

Use of terms like "begottenness" and "procession" might lead one to believe that the Father has some sort of ontological primacy over the other two persons. But this is not what these terms communicate. As Gregory of Nyssa says,

> But in speaking of "cause" and "of the cause" [or, in our case, "Unbegotten" and "Only Begotten"], we do not by these words denote nature . . . , but we indicate the difference in manner of existence. For when we say that one is "caused," and that the other is "without cause," we do not divide the nature by the word "cause," but only indicate the fact that the Son does not exist without generation, nor the Father by generation. . . . To say that anything exists without generation sets forth the mode of its existence, but what exists is not indicated by this phrase. . . . So, . . . when we learn that He is unbegotten, we are taught in what mode He exists, and how it is fit that we should conceive Him as existing, but *what* He is we do not hear in that phrase. When, therefore, we acknowledge such a distinction in the case of the Holy Trinity, as to believe that one Person is the Cause, and another is of the Cause, we can no longer be accused of confounding the definition of the Person by the community of nature.[9]

Thus, according to Gregory, the eternal relations of origin do not distinguish the three persons by dividing their nature into three, for they are all equally and fully God. They all share equally and fully in the divine nature. Rather, the eternal relations of origin distinguish the three persons in terms

9. Gregory of Nyssa, *On "Not Three Gods"* (*NPNF*[2] 5:331–36).

of *how* they exist as one God in three persons, or their individual "modes of existence" (to use Gregory's phrase).

Summary

Although the persons of the Trinity are distinct from each other, their distinction in the Bible does not lie in differences, either by quality or quantity, in attributes, appellations, actions, or adoration. Rather, the one and only way that the persons are distinguished from one another in the Bible is through the language of *eternal relations of origin*. These relations are reflected in the revealed personal names of the three persons of the one God: Father, Son, and Holy Spirit. The Father is eternally unbegotten and eternally begets the Son; the Son is eternally begotten of the Father and, along with the Father, eternally spirates the Spirit; and the Spirit eternally proceeds from the Father and the Son.

REFLECTION QUESTIONS

1. How did you think the persons of God were distinguished from each other before reading this chapter? How has that changed after reading?

2. The doctrine of the eternal relations of origin is not usually discussed or taught in many churches. Why do you think that is the case?

3. The phrase "eternal relations of origin" is not in the Bible—but is the doctrine in the Bible? If so, how?

4. Why is this doctrine important to the Christian life?

5. How would you teach this doctrine to someone who had never heard of it?

QUESTION 27

What Is Meant by the Eternal Generation of the Son?

As we saw in the previous chapter on the eternal relations of origin, the one God exists in three persons who are distinguished from one another by their mode of subsistence in the divine essence. The Father is eternally unbegotten, the Son is eternally begotten or generated from the Father, and the Holy Spirit is eternally spirated from the Father and the Son. In this chapter, we want to explore further the Son's eternal generation from the Father. We will survey the biblical data and discuss its theological implications below.

Biblical Data

In our last chapter we looked at two passages that warrant further comment here: John 5:26 and Proverbs 8:22–31. But before we get to those, we first need to mention perhaps the most crucial biblical argument in the fourth century for the Son's identity and relation to the Father: their divine names. Although Father, Son, and Spirit all share names common to the one God (like Creator, Redeemer, etc.), they are distinguished from one another by their personal names. The Father is the Father and not the Son or Spirit, and so on. These names are not arbitrary; God reveals them to us to reveal something true about himself. What, then, do we learn about God from these personal names?

The fourth-century theologians saw that these scriptural patterns of speaking about the relations of the First and Second Persons of the Trinity are inherently related to generation, or begetting.[1] "Father" and "Son" communicate a particular kind of relation to one another. The fourth-century pro-Nicenes asked, "What does it mean to be father and son?" We could, and they did, point

1. This paragraph is adapted from Matt Emerson, "A Biblical Case for Eternal Generation," *Biblical Reasoning*, June 17, 2017, https://secundumscripturas.com/2016/06/17/a-biblical-case-for-eternal-generation/.

to all sorts of implications of fatherhood and sonship—differences in authority and submission, differences with respect to wealth and inheritance, differences with respect to trade and apprenticeship, and the like. The problem with all those differences is that, if applied to the Father and the Son, they would imply that the Son is less than the Father, even to the point of denying his full divinity. Another problem is that they are not always true of father and son—sons grow up and no longer live under their father's roof and therefore are no longer subject to his authority; fathers die and the son inherits the family's wealth; fathers grow old and their sons take care of them, rather than vice versa; and so on. So, we have to ask again, what does it mean *fundamentally* to be father and son?

The pro-Nicenes recognized that if it means anything to be a son, it means to come from one's father. In other words, sons receive their essence, their being, their nature, from their fathers.[2] To put it simply, the son of a duck is a duck, the son of a human is a human, and the Son of God the Father is God the Son. This pattern of biblical language informed the pro-Nicenes not only about the Son's divine nature but also about the manner of his divinity. To apply this to the Godhead, we say that because he is the Father's Son, the Son's subsistence in the divine nature is communicated from the Father to the Son.[3] This is a thoroughly biblical affirmation, not only in that it exegetes particular texts (which we will see below) but also in that it pays attention to patterns of biblical language.

John 5:26

Several texts that come to mind when we talk about eternal generation. The doctrine has recently experienced a bit of a "theological revival," including a treatment in an edited volume that addresses biblical texts like Micah 5:2 and Hebrews 1, along with patterns of biblical names and the proper translation of the biblical term *monogenēs*.[4] There are more than these we could mention as well. But here we return to John 5:26 and Proverbs 8:22–31.

Regarding the Johannine text, we said in the previous chapter that this passage gives us some clues as to how the divine persons are both same in essence and distinct from one another. Specifically, John 5:26 affirms that both the Father and the Son are said to have "life in himself." While the exact meaning of this phrase has been debated, especially in modern biblical studies, it is difficult

---

2. In human terms, and for many of God's creatures, existence requires both a father and a mother, and, as modern science tells us, "nature" is a gift from both. This is where the analogy to God's own existence breaks down, though; as we have said previously, God is not a creature, and "generation" is not a physical or material act. It is also eternal. There is no "mother" in the Godhead, nor is there physical procreation.
3. Basil of Caesarea, "Third Theological Oration (Oration 29)," in *On God and Christ: The Five Theological Orations and Two Letters to Cledonius*, trans. Frederick Williams and Lionel Wickham, PPS 23 (Crestwood, NY: St Vladimir's Seminary Press, 2002), 123.
4. See Fred Sanders and Scott R. Swain, eds., *Retrieving Eternal Generation* (Grand Rapids: Zondervan Academic, 2017).

to imagine something other than the doctrine of aseity being communicated here. That is, to have "life in himself" seems to imply that neither the Father nor the Son are dependent on anything else in creation for existence. They are both equally and fully *a se*, entirely independent of creatures with respect to their life, their being, their existence. But while John 5:26 affirms that both the Father and the Son are *a se*, this text also distinguishes between exactly *how* both divine persons are independent of creation for their life. For the Father, he "has life in himself" without further elaboration. The Son likewise—"just as"—has life in himself, but it is through the Father giving this life to him.

This "life in himself" that the Son possesses cannot be something he once did not have but now does. Otherwise, he would not always have been fully God, since aseity is a key marker of divinity. Only God is *a se*, and to be otherwise is to be a creature. For the Son to become *a se* would mean that he was formerly a creature and now isn't. This would further entail that there are two gods, one who has always been God and one who became God at some point. All of this is contrary to the biblical truth that there is one and only one God (Deut. 6:4). So for the Son to have "life in himself" simply means that he is *a se* and always has been *a se* just like the Father. But again, John tells us exactly *how* the Son has life in himself—through the Father who gives it to him.

The key to the doctrine of the eternal generation of the Son is its affirmation from biblical texts like John 5:26[5] that the Son subsists in the divine essence by receiving the divine essence from the Father. Of course, this is *eternal* because it never starts and never stops. Otherwise, there would be a time when the Son was not and a time when he came into existence as "god," which is the heresy of Arianism. But eternal generation affirms that the Son is God precisely through his sonship: that is, through eternally receiving the divine nature from his heavenly Father. And this is what John 5:26 teaches us, that "just as the Father has life in himself, so he has given it to the Son to have life in himself."

Proverbs 8:22–31

We also have to work through Proverbs 8:22–31 carefully to understand all its theological import:

> 22 The LORD possessed me at the beginning of his work,
> the first of his acts of old.
> 23 Ages ago I was set up,
> at the first, before the beginning of the earth.
> 24 When there were no depths I was brought forth,
> when there were no springs abounding with water.

5. For more discussion on the biblical warrant, see the previous chapter, as well as the discussion below.

25 Before the mountains had been shaped,
before the hills, I was brought forth,
26 before he had made the earth with its fields,
or the first of the dust of the world.
27 When he established the heavens, I was there;
when he drew a circle on the face of the deep,
28 when he made firm the skies above,
when he established the fountains of the deep,
29 when he assigned to the sea its limit,
so that the waters might not transgress his command,
when he marked out the foundations of the earth,
30 then I was beside him, like a master workman,
and I was daily his delight, rejoicing before him always,
31 rejoicing in his inhabited world
and delighting in the children of man.

Here Lady Wisdom is speaking of her presence with YHWH at creation. While the whole passage is worth careful consideration, there are essentially two verses that concern us here: verses 22 and 25. Both refer to the Lord's "generation" of Wisdom in some sense. What does it mean, then, for God to "generate" or "beget" Wisdom?

First we must determine who Wisdom is, both in this passage and in the rest of Scripture. At least for the early church, there was no doubt that Lady Wisdom is a figurative image for God the Son. This is because Paul in 1 Corinthians 1:24 identifies Christ as "the wisdom of God." Further, Lady Wisdom in this passage is present with YHWH at creation and participates in the act of creation with him. Given the Bible's strong commitment to the Creator/creature distinction, and, in this case, especially with respect to the divine exclusivity of God's act as Creator, Wisdom cannot be a mere creature, even a first creature through whom God creates the rest of creation. Only God creates. Therefore, if Lady Wisdom is present and active at creation (i.e., vv. 27–31), then Wisdom is equal with God. And Wisdom *is* equal with God, because she is a figurative image for God the Son who became incarnate in the person of Jesus Christ, "the wisdom of God" (1 Cor. 1:24).

What does it mean for God to "possess" Wisdom at the beginning of his work (v. 22), or for him to have "brought forth" Wisdom prior to his act of creation (v. 25)? There is some debate over verse 22 in the early church as to whether it refers to God's plan for the Son to become incarnate or whether it refers to the same thing as verse 25. But there is no debate that verse 25 is a clear statement about the eternal generation of the Son. For God to "bring forth" Wisdom, his Wisdom that is equal to him in every way because Wisdom also is present at and participates in the exclusively divine act of creation, is not an act of creation in time. If it were, Wisdom would not be fully God. Further, it would mean that

God was at some point without his Wisdom, which would first of all be a terrible thought and second of all would mean that God changes in his essence.

Whatever "brought forth" means, then, it cannot mean creation in time. Instead, it is a reference to the Father's eternal generation of the Son. The Father "brings forth" the Son eternally—before all of creation, that is, before time itself—which means that he communicates the divine essence of the Son eternally. Wisdom is the Wisdom of God, God's Wisdom, the Wisdom without which God has never existed. To say it slightly differently and by connecting Proverbs 8:25 with 1 Corinthians 1:24, God the Son is the divine son of God the Father, the Father's Son, the Son without whom the Father has never existed.[6]

These two texts, John 5:26 and Proverbs 8:22–31, teach us the same thing: that God the Father eternally begets or generates God the Son. What exactly does this mean theologically?

Theological Implications

There are at least three theological implications from our exploration of these (and other) biblical texts. First, we can say the Son eternally receives the divine essence from the Father. This does not entail any diminishment of the Father's divinity but rather indicates that the Father eternally gives the full divine essence, which he also fully possesses, to his Son. As we have just seen, the Bible uses the language of "generation" or "begetting." But we need to be clear that this analogical language to describe the eternal relation between Father and Son is just that—analogical. It can only take us so far. "Bring forth," "gives," "begotten" is the language we use to describe creaturely realities of conception. But this is the limit of human language in describing God because creaturely generation does not correlate one to one to divine generation. Creaturely generation includes aspects like conception in time, sexual reproduction, and metaphysical distinctions between the one who generates and the one generated. Of course, none of this is true in God. The Father's generation of the Son is eternal, not in time; it does not include anything biological or sexual; and it does not entail any metaphysical distinction between Father and Son. But it is used analogically because at the core of the concept of generation is the passing on of essence from one to another. The son of a duck is a duck, the son of a human is a human, and the Son of God is God. The eternal generation of the Son means—and only means—that the Son receives the fullness of the divine essence from the Father. They are both fully and completely divine but distinct from one another via these eternal relations of origin.

A second theological implication from this discussion of eternal generation concerns the names of God the Son. In the Christian tradition, the Second

6. For more on Proverbs 8:22–31, see Matthew Y. Emerson, "The Role of Proverbs 8: Eternal Generation and Hermeneutics Ancient and Modern," in *Retrieving Eternal Generation*, ed. Fred Sanders and Scott Swain (Grand Rapids: Zondervan Academic, 2017),.

Person of the Trinity possesses four distinct names based on his eternal begottenness from the Father—Son, Word, Wisdom, and Image. These three names are all related to the eternal relation of origin between Father and Son, namely that the Father eternally generates the Son, because they all communicate generation. "Son" is obvious in that sense, but Wisdom, Word, and Image are also related. "Word" communicates the procession of thought to verbalization, "Wisdom" communicates the procession of thought to action, and "Image" communicates the procession of being to visualization. In each case, what is proper to the Father—namely the divine essence—proceeds from him through the Second Person of the Trinity, his Son, Word, Wisdom, and Image.

This brings us the third and final theological implication of the eternal generation of the Son: Trinitarian *taxis* and God's external works. We discuss these concepts in other chapters, so we will not belabor the point. But suffice it to say here that the fact the Son is eternally generated from the Father makes it fitting that the Son is the one who is sent by the Father to become incarnate and, according to his humanity, submit his will to the Father through obedience unto death, even death on a cross.

Summary

Eternal generation is a thoroughly biblical doctrine, derived from such texts as Proverbs 8:22–31 and John 5:46. It, along with the eternal procession of the Spirit, are in many ways the linchpin doctrines of Nicene Trinitarianism. Eternal generation (and procession) allows us to affirm that the Son is fully God alongside the Father while not being the same person as the Father. They together, along with the Holy Spirit, are the one God.

REFLECTION QUESTIONS

1. How does the doctrine of eternal generation help you understand God's oneness?

2. How does the doctrine of eternal generation help you understand God's tripersonal nature?

3. How does the doctrine of eternal generation impact your prayer life?

4. What is a passage in Scripture that has confused you but now seems clearer, based on thinking through the doctrine of eternal generation?

5. How could you teach the doctrine of eternal generation to someone who's never heard of it?

QUESTION 28

What Is Meant by the Eternal Procession of the Spirit?

The eternal procession of the Holy Spirit is one of two processions or emanations (from *emanare*, to flow out) in the life of God that constitute the divine persons in their relations to one another (the other being the eternal generation of the Son, discussed in the previous chapter). As we explore what is meant by the eternal procession of the Holy Spirit, one clarification is important to note at the outset. The word "procession" is used in two different senses in Trinitarian theology. "Procession" is sometimes used as a common term to describe both the origin of the Son from the Father and the origin of the Holy Spirit from the Father and Son. But "procession" is also used to describe what is proper to the Holy Spirit alone: the procession of the Holy Spirit as distinct from the generation of the Son. In order to distinguish the two senses of the term, Western theology has sometimes spoken of the "spiration" of the Spirit from the Father and Son or the "joint spiration" of the Father and Son in the procession of the Holy Spirit. The Father and Son eternally "spirate," or breathe out, the person Holy Spirit as the shared love between them. This chapter will explore the nature of this procession, especially its relation to the mission of the Holy Spirit. This discussion will bring us as well to the perennial debate between Eastern and Western Christianity over the addition of the *filioque* clause to the Nicene Creed: Does the Holy Spirit proceed from the Father alone as his principle or from the Father "and the Son" (*filioque*) jointly?

The Mission and Procession of the Holy Spirit

The language of the Spirit's "procession" is taken from John 15:26: "But when the Helper comes, whom I will send to you from the Father, the Spirit of truth, who proceeds (*ekporeuetai*) from the Father, he will bear witness about me." As we have seen elsewhere, there is an important Trinitarian distinction to be made between the *temporal and economic missions* of the Son and Spirit and their *eternal and immanent processions* in the inner life of God. As Augustine and others have articulated it, the missions, or sendings, of the Son and Spirit reveal who they really are in their eternal relations.[1] But which of the two—mission or procession—is in view in John 15:26? The context appears to be economic. The Son will send the Helper from the Father after the Son himself returns to the Father (16:7). The promised Spirit will not only dwell *with* the disciples but *in* them (14:17).

> And I will ask the Father, and he will give you another Helper, to be with you forever, even the Spirit of truth, whom the world cannot receive, because it neither sees him nor knows him. You know him, for he dwells with you and will be in you. . . . But the Helper, the Holy Spirit, whom the Father will send in my name, he will teach you all things and bring to your remembrance all that I have said to you. (John 14:16–17, 26)

The teaching of John 14–16 appears to be a direct promise of what will happen to the apostles on the day of Pentecost and in the age of the Spirit that it ushers in. Thus, it appears that the context of John 15:26 concerns the Spirit's economic mission, not his eternal procession. Still, the relative clause that Jesus adds in John 15:26—"who proceeds from the Father" (*ho para tou patros ekporeuetai*)—does appear to be saying something further that was not already stated explicitly in the promise of the Spirit's sending. If the only point Jesus was trying to make was economic and not eternal, then his promise, "whom I will send (*pempsō*) to you from the Father," would be sufficient and the further qualification about the Spirit's procession redundant. But interestingly he adds this relative qualifier to the Spirit's identity, "who proceeds from the Father," to tell us just who this Helper is. We might paraphrase Jesus's promise like this: "I will *send* (*pempsō*) from the Father the one who *proceeds* (*ekporeuetai*) from the Father." In short, though the context of John 15:26 is economic, it does not preclude an acknowledgement that the Spirit's procession has an eternal horizon. The one who is economically sent is the one who eternally proceeds.[2]

---

1. Augustine, *The Trinity*, 2nd ed., trans. Edmund Hill ed. John Rotelle, The Works of Saint Augustine 5 (Hyde Park, NY: New City, 2012), 2.5; Thomas Aquinas, *ST*, 1.43.
2. Thomas Aquinas sees the shift to the eternal procession beginning in the phrase just before this one, namely, the apposition "the Spirit of truth." Jesus shows here "the Spirit as related to the Son when he says, the Spirit of truth, for the Son is the Truth. . . . He shows the Spirit as related to the Father when he says, who proceeds from the Father." The third person is the Spirit of both Son and Father. Hence, Thomas sees here evidence for the *filioque*, which we will address more below (Thomas Aquinas, *Commentary on the Gospel of John, Chapters 9-21*, trans. Fabian R. Larcher, Latin/English Edition of the Works of St. Thomas Aquinas (Green Bay, Wi: Aquinas Institute, 2013), 311.).

With this interpretive structure in place, we can better understand all of the passages in Scripture that speak about the promised sending of the Spirit. The Spirit's economic mission presupposes his eternal procession. The historic fulfillment of Christ's promise of the Spirit comes, of course, on Pentecost:

> When the day of Pentecost arrived, they were all together in one place. And suddenly there came from heaven a sound like a mighty rushing wind, and it filled the entire house where they were sitting. And divided tongues as of fire appeared to them and rested on each one of them. And they were all filled with the Holy Spirit and began to speak in other tongues as the Spirit gave them utterance. (Acts 2:1–4)

In addition to this unique historical mission—this visible manifestation of the Holy Spirit—the New Testament also speaks about the gift of the Spirit for all subsequent believers in Jesus Christ. This latter work has sometimes been called the Spirit's "invisible mission."[3] The Spirit is sent and given from the Father and Son to all who believe. First John 4:13 is indicative: "By this we know that we abide in him and he in us, because he has given us of his Spirit" (see also Matt. 3:11; Mark 1:8; Luke 3:16; 11:13; John 1:33; 20:22; Acts 5:32; 2 Cor 5:5). Every new conversion is, in a sense, a new Pentecost, when the Spirit is sent from the Father and Son to indwell believers. And in both the historic sending of Pentecost and these subsequent internal sendings, the Spirit's true personhood is disclosed: He is *sent from* the Father and Son because he *is from* the Father and Son.

The *Filioque* Controversy

Thus far we have assumed without argumentation that the Spirit proceeds eternally from both the Father "and the Son" (Latin, *filioque*). But the addition of the *filioque* clause to the Nicene Creed is debated and was, indeed, the source of the Great Schism between Western and Eastern Christianity. The culminating event of the schism was the mutual excommunications of Pope Leo IX and Patriarch Michael Cerularius in 1054, but the divergence goes back centuries prior. Western Christians had been adding the *filioque* as far back as the fifth century. But the historical and ecclesiastical debate aside, what does the Bible and its Trinitarian logic have to say about the question? There are at least three biblical and theological reasons why the addition *filioque* is justified.

First is the conviction that the divine economy is truly self-revealing. This is the principle explained in the previous section: The missions presuppose and reveal the processions. It is not to say that everything that is true of the

3. See Gilles Emery, *The Trinity: An Introduction to Catholic Doctrine on the Triune God*, trans. Matthew Levering (Washington, DC: The Catholic University of America Press, 2011), 179.

missions can be read back into the processions. For example, the Son, having assumed created humanity, submits to the Father in the economy, but submission is a category error when considering the Son's eternal generation. With this caveat in place, we can still affirm this basic Trinitarian principle: *God is as he reveals himself to be*. The relations revealed in the economy are not arbitrary. They demonstrate who the divine persons really are. The Spirit is clearly said to be sent from both the Father and the Son (John 16:7). The entire structure of the Son's work demands his active participation in the Spirit's sending: It is only as the crucified, risen, and ascended Messiah that the Son gives "gifts to men" (Eph. 4:8–14). So, unless the mission of the Spirit from both Father and Son is purely contingent, purely *ad hoc*, it must reveal something about what God is like, specifically about the eternal relation between the Son and the Spirit.

Second, the Spirit is consistently described in the New Testament as both the Spirit of the Father and the Spirit of Christ. The Spirit of God is the "Spirit of his Son" (Gal. 4:6). He is called "the Spirit of Jesus" (Acts 16:7), "the Spirit of Christ" (Rom. 8:9; 1 Peter 1:11), and "the Spirit of Jesus Christ" (Phil. 1:19). Romans 8:9 weaves the two titles together: "You, however, are not in the flesh but in the Spirit, if in fact the Spirit of God dwells in you. Anyone who does not have the Spirit of Christ does not belong to him." The Spirit of God (the Father) is the Spirit of Christ. So closely does the New Testament connect Jesus and the Spirit that, in one place, Paul simply identifies the two: "Now the Lord is the Spirit, and where the Spirit of the Lord is, there is freedom" (2 Cor. 3:17). The context indicates that the "Lord" to whom believers turn (3:16) is none other than Christ himself (3:15). And Paul identifies the Lord with this Spirit ("the Lord is the Spirit"), but not in such a way that the distinction is lost ("the Spirit of the Lord"). If, then, the Holy Spirit is the Spirit of the Father and of the Son, this identification points in the direction of his procession from both.

Third, if the Spirit proceeds only from the Father and not from the Father and Son jointly, then it becomes difficult to distinguish the two processions or emanations in the life of God. If the Father is the sole source of the Spirit, then are generation and procession the same relation? Does God then have two Sons, twins, as it were? The Orthodox certainly wish to assert the distinction between generation and procession, but it is difficult to see what explanation might be given for the difference between the two. The joint spiration of the Spirit from the common principle of the Father and the Son not only seems most consistent with the biblical witness, but it also provides a theological accounting for how we might distinguish the two eternal processions.[4]

4. In addition to reasons such as these, some Western theologians have also posited the essential unity of the Father and Son as grounds for the Son's equal participation in the procession of the Spirit. But this argument proves too much. In seeking to guard the unity of the first two persons, the third person is left in the lurch, as it were. Is the Spirit not essentially

Further, if the Father alone is the principle of the Spirit, then what eternal relation exists between the Son and the Spirit? Are they only indirectly related through a common source?

So, what kind of arguments have Eastern theologians marshaled in opposition to the *filioque*? Part of the divergence between East and West concerns the ground of the unity of the Trinity.[5] Eastern theologians insist that the unity is grounded not in the divine nature taken in the abstract but in the monarchy (one origin) of the Father alone. If the Son is introduced as the principle of the Spirit, then we are faced with the dilemma of two principles or two sources in the Godhead, which undermines the divine unity. The unity of the divine nature is grounded in the prior singularity of the Father's monarchy. As the origin of the other two divine persons, the Father eternally confers his very nature upon them. Western theologians can appreciate the concern here and can even affirm the core of what the Orthodox assert: The Father is indeed the unique and unbegotten source of the other two persons. Nevertheless, the Son's participation in the procession of the Spirit does not introduce a second origin or source to the Trinity because, being one with the Father, the Son functions along with the Father as a singular and common principle of the Spirit's personhood. The primal relation is the Son's generation from the Father but entailed in that relation is a second relation of the shared Spirit between the Father and Son. So, the Father retains his primacy as the sole principle of the Godhead, but the Spirit is related to both Father and Son in his eternal procession. Some have suggested that the formula "from the Father through the Son" might capture something of the shared consensus between Eastern and Western Christianity on this point, and perhaps it does. Still, the debate is not insignificant, and in our opinion the Western addition of the *filioque* has strong biblical and theological warrant.

Summary

Trinitarian theology uses the word "procession" in two different ways. It can describe the two eternal emanations in the life of God: the eternal generation of the Son and the eternal spiration of the Holy Spirit. But it can also be used in a narrower sense to describe just the latter procession: the Spirit's eternal *coming forth* from the Father and Son. The NT clearly teaches that the Holy Spirit is sent by both Father and Son, and this economic mission reveals his eternal procession. God is as he reveals himself to be. There are good biblical

---

one with the Father as well? Does that mean he participates in the Son's eternal generation? Or even in his own procession?

5. For a modern defense of the Eastern view, see Vladimir Lossky, *The Mystical Theology of the Eastern Church* (Yonkers, NY: St Vladimir's Seminary Press, 1997). For a contemporary exposition of the Western view, see Thomas Joseph White, *The Trinity: On the Nature and Mystery of the One God*, Thomistic Ressourcement Series 19 (Washington, DC: The Catholic University of America Press, 2022), 483–503.

and theological reasons to affirm the Western addition to the Nicene Creed, namely, that the Spirit proceeds from the Father "and the Son" (*filioque*): The Spirit is sent by both Father and Son, and this sending reveals who he really is; in the New Testament, the Holy Spirit has reference to both Father and Son as their shared Spirit; and finally, the Spirit's procession from the joint spiration of Father and Son can provide a way to distinguish this eternal procession from the eternal generation of the Son.

REFLECTION QUESTIONS

1. What does the Holy Spirit's personal name ("Spirit") tell us about his unique personhood?

2. What do you think about the debate between Eastern and Western Christianity on the *filioque* clause? Which side has the stronger arguments? Why does this doctrine matter?

3. What are ways that considering the Spirit's eternal procession helps your prayer life?

4. What is a passage in Scripture that has confused you but now seems clearer based on thinking through the eternal procession of the Spirit?

5. How would you teach the eternal procession of the Spirit to someone who has never heard of it?

QUESTION 29

What Is Meant by Perichoresis?

The term *perichoresis* signifies the mutual indwelling of the three divine persons. Each of the divine persons is *in* the others. There is a mutual *interpenetration* or *coinherence* among the three persons. This doctrine is a theological entailment of the *homoousion*, the essential unity of Father, Son, and Holy Spirit. But the doctrine can also be borne out by biblical exegesis. The doctrine of *perichoresis* paints a beautiful picture of the inter-Trinitarian fellowship and love and has important implications for thinking about the being and action of the triune God.

Defining Perichoresis

Gregory of Nazianzus coined the Greek term perichoresis in the fourth century to describe how the two natures of Christ relate to one another.[1] Without losing their distinct properties, the two natures of Christ flow together (literally "go around," *peri* + *chōrein*) in the person of Christ. This reality underwrites the *communicatio idiomatum*, the doctrine that states that the names and titles of each of Christ's two natures can be appropriated to the singular person of the Son. But this theological conception also came to be applied to the mutual coinherence of the three divine persons as well. The Latin equivalent of perichoresis is *circumincessio*: the three persons "go along and around" or "encircle" one another.

From a theological point of view, this doctrine is simply an entailment of the *homoousion* and of monotheism. There is only one God. The three divine persons are not three distinct gods or three discrete divine agents. Each is equally and eternally the selfsame God. Likewise, the doctrine of perichoresis is an entailment of the eternal relations of origin. The processions of the Son and Spirit from the Father do not produce a second and third God. They

1. For a fuller discussion of this usage, see Verna Harrison, "Perichoresis in the Greek Fathers," *St Vladimir's Theological Quarterly* 35 (1991): 35–54.

remain in the Father, sharing the identically same divine essence. Hence, the divine persons are coequal and coeternal. It is not the case that God the Father *chose* to be the origin of the other two persons. If that were the case, then the Father would not be Father by nature. But as it is, the Son is generated from the Father and the Spirit "spirated" by the Father and Son by nature. So the mutual love and reciprocity they enjoy is constitutive of God's own being and nature. They differ according to their eternal relations of origin, which are extended in their distinct modes of action in the world. But there is, in God, only one divine being, and there is, in God's external actions, only one indivisible divine action. Three persons are only one God. And so, they each can be said to be *in* the others, because they each are the one divine essence.[2]

The Biblical Teaching on Perichoresis

The doctrine of perichoresis can be demonstrated from biblical exegesis as well. When Philip asks Jesus to show the apostles the Father, Jesus rebukes his slowness to understand:

> Jesus said to him, "Have I been with you so long, and you still do not know me, Philip? Whoever has seen me has seen the Father. How can you say, 'Show us the Father'? Do you not believe that I am in the Father and the Father is in me? The words that I say to you I do not speak on my own authority, but the Father who dwells in me does his works. Believe me that I am in the Father and the Father is in me, or else believe on account of the works themselves." (John 14:9–11)

Both unity and distinction are on display in this passage. Whoever sees the Son sees the Father, not because the Son is the Father in his personal property but because the Father dwells in the Son. And the obverse is true as well: The Son is in the Father. The doctrine of inseparable operations is also exhibited here. When the Son does his works, so does the Father. Again, perichoresis underscores both their essential unity and their operational unity.

Jesus then extends this principle of mutual indwelling to the Holy Spirit, who will come to indwell believers. He promises to send "another Helper," the Holy Spirit to dwell within believers:

> If you love me, you will keep my commandments. And I will ask the Father, and he will give you another Helper, to be with you forever, even the Spirit of truth, whom the world cannot

2. For a helpful treatment of the grounds of perichoresis in the thought of Thomas Aquinas, see Thomas Joseph White, *The Trinity: On the Nature and Mystery of the One God*, Thomistic Ressourcement Series 19 (Washington, DC: The Catholic University of America Press, 2022).

> receive, because it neither sees him nor knows him. You know him, for he dwells with you and will be in you. (John 14:15–17)

Jesus then makes clear that this promised Helper will be an extension of his own presence with the disciples: "I will not leave you as orphans; I will come to you. Yet a little while and the world will see me no more, but you will see me. Because I live, you also will live. In that day you will know that I am in my Father, and you in me, and I in you" (John 14:18–20). Though in some sense Jesus will leave his disciples in his death and eventually in his ascension to the Father, he will come to them precisely in the promised Holy Spirit. The perichoretic relations of the Father, Son, and Holy Spirit are unique, but astonishingly, the indwelling Holy Spirit will envelop believers into this same fellowship. As the church fathers often put it, what the Son is by nature we become by grace. And all this takes place precisely by the indwelling Spirit, who in Paul's language is the "Spirit of adoption," producing in our hearts the cry of a son: "Abba! Father!" (Rom. 8:15; cf. Gal. 4:6–7).

Jesus then makes the point even clearer: The indwelling Holy Spirit brings with him the presence of the Father and the Son as well: "If anyone loves me, he will keep my word, and my Father will love him, and we will come to him and make our home with him" (John 14:23). Note the parallels to Jesus's earlier words in John 14:15–17. The conditions are the same: loving and being loved by Jesus and keeping his commandments/word. In verses 15–17, the consequence is the sending and receiving of the other Helper, the Holy Spirit. Here in verse 23 the consequence is the reception of the Father and Son, who make their home with the disciples. To be indwelt by the Spirit, then, is to be indwelt by the Father and Son as well. The mystery of the gospel brings an unimaginable gift: the indwelling of the Holy Trinity in the hearts of believers. And all of this is made possible because of the doctrine of perichoresis: The Father is in the Son and his works; the Son is in the Father, and the coming of the Holy Spirit brings the first two divine persons as well.

The apostle Paul likewise taught a doctrine of perichoresis. We have already seen how, for Paul, the reception of the Spirit includes the believer in the sonship of the unique Son. The glories of Christ are revealed to believers through a revelation from the Father through the Holy Spirit: "For the Spirit searches everything, even the depths of God" (1 Cor. 2:10). Paul draws an analogy to the spirit within a human person. "For who knows a person's thoughts except the spirit of that person, which is in him? So also no one comprehends the thoughts of God except the Spirit of God" (1 Cor. 2:11). The Spirit of God is in God (the Father) in a similar way that the spirit or mind is within an individual human being.

Elsewhere, Paul simply equates the Lord with the Spirit, who removes the veil over our hearts: "Now the Lord is the Spirit, and where the Spirit of the Lord is, there is freedom. And we all, with unveiled face, beholding the glory of the Lord, are being transformed into the same image from one degree of glory to another. For this comes from the Lord who is the Spirit" (2 Cor. 3:17–18). Once again, we see the coinherence of the divine persons. It is difficult to tell whether the "Lord" here references the Father or to Christ, but in either case, to see the vision of glory of the Lord is made possible by the Lord himself, who is the Spirit.[3] Again we see the unity of the divine persons in their being and action because they mutually indwell one another.

Uses and Implications of the Doctrine

As we will see in another chapter, some modern expositions of the Trinity can be characterized as "social" models. Social Trinitarianism often portrays the divine persons in ways that very closely mirror human personal relationality, such that the divine persons are conceived of as distinct centers of consciousness and will. This way of rendering the Trinity raises an obvious question: How are the three persons not then three distinct beings or three distinct gods? Let us call it the *monotheism problem* for social Trinitarianism. Some have sought to secure the unity of the divine persons by means of perichoresis. Though the persons are three distinct psycho-volitional subjects, they remain one because they each mutually inhere the others. There are three divine minds, but they each have access, as it were, to the other divine minds. But, as we have seen, this reverses the order of the doctrinal and biblical logic. Perichoresis is grounded ultimately in the essential unity, coeternality, and relations of the three persons. Mutual indwelling is a consequence of their oneness; it cannot, as a stand-alone doctrine, secure that oneness. In short, we should avoid asking perichoresis to bear the entire weight of divine unity. Perichoresis is, instead, an entailment or implication of the divine unity. The three persons are one in mind and will in virtue of the *homoousion*. It is a mistake to envision three divine minds and wills that are united only in virtue of a subsequent mutual indwelling.[4]

But if perichoresis cannot be used, so to speak, to secure the unity of the divine persons, that does not mean that the doctrine of perichoresis has no use at all in our Trinitarian theology. We have already seen in Jesus's teaching on perichoresis how the doctrine of mutual indwelling expands, by an act and analogy of God's grace, to envelop those who are united to Christ by the Helper, the Holy Spirit, such that we become the adopted children of the Father. So, we can say that the major entailment of the doctrine of perichoresis

3. Gordon Fee teases out the Trinitarian implications of this passage: "In the freedom that the Spirit provides, we have seen the glory of God himself—as it is made evident to us in the face of our Lord Jesus Christ—and we have come to experience that glory, and will do so in an ever-increasing way until we come to the final glory" (*God's Empowering Spirit: The Holy Spirit in the Letters of Paul* [Grand Rapids: Baker Academic, 2019], 319).
4. See Karen Kilby, "Perichoresis and Projection: Problems with Social Doctrines of the Trinity," *New Blackfriars* 81 (2000): 432–45.

is that it gives us assurance that when we encounter one divine person in the economy of redemption, we are also encountering the others as well.

In Question 31 we will consider the doctrine of inseparable operations, the belief that in all of God's external acts he acts indivisibly as Father, Son, and Holy Spirit. When God creates, he creates as Father, Son, and Holy Spirit. When he sustains and governs the world, he does so as Father, Son, and Holy Spirit. The same holds true for his acts of salvation, sanctification, judgment, and so on. To be sure, in each external act of the Trinity, each of the divine persons is operative according to his own personal mode. There is an ordering within (Greek, *taxis*) the one activity of the triune God. So, the one act of God comes from the Father, through the Son, and by the Spirit. But these three modes of action do not constitute three distinct (even if harmonious) actions. There is, rather, only one divine action in three distinct personal modes.

Summary

All of this means that when one person acts, the other two persons are with and in that person's act. As Jesus tells us, the Father dwells in the Son such that when we see the Son acting we also see the Father acting. The incarnation introduces the need for some important qualifications to this teaching. Only the Son is incarnate. Only the Son suffers and dies. But because the Son is both divine and human, in all of the Son's human actions, the Father and Spirit are with him. We will explore in a later chapter how all of this works out with regard to the death of Christ (question 34), but for now we can state that while only the Son dies (and then only in virtue of his human nature), he does so as a divine person in union and communion with the other two divine persons. Mutual indwelling, then, secures the divine efficacy of Christ's death. When Christ dies, the triune God is making atonement by substituting a divine person as a substitute and representative of fallen humanity.

REFLECTION QUESTIONS

1. What is the meaning of perichoresis?

2. How does this doctrine relate the *homoousion*, the shared common essence of the Trinity?

3. What are the potential uses and misuses of the doctrine of perichoresis?

4. What are ways that considering perichoresis helps your prayer life?

5. What is a passage in Scripture that has confused you but now seems clearer based on thinking through perichoresis?

QUESTION 30

What Are the Divine Missions?

We have spent the last few chapters discussing God's life apart from his external works of creation and redemption, but we now need to turn to how the Bible describes his life in relation to his creation. These are not fundamentally distinct from one another but mutually inform who God is (even while God's immanent life takes conceptual precedence). As Karl Rahner put it, the immanent Trinity is the economic Trinity and the economic Trinity is the immanent Trinity. Of course, this statement needs quite a bit of qualification and explanation (see question 25), but the basic point is simple and true—there is no "different God" behind who God is in the economic acts of creation of redemption. The God who exists from eternity is the same God who makes us and saves us.

But it is important to press into exactly what this means. Much heretical and heterodox ink has been spilt moving backward from the economic Trinity to the immanent Trinity in ways that are not justified by Scripture or its inherent theo-logic. Most often this happens when subordinationists of various stripes read Jesus's needs for food and sleep and the like, as well as his submission to the Father, as indication of his eternal inferiority to the Father. In order to avoid this and other heretical and heterodox errors, we must clarify this relation between immanent and economic, between God *ad intra* and *ad extra* beyond the basic affirmation that it is the same God. This is why the doctrine of the divine missions is important.

Defining the Divine Missions

The doctrine of the divine missions states explicitly that God's eternal relations of origin—the divine processions—are displayed to his creation in the divine missions. To say it in the obverse, the *taxis* (or order) of the divine missions is fitting due to their origin in the divine processions. Another way to put it is that the doctrine of the eternal processions describes the invisible/inner life of God, while the doctrine of the external missions describes the visible/external works of God. This is the most basic definition of the doctrine, that the divine missions are the external operation of the Trinity appropriated to each person according to their eternal relations of origin. Of course, that's a lot of big words, to put it mildly. So to try and put it more simply:

> The divine missions are how God relates to his world. Because he is one God in three persons, each divine person's mission is a revelation of his personal property: that is, his eternal relation(s) of origin, to creation.

So, for instance, the Father's mission is to send the Son, because the Father is the unbegotten who eternally begets the Son. We will talk more about the distinct missions of each person in a moment. For now, it is important to understand the foundational truth of this doctrine, that the divine missions are how we describe each divine person's relation to the world in the one God's acts of creation and redemption.

Like other aspects of Trinitarian theology, this concept is thoroughly biblical. We could point to texts in the gospel of John that indicate the divine missions (like John 15:26). We could also exposit Pauline texts like Galatians 4:4–6 and Romans 5:5, texts on which, for instance, Thomas Aquinas relies in his explanation of the divine missions. The former states that "in the fullness of time, God sent his Son," while in the latter Paul describes the Holy Spirit as the one who is given to us by God. Another important text (also cited by Thomas[1]) is John 8:16, where Jesus says that it is not he alone who judges but he and "he who sent" Jesus, that is, the Father. Notice that in this text the external mission ("he who sent me") is placed alongside an indication of the eternal procession, namely the Son's equality with the Father in the divine act of judging and the divine attribute of authority that is required to act as Judge.

Distinguishing the Divine Missions

Given the definition above, the most obvious way to distinguish the divine missions is simply to work through Trinitarian *taxis*. As Fred Sanders puts it, "Eternal processions ground temporal missions which ground full salvation."[2] The Father is eternally unbegotten, and the one who eternally begets the Son,

1. On Thomas's use of these and other texts, see Gilles Emery, *The Trinitarian Theology of Saint Thomas Aquinas*, trans. Francesca Aran Murphy (Oxford: Oxford University Press, 2007), 364. He is particularly noting Thomas's citation of these passages in *ST* I, q. 43, a. 1, sed contra; a. 2, sed contra; a. 3, arg. 2. Emery makes the interesting comment, "The *Summa* does not do word-by-word analyses of specific scriptural passages, but rather gives us a theological synthesis of Thomas's reading of the New Testament; the back-up for what he does here can be found in his biblical commentaries" (364).
2. Fred Sanders, *Fountain of Salvation: Trinity and Soteriology* (Grand Rapids: Eerdmans, 2021), 100.

and the one from whom proceeds the Holy Spirit through the Son. This means that the Father can be referred to as the "fount of divinity," in the sense that he is the one who communicates the divine essence to the Son in eternal generation and to the Spirit with the Son in eternal spiration. He does not possess more of the divine essence or a better version of the divine essence than the Son or the Spirit, nor does he possess distinct attributes of the divine essence that the Son and Spirit do not equally possess. Nevertheless, it is proper to acknowledge his unbegottenness and, therefore, the fact that he is the "fount of divinity" in the Godhead.

Fittingly, then, the mission of the Father in the acts of creation and redemption is to direct them through the Son and by the Spirit. In the act of creation, this is seen in the Father's creation of the world through his Word (his Son; Gen. 1:3, 6, 9, 11, 14, 20, 24, 26) and by his Spirit (Gen. 1:2). In the act of redemption, this is seen through the Father sending the Son by his Spirit (e.g., John 7:28) and in sending the Spirit through the Son (e.g., John 15:26). We could expand this discussion to include more specific acts, like predestination (Eph. 1:3) and providence, but we will save those for the next chapter. For now, it is important simply to understand that the mission of the Father accords with the intra-Trinitarian *taxis* of the divine life, the *taxis* in which the Father is the "fount of divinity." The external mission reveals to us the internal procession.

Likewise, the external mission of the Son reveals the eternal procession of the Son. The Son's mission is to be sent by the Father, both as his Word, the means of creation in the act of creation, and as the incarnate Son, Jesus of Nazareth, the means of redemption in the act of redemption. Again, we could expand this description to include more specific acts within creation and redemption, such as the Father sending the Son to the cross. For now, again, it is important simply to understand that the mission of the Son accords with the intra-Trinitarian *taxis* of the divine life, the *taxis* in which the Son is from the Father. The external mission of the Son's "sent-ness" reveals to us the internal procession of the Son's begottenness.

Finally, and similarly, the external mission of the Spirit reveals the eternal procession of the Spirit. The Spirit's mission is to be the agent of the Father's direction of creation and redemption through the Son. So, in creation, the Father creates through his Word and by his Spirit. In redemption, the Father saves through his Son, whom he sends through his Spirit. Once again, we could be more specific here; for instance, the sending of the Son by the Spirit includes the anointing of the incarnate Son at his baptism. For now, it is important simply to understand that the mission of the Spirit accords with the intra-Trinitarian *taxis* of the divine life, the *taxis* in which the Spirit proceeds from the Father and the Son. The external mission of the Spirit's agency in the Father's sending of the Son and of the Spirit's "sent-ness" by the Father and the Son reveals to us the internal procession of the Spirit's spiration by the Father and the Son.

To end this section as we began it, with a quote from Fred Sanders, we can summarize the relation between mission and procession this way:

> When we speak of missions revealing processions, we are not speaking of any sending. Not all sending reveal eternal processions. God sends prophets, apostles, servants, angels, and all manner of other emissaries. But when God the Father sends the Son and the Spirit, we meet God in sendings that have an infinite depth behind them: self-sendings in which God sends God; sendings in which God is God with us. This is the economic Trinity, in which we see that the 'of' in the locution 'Spirit of God' goes all the way back into the depths of God. For a doctrine of God to be in earnest, it must take this step, seeing the processions behind the missions, or, in modern idiom, confessing in the economic Trinity the revelation and presence of the immanent Trinity.[3]

Summary: Distinguishing Missions, Differentiating Persons

Given the fittingness of the divine missions according to the divine processions, we may be tempted to press the distinctions between the persons further than we should. In other words, we may be tempted to say, "*only* the Father can send the other two persons of the Godhead," or "*only* the Son could become incarnate," or "*only* the Spirit can be sent as the agent of God's acts." This would be a mistake. While the missions are fitting to the eternal processions of God's divine life, they are not indications of some kind of hard distinction between the persons' attributes, agency, or authority.

Instead, they reveal the eternal processions, the eternal relations of origin, which are taught in Scripture and confessed by the church precisely because they and they alone are able to distinguish between the divine persons in such a way that their essential oneness is not compromised. If we "read back" the economic Trinity into the immanent Trinity in such a way that the three persons are distinguished ultimately by their external acts instead of firstly by their eternal relations of origin, we risk treating God's economic activity "as the actions of three different agents doing three distinct things."[4] Or, as Thomas puts it,

> Mission implies inferiority in the one sent, [only] when it means procession from the sender as principle, by command or counsel; forasmuch as the one commanding is the greater,

3. Sanders, *Fountain of Salvation*, 120–21.
4. Sanders, *Fountain of Salvation*, 119.

> and the counsellor is wiser. In God, however, it means only procession or origin, which is according to equality, as explained above. [Q. 42, AA. 4, 6][5]

To return to Rahner's rule, the economic Trinity surely is the immanent Trinity, but in such a way that the inner life of God, the immanent Trinity, is revealed to creation in the activity of God's external acts, the economic Trinity. We cannot reverse the order here without risking either tritheism or subordinationism or both.

REFLECTION QUESTIONS

1. How does the doctrine of divine missions help you understand God's oneness?
2. How does the doctrine of divine missions help you understand God's tripersonal nature?
3. How does the doctrine of divine missions impact your prayer life?
4. What is a passage in Scripture that has confused you but now seems clearer based on thinking through the divine missions?
5. How would you teach the doctrine of the divine missions to someone who's never heard of it?

---

5. homas Aquinas, *ST*, I.43.2, Reply Obj. 1. 438.

QUESTION 31

What Is the Doctrine of Inseparable Operations?

In the last chapter we saw that the divine processions are revealed in the external missions of the persons of the Trinity. The eternally unbegotten Father sends his only, eternally begotten Son, and the eternally unbegotten Father and his only, eternally begotten Son send the Spirit who eternally proceeds from them both. We ended that chapter clarifying that the external missions are just that—the visible revelation of who God is in himself to his creatures. But further clarification is needed. Namely, we need to be crystal clear on the fact that the missions are not three separate activities undertaken by three distinct agents but instead the revelation of the one triune God through his acts of creation and redemption, acts that are singular in their willing because there is one and only one God. This is the clarification provided by the doctrine of inseparable operations.

Defining Inseparable Operations

The doctrine of inseparable operations is historically stated this way: *opera Trinitatis ad extra indivisa sunt*, that is, "the external works of the Trinity are undivided." As Adonis Vidu points out, this is a "*dogmatic rule*," a safeguard to keep our language in line as we creatures attempt to describe divine action, that which is "unspeakable" and "indescribable."[1] Its most basic function is to maintain, in faithfulness to and in keeping with biblical patterns of language, that all of God's actions are one. To state it negatively, there is no action undertaken by one divine person that is not also undertaken by each of the other two divine persons. When we say that "God creates," the doctrine of inseparable operations reminds us that what we mean by that state-

1. Adonis Vidu, *The Same God Who Works All Things: Inseparable Operations* (Grand Rapids: Eerdmans, 2021), xiv.

ment is that the one God, the triune God who is Father, Son, and Holy Spirit, creates. It is not just one of the divine persons who performs any particular divine action but all three divine persons, because all three divine persons are the one God.

Ultimately, this unity of action is required by the unity of essence in the Godhead. "In the same way that the persons *exist* indivisibly, so they *act* undividedly," says Gilles Emery.[2] It is worth quoting at length Emery's summary of Aquinas's commentary on John in relation to inseparable operations:

> . . . *the works manifest the nature of the one who acts.* By carrying out the Father's own works, Christ shows himself to be of the same nature as the Father, since "the clearest indication of the nature of a thing is from its works." Thus, *the divine activities of the Son induce one to recognize that unity of nature through which he is in the Father, and conversely.* The Son's action is not "diverse" or different from the Father's, but rather the persons act within one single operation. The Father who acts is in the Son and Holy Spirit, the acting Son is in the Father and the Holy Spirit, the Spirit who acts is in the Father and in the Son. *The undivided operation of the three persons thus constitutes one aspect of their communal "in-being."*[3]

The point is, as Emery says at the beginning, that the tripersonal unity of God's being requires the tripersonal unity of the divine acts. Because God is one, his acts are one. In the next chapter, we will make sure to state the corollary of this doctrine clearly—that because God is one God *in three persons*, his acts are also one *in such a way that the three persons are revealed*. In this chapter, however, we want to start where Trinitarian theology starts, and indeed where the Bible starts—with the oneness of God and thus the oneness of his action.

Defending Inseparable Operations

Biblical Support

As we have stated throughout this book, the categories of classical Trinitarian theology are thoroughly biblical. This is as true for inseparable operations as

2. Gilles Emery, *The Trinitarian Theology of Saint Thomas Aquinas*, trans. Francesca Aran Murphy (Oxford: Oxford University Press, 2007), 309, emphasis original.
3. Emery, *The Trinitarian Theology of Saint Thomas Aquinas*, 309 (emphases added). Emery is summarizing and quoting Aquinas' *In Ioan.* 10.38 (nos. 1465–1466); 5.19 (no. 752); and 14.10 (no. 1893).

it is for any other category we have discussed or will discuss. We have already covered this in some ways in the chapters on the Bible's teaching about the Trinity. For instance, we have noted throughout that the three persons are equally God because they and they alone share in exclusively divine attributes, actions, appellations, and adoration. The second category, divine action, concerns us here. The doctrine of inseparable operations simply codifies in systematic form the biblical pattern of language that attributes divine action clearly and wholly to each of the divine persons.

To expand on what we've noted in earlier chapters, Scripture teaches that each of the persons, together as the one God, perform every divine action. The classical text for teaching inseparable operations comes at the end of John 5:19, where Jesus says, "For whatever the Father does, that the Son does likewise" (cf. also 14:10). This is a straightforward statement about divine action, at least as far as the Father and the Son are concerned. And, from context, Jesus is referring to explicitly *divine* actions—raising the dead (5:21), judgment (5:22), receiving glory (5:23), and, most importantly, possessing life in himself (5:26). What the Father does, the Son does—inseparably.

But while this one text would be sufficient to build the doctrine of inseparable operations, there are other ways the Bible teaches it. One of the most obvious is that, with respect to several of God's activities, the Bible attributes particular divine actions to two or more of the divine persons. For instance, regarding the atonement, and especially Jesus's crucifixion, the Bible says the following:

- He [the Father] who did not spare his own Son but gave him up for us all. (Rom. 8:32)
- No one takes it from me, but I [the incarnate Son] lay it down of my own accord. (John 10:18)
- How much more will the blood of Christ, who through the eternal Spirit offered himself without blemish to God, purify our conscience from dead works to serve the living God. (Heb. 9:14)

In these verses we see that the Father gave up his Son, who gave his life of his own accord through the power of the Holy Spirit. The crucifixion is an act of all three divine persons, because God is one God, existing in three persons, who acts inseparably.

Another related example is the resurrection of Jesus. Again, Scripture attributes this act to each of the three divine persons, as we see from the following verses (among others):

- *Resurrection attributed to the Father:* "Paul, an apostle—not from men or by man, but by Jesus Christ and God the Father who raised him from the dead" (Gal. 1:1 CSB); "Through him you believe in God , who raised him from the dead and gave him glory, so that your faith and hope are in God" (1 Peter 1:21 CSB).

- *Resurrection attributed to the Son:* "Jesus answered them, 'Destroy this temple, and I will raise it again in three days.' They replied, 'It has taken forty-six years to build this temple, and you are going to raise it in three days?' But the temple he had spoken of was his body" (John 2:19–21 NIV); "No one takes it from me, but I lay it down on my own. I have the right to lay it down, and I have the right to take it up again. I have received this command from my Father" (John 10:18 CSB).
- *Resurrection attributed to the Spirit:* "And if the Spirit of him who raised Jesus from the dead lives in you, then he who raised Christ from the dead will also bring your mortal bodies to life through his Spirit who lives in you" (Rom. 8:11 CSB); "He was put to death in the flesh but made alive by the Spirit" (1 Peter 3:18b CSB).[4]

We could multiply these examples for other divine actions, such as creation, salvation, judgment, being glorified, new creation—basically any divine action we can list is attributed in some way to each of the divine persons in Scripture.[5] Once again with the doctrine of the Trinity we have here a pattern of biblical language—attributing divine actions to each of the divine persons—that supports a particular theological conclusion, namely that God acts inseparably.

Theological Logic

In addition to the clear teaching of Scripture that gives us the doctrine of inseparable operations, we also need to note that there is a certain theological logic to this doctrine. If God is one God and not three gods, then his attributes, adoration, appellations, and here, actions must also be one and not three. In other words, if we did not have the doctrine of inseparable operations and instead posited a situation where the Father does some things, the Son does other things, and the Spirit does things other than either the Father or the Son, we would have three gods and not one God. Gregory of Nyssa states it this way:

> But in the case of the Divine nature we do not similarly learn that the Father does anything by Himself in which

4. I am indebted to Brandon D. Smith for this list of Scriptures and its relation to the doctrine of inseparable operations. See Brandon D. Smith, "Who Raised Jesus from the Dead?," *The Center for Baptist Renewal*, April 5, 2022, https://www.centerforbaptistrenewal.com/blog/2022/4/5/trinitarian-unity-and-christs-resurrection.
5. For further discussion of the inseparability of each divine action in the economy of creation and redemption, see Matthew Y. Emerson and Brandon D. Smith, *Beholding the Triune God: The Inseparable Work of Father, Son, and Spirit* (Wheaton, IL: Crossway, 2024).

> the Son does not work conjointly, or again that the Son has any special operation apart from the Holy Spirit; but every operation which extends from God to the Creation, and is named according to our variable conceptions of it, has its origin from the Father, and proceeds through the Son, and is perfected in the Holy Spirit. For this reason the name derived from the operation is not divided with regard to the number of those who fulfil it, because the action of each concerning anything is not separate and peculiar, but whatever comes to pass, in reference either to the acts of His providence for us, or to the government and constitution of the universe, comes to pass by the action of the Three, yet what does come to pass is not three things. We may understand the meaning of this from one single instance. From Him, I say, Who is the chief source of gifts, all things which have shared in this grace have obtained their life. When we inquire, then, whence this good gift came to us, we find by the guidance of the Scriptures that it was from the Father, Son, and Holy Spirit. Yet although we set forth Three Persons and three names, we do not consider that we have had bestowed upon us three lives, one from each Person separately; but the same life is wrought in us by the Father, and prepared by the Son, and depends on the will of the Holy Spirit. Since then the Holy Trinity fulfils every operation in a manner similar to that of which I have spoken, not by separate action according to the number of the Persons, but so that there is one motion and disposition of the good will which is communicated from the Father through the Son to the Spirit (for as we do not call those whose operation gives one life three Givers of life, neither do we call those who are contemplated in one goodness three Good beings, nor speak of them in the plural by any of their other attributes); so neither can we call those who exercise this Divine and superintending power and operation towards ourselves and all creation, conjointly and inseparably, by their mutual action, three Gods.[6]

Notice that Gregory relies on three crucial pieces of logic here. First, because the *result* of the action is one, the action itself is one ("we do not consider that we have had bestowed upon us three lives, one from each Person separately; but the same life is wrought in us by the Father, and prepared by

---

6. Gregory of Nyssa, *On "Not Three Gods,"* (*NPNF*[2] 5:334).

the Son, and depends on the will of the Holy Spirit"). Second, to speak of three separate actors would imply three gods ("neither can we call those who exercise this . . . operation . . . three Gods"). In these first two pieces of logic we have the fundamental argument for inseparable operations—the presence of these three actors implies three gods, and three actors would entail two or more of the same action with two or more of the same results, depending on which divine persons are acting. This just doesn't make sense of the biblical witness regarding who God is and what he does.

The third and final piece of logic that Gregory uses here is to refer to the singular divine will: "Since then the Holy Trinity fulfils every operation in a manner similar to that of which I have spoken, not by separate action according to the number of the Persons, but so that there is one motion and disposition of the good will which is communicated from the Father through the Son to the Spirit." To put this point simply, for God to be one, his essence must be singular, and so, because the divine will is proper to the divine essence, there can only be one will. For there to be more than one divine will, that is, for there to a divine will for each of the divine persons, would imply three gods.

This logic relies on the doctrine of divine simplicity, which states that God cannot be composed of parts. If he were, his attributes, including his essence, would be logically prior to his existence—his parts would have to be "put together" for him to exist. Even if they've always been "put together" from eternity, we can conceive of a scenario in which they haven't been, which is to say we could conceive of some things prior to God himself. That's not how the Bible describes God. He is *a se*, needing nothing else—including his parts being put together, logically or ontologically—to exist (John 5:26). With respect to the divine will, this means two things. First, the divine will is not a "part" of God but just is his essence, as is the case with his other attributes. Second, for each divine person to possess their own will would imply that they possess an attribute distinct from one another, which would mean they do not each share in the same essence. This is tritheism.

Summary

So, back to inseparable operations—we have to say that God acts as one, inseparably, because he *is* one. To say anything else would mean that each divine person has a distinct will that performs distinct actions, which does not fit the biblical picture of Trinitarian monotheism. Of course, there is a certain *taxis* to God's external acts, an order that follows the order of the relations of origin. As Gregory says above, every divine action can be described as "from the Father through the Son by the Spirit." This mirrors the divine life, in which the Father begets the Son and the Father and the Son spirate the Spirit. As we said in the last chapter, divine missions reflect divine processions, and in the divine missions each act is inseparably triune.

REFLECTION QUESTIONS

1. How does the doctrine of inseparable operations help you understand God's oneness?
2. How does the doctrine of inseparable operations help you understand God's tripersonal nature?
3. How does the doctrine of inseparable operations impact your prayer life?
4. What is a passage in Scripture that has confused you but now seems clearer based on thinking through inseparable operations?
5. How would you teach the doctrine of inseparable operations to someone who's never heard of it?

QUESTION 32

What Is the Doctrine of Appropriations?

In the last chapter we explored the doctrine of inseparable operations, which states that each divine act is carried out inseparably by each of the three persons of the one God. In Latin, this doctrine is stated as *opera Trinitatis ad extra indivisa sunt*, translated as "the external works of the Trinity are indivisible." It is important to maintain this emphasis on the unity of divine action because, if we do not, we will fall into tritheism. Nevertheless, the one God exists in three persons, and so there is a corollary statement necessary. Even as "the external works of the Trinity are indivisible," this is true while "preserving, of course, the properties of each person" (Latin: *scilicet servata cuiusque personae proprietate*).[1]

Explaining Appropriations

These "properties of each person" are the divine persons' individual properties, which is to say, their eternal relations of origin. The Father, Son, and Spirit do not have distinct attributes or wills from one another, because that would imply three gods. Instead, they each fully possess the divine essence and are only distinguished by their personal properties, their eternal relations of origin. As we saw in earlier chapters, the eternal relations of origin are thus: The Father is eternally unbegotten, the Son is eternally begotten from the Father, and the Spirit eternally proceeds from the Father and the Son.

So, when the doctrine of appropriation states that the external works of the Trinity are indivisible, *preserving, of course, the properties of each person*, it is stating simply that the Father, Son, and Spirit remain who they each are as they act indivisibly in creation and redemption. Because in his external works

1. On this phrase and its history, see Fred Sanders, "'Preserving, of Course, the Properties of Each' (Beckwith)," *Scriptorium Daily*, November 2, 2016, https://scriptoriumdaily.com/preserving-of-course-the-properties-of-each-beckwith/.

God remains the same—that is to say, he remains triune—we can speak of his actions in a way that reflects the divine processions. As we heard Gregory of Nyssa state in the last chapter, divine action is "from the Father, through the Son, and by the Spirit."

In their book *Biblical Reasoning*, Bobby Jamieson and Tyler Wittman introduce truths about the doctrine of God and its foundation in Scripture using what they call Trinitarian principles and rules. Regarding the interrelation between the triune God's oneness in essence and in action, they state their principle and rules as follows:

> **Principle 5:** The one true and living God is eternally Father, Son, and Holy Spirit, distinct in their relations to one another and the same in substance, power, and glory.
>
> **Rule 5:** The external works of the Trinity are indivisibly one, just as God is one. Whenever Scripture mentions only one or two divine persons, understand that all three are equally present and active, undertaking the same actions in ways that imply their relations to one another. In this way, learn to count persons rather than actions.
>
> **Rule 6:** Scripture sometimes attributes to only divine person a perfection, action, or name common to all three, because of some contextual fit or analogy between the common attribute and the divine person in question. Read such passages in a way that does not compromise the Trinity's essential oneness and equality.[2]

So, again, because God is one, his actions are inseparable. Because God is one God in three persons, his inseparable actions reflect his triune nature. Because the Father is unbegotten, theologians have deemed it appropriate to refer to him as *font divinitas*, the fount of divinity. The Son and Spirit are both *from* the Father (and the Spirit is also from the Son), so, as we see in John 5:26, it is biblically accurate to say that the Father gives, or communicates, the divine essence to the Son and, along with the Son, to the Spirit. This act is eternal, so this just is who God is. But this *from-ness* in the divine processions is reflected in the *taxis*, the order, of the divine missions, so that we can say that divine action is *from* the Father. Likewise, because the Son is the Father's Word (John 1:1), Wisdom, and Power (1 Cor. 1:24), it is appropriate to say that divine action happens *through* the Son. And because the Spirit proceeds

---

2. R. B. Jamieson and Tyler R. Wittman, *Biblical Reasoning: Christological and Trinitarian Rules for Exegesis* (Grand Rapids: Baker Academic, 2022), 106.

from the Father and the Son, because he is the Spirit *of* the Father and the Son, it is appropriate to say that divine action happens *by* the Spirit.

Appropriations in Scripture

We saw two examples of this kind of ordering in the last chapter, when we cited Scripture's description of God's activity in the crucifixion and the resurrection. The Father sent the incarnate Son to the cross to atone for sin; the incarnate Son gave up his own life at the direction of the Father to atone for sin; and the incarnate Son offered up himself to atone for sin through the eternal Spirit. With respect to the resurrection, we saw similar patterns of speech—the Father raised Jesus from the dead; Jesus took up his own life that he also laid down of his own accord; and the Spirit raised Jesus from the dead. Jesus's death and resurrection can both rightly be said to be from the Father, through the Son, by the Spirit. Like inseparable operations, we could multiply examples here. Creation, for instance, is from the Father; through the Son, his Word, through whom he speaks and thus through whom he creates (e.g., the multiple instances in which Genesis states, "And God said . . . and there was"); and by the agency of the Spirit, who hovers over the face of the waters (Gen. 1:2). The doctrine of appropriation thus commits us to a pattern of speech that at one and the same time acknowledges the inseparability of the one God's actions and also the inherent Trinitarian shape to the one triune God's actions. Both of these commitments are rooted in God's own inner life because he is one God in three persons.

But the doctrine of appropriations does more than this. It also recognizes that Scripture can and does attribute, or appropriate, certain divine actions to a particular person of the Godhead, and it does so in keeping with the basic *taxis* of the divine processions and missions. Because the doctrine of appropriations is tied to the doctrine of inseparable operations, it warns us against taking these instances in Scripture as an indication that a divine person acts alone in some particular work. So, for instance, even though Ephesians 1:3–14 repeatedly mentions the Father's activity in predestination and providence, inseparable operations reminds us that it is not the Father alone who does this. Nevertheless, appropriations reminds us at the same time that it is apt to attribute, or appropriate, these particular works to the Father because they reflect the fact that all things are *from* him.

With respect to the Son, Paul in Ephesians 1:3–14 repeatedly indicates that the actions planned by the Father are carried out *through* the Son. The Father has "blessed us *in Christ* (v. 3), chosen us *in* Christ" (v. 4), adopted us "to himself as sons *through* Jesus Christ" (v. 5), blessed us "*in* the Beloved" (v. 6), redeemed us "*through* [Christ's] blood" (v. 7), set forth his purpose "*in* Christ" (v. 9), and united "all things *in* [Christ]" (v. 10). The work of salvation is planned by the Father and accomplished *through* (or *in*) the Son. This is a reflection of the divine processions, in which the Son is eternally begotten from the Father. The eternally unbegotten Father who eternally generates the eternally only begotten Son works through his Son in creation and redemption.

Finally, with respect to the Holy Spirit, Paul's language in Ephesians 1:3–14, and, in particular, verses 13–14, reflects the Spirit's eternal procession from the Father and the Son. Because the Holy Spirit eternally proceeds from the Father and the Son, this intra-Trinitarian *taxis* is reflected in the divine missions, namely the fact that God's external works can be said to be accomplished *by* the Holy Spirit. The language of "agent" is often used to describe the Holy Spirit's mission in God's acts of creation and redemption. In Ephesians 1:13–14, Paul says that the work of salvation that comes from the planning of the Father and through the redemptive work of the Son is "sealed *with* [or *by*] the promised Holy Spirit, who is the guarantee of our inheritance until we acquire possession of it, to the praise of his glory." In sum, Paul says in this passage that salvation is providentially *from* the Father, accomplished *through* the Son, and applied to believers *by* the Holy Spirit.

Summary

Here we see Trinitarian *taxis*, the relation between the divine processions and missions, inseparable operations, and appropriation all at work. The language of "from, through, and by" demonstrates the order of Trinitarian activity, whether in the processions *ad intra* or the works *ad extra*. Paul also appropriates particular actions to particular divine persons, namely the providential ordering of salvation to the Father, the accomplishment of salvation to the Son, and the application of the Son's saving work to the Holy Spirit. But, according to the rule of inseparable operations, we would be remiss to say that these are the works of those distinct persons *alone*. All three persons of the Trinity providentially order salvation, accomplish salvation, and apply salvation to the believer because there is one and only one God. As we saw in the last chapter, the Bible speaks distinctly about distinct persons accomplishing distinct works, but we can find different passages that speak of each of the persons for particular acts—the Father raises the incarnate Son from the dead, the incarnate Son raises himself from the dead, and the Spirit raises the Son from the dead. God's works are inseparable. Nevertheless, it is appropriate to appropriate particular actions to particular persons, especially as we see in Ephesians 1:3–14, where Paul describes the work of the three persons in redemption as *from* the Father, *through* the Son, and *by* the Spirit.

REFLECTION QUESTIONS

1. How does the doctrine of appropriations help you understand God's oneness?

2. How does the doctrine of appropriations help you understand God's tripersonal nature?

3. How does the doctrine of appropriations impact your prayer life?

4. What is a passage in Scripture that has confused you but now seems clearer based on thinking through the doctrine of appropriations?

5. How would you teach the doctrine of appropriations to someone who has never heard of it?

SECTION B

Historical and Contemporary Questions About the Trinity

QUESTION 33

Does the Son Submit to the Father from All Eternity?

A popular view among evangelicals is that God the Son eternally submits to the Father, not according to his essence or being but only according to his function or role in the Godhead. In this view, the Father is the source of authority in the Godhead, and it is to him that the Son and the Spirit willingly submit. While this view continues to shift and change, it is fair to say that this position arises from at least two sources. First, advocates of Eternal Relations of Authority and Submission (ERAS) have not seen clear and explicit biblical support for the eternal relations of origin, whereas they do see clear and explicit support for ERAS. Although the two main advocates of this position, Wayne Grudem and Bruce Ware, have both shifted a bit on this and have now clearly affirmed that the eternal generation of the Son is taught in Scripture, they still argue that ERAS is the clearer teaching of Scripture and its primary point of emphasis in articulating the distinction between the three persons of the Godhead.

Second, advocates of ERAS are concerned to root gender roles in the Godhead, such that there is an analogy between the relation of a wife to her husband and the relation of the Son and Spirit to the Father. Regarding human beings, the position called complementarianism argues that men and women are equal in worth and image bearing but distinct in their roles in the home and church, and namely in the woman's role to submit to her husband in the home and in the limitation of the office of elder in the church to men. According to ERAS proponents, this equality in essence and distinction in roles is analogous to the Trinity, where, they argue, the Son and Spirit are equal in essence to the Father but distinct in their roles within the Godhead and namely in their submission to the Father (and the Spirit's submission to the Son as well).

Many (including the authors of this book) have written extensively about this issue elsewhere and do not wish to rehash the entire debate. Suffice it to say that we do not believe the ERAS position is the best explanation for the biblical data regarding the relation between the persons of the Godhead, nor do we believe that it deals adequately with necessary theological questions.[1] Below we will work through our three primary objections in order to argue that the Son (and Spirit) does not submit to the Father from eternity.

Biblical Data

The most important reason for rejecting this position is that it is not supported by Scripture. Despite the protestations of ERAS proponents to the contrary and their claims that ERAS is more explicitly taught in Scripture than the eternal relations of origin, the reality is that the classical doctrine of the Trinity is the more biblical articulation.

We have already surveyed the biblical data regarding the classical doctrine of the Trinity in the chapters in part 2 and have repeatedly noted biblical support for the theological positions noted in part 4 so far. The key distinction between this model and ERAS is twofold. First, ERAS proponents agree that the Bible teaches that there is only one God and this God exists in three persons, but they do not see sufficiently clear and overwhelming exegetical evidence for the eternal relations of origin. To be clear, neither Grudem nor Ware has ever explicitly denied this doctrine, but they have questioned its exegetical support and have instead posited that the better, clearer, and biblically explicit way to distinguish the divine persons is through ERAS. The second distinction between classical Trinitarianism and ERAS is that the latter does not partake in partitive exegesis. Instead of distinguishing between passages that speak of the incarnate Son's obedience and submission according to his humanity and those that speak of the Son according to his divinity, ERAS proponents argue that the Bible's language about the Son's obedience and submission refers to both his incarnation and his divine life apart from creation.

To this particular thesis we wish to respond biblically in this section but also theologically and historically in the rest of the chapter. Regarding the biblical data, we want to emphasize as we did in earlier chapters that the doctrine of the eternal relations of origin is thoroughly biblical. Texts like John 5:26 and Proverbs 8:22–31, as well as the biblical pattern of naming the three persons, provide ample support. But there is more to say than this regarding

---

1. For a fuller treatment of and response to this position, see Matthew Y. Emerson and R. Lucas Stamps, "On Trinitarian Theological Method," in *Trinitarian Theology: Theological Models and Doctrinal Application*, ed. Keith S. Whitfield (Nashville: B&H Academic, 2019), 95–128, as well as our "Response to Malcolm B. Yarnell III," 157–74. See also Matthew Y. Emerson and R. Lucas Stamps, "On the Biblical and Historical Doctrine of the Trinity: A Response to Wayne Grudem," in *Word by Word*, February 12, 2021, https://www.logos.com/grow/on-the-biblical-and-historical-doctrine-of-the-trinity-a-response-to-wayne-grudem/#. This is our response to Grudem's engagement with our critiques of ERAS in the second edition of his *Systematic Theology*. See Wayne Grudem, *Systematic Theology*, 2nd ed. (Grand Rapids: Zondervan Academic, 2020), 301–11.

ERAS's claims. First, despite biblical texts that may at first appear to support ERAS, such as the "sending" texts in John (e.g., John 8:42) and the prepositional order of "from the Father . . . through the Son,"[2] there are texts that say the exact opposite *if these biblical texts should be read as supporting ERAS*. So, for instance, with respect to the idea that Jesus's sending ought to be understood as submitting to the Father's distinct volition, there are other texts that indicate the Son's own agency in his incarnation, namely the "I have come" statements in the Synoptic Gospels (e.g. Mark 1:38; Matt. 9:13; Luke 12:49). Further, as we have seen in the previous chapters, both the "sending" language and the prepositions used to describe the relation between the divine persons in their common activity are reflections of the divine missions, which in turn are rooted in the eternal processions. Rather than indicating differences in authority and submission, they are instead reflections of the divine relations between the persons, relations that are not differences in attributes (i.e., authority or will), actions, appellations, and adoration but only and exclusively differences in the mode of subsistence in the divine essence.

Second, ERAS proponents do not adequately reckon with Philippians 2:5–11:

> Have this mind among yourselves, which is yours in Christ Jesus, who, though he was in the form of God, did not count equality with God a thing to be grasped, but emptied himself, by taking the form of a servant, being born in the likeness of men. And being found in human form, he humbled himself by becoming obedient to the point of death, even death on a cross. Therefore, God has highly exalted him and bestowed on him the name that is above every name, so that at the name of Jesus every knee should bow, in heaven and on earth and under the earth, and every tongue confess that Jesus Christ is Lord, to the glory of God the Father.

The key phrases occur in verses 7 and 8. After articulating the Son's equality with God (the Father) in verses 5–6, Paul explains that he "[took] the form of a servant"; that is, the Son became incarnate. This is the moment in time in which the incarnate Son can be said to be submissive, a servant, at the moment of his conception. Not before, not from eternity, but at conception as a human being. And that last phrase is also the teaching of this text, that "form of a servant" is a reference to the incarnate Son's humanity, as Paul clarifies in the next verse: "And being found in human form." The Son takes on a human nature in the incarnation, and it is according to that human nature—"being found in human form"—that

2. Both Wayne Grudem and Bruce Ware make much of both of these examples. See Grudem, *Systematic Theology*, 299–305; and Bruce Ware, "Unity and Distinctions Between the Divine Persons," in Whitfield, *Trinitarian Theology*, 35–45.

the Son can be called "servant" and that the Son can "[become] obedient to the point of death, even death on the cross." Further, it is according to his humanity that the Son receives the "name that is above every name," so that the "name of Jesus" is now equal to the "name that is above every name" (that is, YHWH; Phil. 2:10–11). As God the Son, he already possessed that name. But now as the incarnate Son, Jesus Christ, he possesses it as Israel's Messiah and Lord.

This passage of Scripture, then, provides clear reading strategies for those other texts in Scripture that speak of the Son's submission to the Father. These texts must be read in reference to the Son's incarnation, and particularly to his actions according to his humanity, and not as references to his life in eternity and apart from God's acts of creation and redemption. Texts like John 6:38, 8:42, or 10:36 are not prooftexts for ERAS but instead the opposite. As we noted in earlier chapters, the practice of reading Scripture according to this distinction is called "partitive exegesis." It is rooted in Philippians 2:5–11 and is also crucial for maintaining the (theo)logical coherence of the doctrine of the Trinity. It is from this theo-logic that our next objection to ERAS comes.

Theo-Logic

Aside from its clearly biblical warrant, one of the primary reasons for employing partitive exegesis is that it helps to explain passages that otherwise would not fit with the classical doctrine of the Trinity. Another way to say that is that the theological logic of classical Trinitarianism requires the kind of reading strategy that Philippians 2:7–8 supports. This is because God's oneness in essence and threeness in person can only be explained via the eternal relations of origin. Or, to put it differently, if the persons of God are distinguished by anything other than the eternal relations of origin—whether it be by distinctive attributes, actions, appellations, or adoration—then they are not one in essence but multiple.

Even though ERAS proponents explicitly affirm the Nicene commitment to *homoousios*, the oneness of God's essence, to do so at the same time as positing a distinction between the Father on the one hand and the Son and Spirit on the other in terms of authority (and, in many cases, glory and will) is nonsensical according to Nicaea's (and ultimately the Bible's) theo-logic. What the Bible teaches, and the pro-Nicenes affirmed and articulated theologically, is that God's oneness is utterly simple. There is no variation, change, or distinction in God or between the persons of God in terms of attributes, actions, appellations, or adoration. For there to be otherwise would mean that God is somehow made up of parts, which would in turn mean that he is a composite being, someone made up of something or some things different from himself.

Further, to say that there is a difference in authority (or glory, or will, etc.) between the persons would be to deny the fundamental means of affirming the divinity of the Son and the Spirit. In the arguments against the subordinationists of the fourth and fifth centuries, pro-Nicenes like Athanasius and Gregory of Nazianzus defended both the Son's and the Spirit's divinity by demonstrating that there is absolutely no difference between them and the Father in Scripture *except* in their eternal relations of origin. They possess the same attributes, the attributes that only God possesses. They perform the same actions, the actions that only God performs. They share the same appellations, the names by which only God is called. And they receive the same adoration, the worship and glory of which only God is worthy.

Particularly important here is that the divine persons perform the same actions and share the same attributes. ERAS proponents distinguish between the persons at least on the basis that they perform different roles in God's acts, even if they do so as the one God. And this distinction in role contains an element of submission as well, where the Son and Spirit are essentially responding to the Father's command. There is thus also a distinction in the divine will. While ERAS proponents vigorously deny that their position entails three wills in the Godhead, it is hard to see how they avoid such an entailment in their position. All of this amounts to differentiating power, authority, and glory in the Godhead. While ERAS proponents are quick to affirm *homoousios* and the Son's and Spirit's equality to the Father in terms of the divine essence, it is theo-logically inconsistent, to put it mildly, to simultaneously argue for a distinction between the persons in attributes and actions. This is true even if it is only a difference functionally and not ontologically.

As we argued in questions 31 and 32 on inseparable operations and appropriation, for God's actions to be one he must only have one will. To say that the Son submits to the Father is to come very close to saying that the Son has a separate will from the Father. And even if one wants to deny that charge, there has still been no adequate explanation for how it is to be avoided given the logic of ERAS. Further, to say that there is a functional difference between the authority (or glory) of the Father and the Son in eternity is again theo-logically inconsistent (at best). For there to be even a functional difference between the persons with respect to the attributes of God is to introduce variation precisely where there cannot be any for the Nicene judgment of *homoousios* to be upheld.

Submission as *Taxis*

This is all not to say that the language of submission cannot be used about Trinitarian relations *ad intra*. To the contrary, the Christian tradition has used such terms frequently but *only* in reference to the eternal relations of origin. Classical Trinitarianism teaches a doctrine known as *taxis*, which we covered in question 30. *Taxis* is a helpful way of explaining both the Bible's teaching on the eternal relations of origin and the tradition's use of terms like "submission" to describe the relation of the Son to the Father. Regarding the Bible's language, passages and patterns that teach the eternal relations of origin do teach a certain order to these relations. The Father is eternally unbegotten, the Son is eternally begotten from the Father, and the Spirit is eternally spirated from the Father and the Son. The Father, in this *taxis*, is the "fount of divinity," the divine person from whom the other two persons eternally proceed.

It is in this sense, secondly, that the tradition is comfortable using the term "submission" to refer to the relation between the Father and the Son. We cannot simply use "Ctrl + F" to find instances of "submission" in the early church and assume that means they taught ERAS. Actually, to the contrary, if one reads these ancient texts in context, we quickly find out that they meant the exact opposite of ERAS and were instead simply articulating the classical doctrine of the Trinity. We have written elsewhere to defend this claim, but it is important to state here again that ERAS was not a theological position attested to in the church until the mid- to late-twentieth century (see the references in the first footnote of this chapter). While the language of ERAS bears some semblance to classical Trinitarian writings in the sense that it uses the language of "submission" to describe the relation between the Father and the Son, its theo-logic is almost entirely alien to it.

Summary

For these reasons—biblical, theological, and historical—we do not affirm that the Son submitted to the Father from eternity. In fact, we argue that ERAS is fundamentally at odds with the logic of Nicene, classical, biblical Trinitarianism, even while its proponents explicitly affirm the Nicene judgment of *homoousios*, argue that their position is at least in line with if not a rearticulation of the classical position, and contend that their doctrine is the right reading of Scripture. We appreciate proponents of ERAS as fellow laborers in the kingdom and followers of our Lord Jesus Christ. We are also glad they affirm Nicaea's core theological commitment, that the Father, Son, and Holy Spirit equally and fully share the one essence of God and so are *homoousios*. We do not believe, however, that their position reflects the biblical and theological logic of Nicaea's affirmation of *homoousios* or, ultimately, that it is warranted from Scripture, tradition, or logic.

REFLECTION QUESTIONS

1. What are the dangers in getting this question wrong?
2. How do popular Christian songs and writings form our thinking about this question?
3. What are ways that considering this issue helps your prayer life?
4. What is a passage in Scripture that has confused you but now seems clearer based on thinking through this issue?
5. How would you address this issue with someone who has never heard of it?

QUESTION 34

What Happened to the Trinity at the Cross?

"The Father turns his face away." This is a popular line in a hymn that we enjoy singing. But does it accurately reflect the nature of the cross and especially the meaning of one of Jesus's last sayings, the cry of dereliction? When he utters, "My God, my God, why have you forsaken me?" (Mark 15:34) and then breathes his last, does this mean that God the Son has been abandoned by God the Father? Is there some kind of existential or even deeper separation between the Father and Son on the cross? Is God the Father pouring out his wrath on God the Son? Where is the Holy Spirit during all this? These are the kinds of questions that occur to careful readers of Scripture who also affirm the Trinity. To sum up the question, what happened to the Trinity at the crucifixion of Christ?

Rather than keeping you guessing until the end of the chapter, a summary of our position is as follows: On the cross, Jesus Christ bore the ultimate penalty for sin—God's wrath—on behalf of all sinners who come to him in faith and repentance. He did so as the God-Man, one person with two hypostatically united natures, human and divine. According to his humanity and as Israel's Messiah, he suffered God's wrath and died. According to his divinity, he, along with the Father and the Spirit, poured out the one wrath of the triune God. As the one person of Jesus Christ, he both bore the penalty for sin and poured out that same penalty. Or, to put it another way, God satisfied his own justice by substituting himself for sinners on the cross in the person of Jesus Christ.

Theological Parameters[1]

Each year during Holy Week, most Christians have their hearts turned toward

1. This section is adapted from Matthew Y. Emerson, "Parameters for Talking about the Cry of Dereliction," *Biblical Reasoning*, March 27, 2018, https://secundumscripturas.com/2018/03/27/parameters-for-talking-about-the-the-cry-of-dereliction/.

Golgotha. There is so much confusion, though, about one biblical passage that describes the crucifixion—the cry of dereliction, Jesus's quotation of Psalm 22:1 from the cross. In our view, this cry needs to be understood in thoroughly Trinitarian, non-Nestorian, and Messianic fashion.

First, anything we say about the cry of dereliction needs to retain the oneness of the Godhead, both with respect to rejecting any ontological or relational division between Father and Son and with respect to affirming inseparable operations. The cross does not produce division between Father and Son, and it is not only the Father who acts in the crucifixion. It is appropriate to talk about the Father pouring out his wrath, but, according to the doctrine of appropriations, ascribing an action to one person of the Trinity does not deny that the other persons are acting inseparably. It is not only the Father who pours out wrath; the Son and the Spirit, as the other two persons of the one God, also pour out the one wrath of the one God.

Second, anything we say about the cry of dereliction needs to retain the oneness of the person of Jesus Christ. That is, it needs to avoid the heresy of Nestorianism.[2] He is one person with two natures, divine and human, and he goes to the cross as one person. In other words, the Son cannot die in virtue of his divinity, but by virtue of the hypostatic union we can also say that God dies on the cross in virtue of his humanity.

Third, anything we say about the cry of dereliction needs to retain the covenantal and therefore relational unity between God and his Messiah. Psalm 22 is a lament psalm that *ends with a confession of covenantal hope*. Jesus is (most likely) quoting Psalm 22 metaleptically, that is, quoting one line of the psalm but assuming its entire context.[3] Jesus's lament comes in a covenantal context, a context in which he is the messianic Son chosen by YHWH to deliver his people Israel by suffering on their behalf. God pours out his wrath on Jesus as his anointed Son who suffers in his people's place.

Canonical Parameters[4]

There are also canonical parameters for the cry of dereliction. Jesus's guttural utterance from the cross, "My God, my God, why have you forsaken me?" (Mark 15:34) ought to be taken in its immediate, surrounding, and, ultimately, canonical contexts.

The first contexts for the cry of dereliction are its immediate and surrounding contexts in Mark's gospel. Mark and Matthew (27:46) are the only

2. Nestorianism separates the two natures of Christ to such an extent that, rather than one person with two natures, we end up speaking of two persons, each with a distinct nature.
3. See, for instance, Michael B. Shepherd, *An Introduction to the Making and Meaning of the Bible* (Grand Rapids: Eerdmans, 2024), 38.
4. This section is adapted from Matthew Y. Emerson, "Canonical Parameters for Talking about the Cry of Dereliction," *Biblical Reasoning*, April 3, 2018, https://secundumscripturas.com/2018/04/03/canonical-parameters-for-talking-about-the-cry-of-dereliction/.

Gospels that include it, and Mark includes no other sayings of Jesus from the cross in his gospel. Regarding the immediate context, there are a few things to note. First, the temple veil is torn in two (Mark 15:38) and the Roman centurion confesses that "truly, this man was the Son of God" (Mark 15:39) immediately after Jesus's cry and subsequent death. Second, this cry stands as the culmination of "the hour," spoken of repeatedly in Mark 13 and fulfilled in the events of Mark 14.[5] This "hour" is for "the Son of Man," who "will come riding on the clouds in glory" (Mark 13:24–27). Third, the cry from the cross is answered preliminarily in his royal, Jewish burial by Joseph of Arimathea (Mark 15:42–47) and ultimately by the empty tomb (Mark 16:1–8). Regarding the surrounding context (i.e., the context of the entire book), Jesus's reference to Psalm 22:1 stands as the culmination of a long line of references to the Old Testament's Suffering Servant in Mark's gospel.[6] Most of these come from Isaiah, but in both the Psalms and Isaiah the Suffering Servant songs are intended to convey lament over present circumstances *in the context of* trust in God's covenant promises, and specifically his promise to bring Israel's new exodus *through* the Suffering Servant. In other words, in Mark, the cry of dereliction, a cry of pain, anguish, suffering, and abandonment, is couched within the self-identification of Jesus as the divine and royal Son of Man, trust in God's covenantal promises, the fulfillment of those promises in the penal substitutionary death of the Messiah, and the vindication of his death as a substitute for sinners in the temple curtain's tearing, the centurion's exclamation, Jesus's royal burial (rather than a criminal's burial) by Joseph of Arimathea, and ultimately the empty tomb.

In addition to Mark's context, we also need to pay attention to the canonical context of the four Gospels, and specifically to Jesus's other sayings from the cross. We are here not so concerned about chronological order for the seven sayings as I am about how to read them together. Jesus cries "my God, my God why have you forsaken me?" in the context of also saying, "Father, forgive them, for they know not what they do" (Luke 23:34), (to the thief) "Truly, I say to you, today you will be with me in paradise," (Luke 23:43), "Woman, behold your son. Son, behold your mother" (John 19:26–27), "I thirst" (John 19:28), "It is finished" (John 19:30), and "Father, into your hands I commend my spirit" (Luke 23:46). Notice a few things about these other sayings. First, the initial and final sayings are prayers *to the Father*. While Jesus experiences abandonment here, it is not in such a way that he believes that the Father will not hear his prayers. Second, whatever we say about abandonment needs

5. See Peter Bolt, *The Cross from a Distance: Atonement in Mark's Gospel*, NSBT 18 (Downers Grove, IL: IVP Academic, 2004), 85–115.
6. See, for example, Rikki E. Watts, *Isaiah's New Exodus in Mark*, Biblical Studies Library (Tübingen: Mohr Siebeck, 1997; repr., Grand Rapids: Baker Academic, 2000), 295–368.

to include not only Jesus's continued prayers to the Father but also his continued speech to those around the cross. He cares for his mother and friend (John 19:26–27), and he speaks to the soldiers ("I thirst"). Third, and most importantly, these other sayings indicate that Jesus's actions are intended as a propitiatory, *acceptable* sacrifice (John 19:28, 30). As the Suffering Servant, he experiences distress on the cross (John 19:28; cf. Ps. 69:21) and finishes the work needed to be done to redeem God's people (John 19:30). Therefore at death, in anticipation of the ultimate vindication of the resurrection, Jesus's righteous life and sacrificially satisfactory death will be vindicated when he enters the intermediate state in the righteous place of the dead, Paradise (Luke 23:46).

A third canonical context for the cry of dereliction is Psalm 22. While we should affirm that Jesus quotes this in a moment of intense suffering, and therefore has the abandonment mentioned in 22:1 fully in view, the NT authors (and Jesus in his ministry) often quote Scripture metaleptically.[7] That is, when they quote one verse they have the entire context of that one verse in view. Given both Mark's use of the Suffering Servant motif and the other sayings from the cross, as well as a proper understanding of the lament genre,[8] it is likely that Jesus has the entirety of Psalm 22 in view even though he only quotes verse 1. When we look at Psalm 22, we find that this righteous man who suffers unjustly is ultimately vindicated and that his feeling and experience of abandonment to death take place in the context of God's covenant faithfulness.

Finally, we need to understand that Jesus's cry of dereliction stands at the apex of the biblical story, which is Israel's story. Israel is promised exile in the Old Testament. They are told that, on the day of the Lord, God will send them out of the promised land. God departs from the temple at the beginning of Ezekiel (cf. 1:1–28; 3:12–15) in anticipation of its and Israel's destruction. In other words, exile is divine abandonment. It is judgment on sin. Israel deserves it because they have not repented and trusted in YHWH. But when we look at the narratives concerning exile, YHWH is not only the God who judges but also the God who saves. As he sends Israel's enemies to crush them and to remove them from the land, he also remains with them. He abandons Israel in 1 Samuel 5, when the ark is taken by the Philistines. But he also in that story is working on their behalf, going into exile *on their behalf* and defeating their enemies for them in the midst of that self-imposed exile by knocking over the idol of Dagon. In Ezekiel (1:1–28; 3:12–15), as he pronounces judgment on Israel by abandoning the temple, his presence goes *with Israel* into exile. Exile is real, but so is the promise of return. And

7. See, for example, Shepherd, *An Introduction to the Making and Meaning of the Bible*, 37–39.
8. Laments cry out to God about unjust, current circumstances but also remind the reader of God's past covenantal faithfulness and, therefore, express hope for future deliverance.

in God, mercy triumphs over judgment (James 2:13). Return triumphs over exile. Resurrection triumphs over death. The judgment that takes place on the cross is real, but it is judgment in a covenant context that anticipates vindication through resurrection.

Summary: The End of the Matter

None of these parameters deny penal substitution. We want to state clearly that we affirm penal substitution. Jesus bore the wrath of God that sinners deserve on the cross. But our description of how that happened—the crucifixion's metaphysical mechanics, so to speak—needs to fall within the parameters listed above.

Again, we wholeheartedly affirm penal substitution. God pours out his wrath toward sinners on Jesus at the cross. Those who repent of their sins and believe Jesus is Lord and that God raised him from the dead (Rom. 10:9) receive life instead of death because Jesus took the curse that we deserve (Gal. 3:13). Jesus became sin so that we might become the righteousness of God (2 Cor. 5:21). In all these ways we affirm penal substitution. But in describing this mystery we must ensure we do not cross the dogmatic boundaries of Nicaea and Chalcedon or, ultimately, the canonical boundaries of Holy Scripture.

REFLECTION QUESTIONS

1. How have you heard the cry of dereliction interpreted in the past? Was it connected to the doctrine of the Trinity?

2. How has understanding the doctrine of the Trinity supported, challenged, or changed your understanding of the cry of dereliction?

3. Are there lines in songs or hymns about the cross that we should change based on a better understanding of the doctrine of the Trinity?

4. What are ways that considering this issue helps your prayer life?

5. What is a passage in Scripture that has confused you but now seems clearer based on thinking through this issue?

QUESTION 35

What Is Social Trinitarianism?

As we mentioned in question 22, one of the characteristic features of the twentieth-century "revival" of Trinitarianism was the tendency to view the Trinity as a society of individuals and to tease out the social implications of such a doctrine. This chapter explores these various social Trinitarianisms in closer detail. It will seek to define precisely what is meant by social Trinitarianism, to examine some of the major proponents of these views, and to provide a biblical and theological evaluation of their strengths and weaknesses.

What Is Social Trinitarianism?

For a time in the late twentieth century, social Trinitarianism was *en vogue*. Scholars as diverse as feminist theologians and conservative evangelicals could be found defending views that fit broadly within the social Trinity scheme. In more recent years, the approach has fallen out of fashion, especially in circles that prize the theological retrieval of the church fathers. In some cases, the label can be seen as an epithet, with any whiff of social sounding themes a sure sign of heterodoxy. In such cases, the mere accusation of social Trinitarianism can sometimes be a conversatio stopper. For these reasons, it is crucially important to make clear precisely what counts as a social view of the Trinity.

As other scholars have noted, social views of the Trinity tend to include several different emphases.[1] First, and foundationally, social Trinitarians understand the divine persons as distinct centers of consciousness and will. Whereas the patristic doctrine understood these faculties as belonging to the shared, simple divine essence of the Godhead, social Trinitarians maintain that consciousness and will belong properly to persons, and since there are

1. See, for example, Karen Kilby, "Perichoresis and Projection: Problems with Social Doctrines of the Trinity," *New Blackfriars* 81 (2000): 432–45.

three persons in the Trinity, there must be three distinct psycho-volitional centers. "Person," as it is understood in social Trinitarianism, must be sufficiently similar to our common understanding of persons, understood more generically, in order for the language to be intelligible. One obvious concern for social views is the need to secure monotheism. If the divine persons are distinct in mind and will, then how can they constitute one God? Many proposals have been offered, but one common approach involves an appeal to the doctrine of *perichoresis*, the mutual indwelling of the divine persons (see question 29 for more on this maneuver).

Second, social Trinitarians have tended to seek support for their understanding of divine personhood in the Greek fathers. According to one standard story told about the patristic era (the so-called de Régnon thesis), the Latin Fathers tended to "begin" with the *oneness* of the divine essence and then to work toward securing the *threeness* represented by the divine persons, whereas the Greek fathers tended to "begin" with threeness and then work toward securing oneness.[2] Social Trinitarians have claimed to find support for their views in the writings of the latter.

Third, social Trinitarians then seek to apply this social doctrine to human social problems and concerns. Sometimes these applications have been political, with theologians seeking support in the Trinity for particular sociopolitical arrangements.[3] In other cases, the application has been ecclesial in nature, with theologians seeking to underwrite a particular church polity.[4] In still other cases, a social doctrine of the Trinity has been applied to gender relations, with some theologians using the Trinity as support for egalitarian views on gender and others arriving at opposite and more traditional views on gender.[5] Despite the diversity, social Trinitarianism tends to be marked by some combination and articulation of these three characteristics: divine persons as distinct centers of consciousness, appeal to the Greek fathers, and social applications of the doctrine.

Varieties of Social Trinitarianism

Given their diversity of perspectives, it is perhaps best to refer to *social Trinitarianisms* (plural) rather than to treat this family of approaches under a single

---

2. This perspective is referred to as the "de Régnon thesis" because of its articulation by Theodore de Régnon (1831–1893). For an evaluation of de Régnon, see Michel Barnes, "De Régnon Reconsidered," *Augustinian Studies* 26 (1995): 51–79.
3. Jürgen Moltmann, *The Trinity and the Kingdom: The Doctrine of God*, trans. Margaret Kohl (Minneapolis: Fortress, 1993).
4. John D. Zizioulas, *Being As Communion: Studies in Personhood and the Church*, Contemporary Greek Theologians Series 4 (Yonkers, NY: St Vladimir's Seminary Press, 1997).
5. For a collection of essays on these debates, see Dennis W. Jowers and H. Wayne House, eds., *The New Evangelical Subordinationism: Perspectives on the Equality of God the Father and God the Son* (Eugene, OR: Wipf & Stock, 2012).

rubric.[6] At the risk of oversimplification, we can speak of a typology of social Trinitarianisms in the following three categories: revisionist social Trinitarianism, analytic social Trinitarianism, and evangelical social Trinitarianism. The first category includes major Trinitarian thinkers in the so-called Trinitarian revival of the twentieth century, such as Jürgen Moltmann. The second category includes several prominent analytic theologians, that is, those who utilize the tools of analytic philosophy in the service of doctrinal formulation. The third category includes proponents of the eternal functional subordination (EFS) of the Son and Spirit, such as Wayne Grudem. There is certainly overlap in these categories, but they represent distinct varieties of the social approach to the doctrine of the Trinity.

Revisionist Social Trinitarianism

As we discuss in question 22, the so-called revival of Trinitarianism in the twentieth century often involved major revisions to the classical doctrine. The German Reformed theologian Jürgen Moltmann represents one influential example of this tendency. In his many writings on the subject, Moltmann expresses dissatisfaction with traditional renderings of the Trinity, especially those dependent upon the great North African bishop, Augustine of Hippo. Moltmann believes that the Augustinian appeal to human psychology as an analogy for the Trinity is particularly destructive to the development of a doctrine that is sensitive to God's actions in history. He writes, "In contrast to the psychological doctrine of the Trinity, we are therefore developing a social doctrine of the Trinity, and one based on salvation history."[7] God is to be understood not simply as one psycho-volitional subject but as a fellowship of persons in loving relationships with one another:

> The reduction of the Trinity to a single identical subject (even if the subject is a threefold one) does not do justice to the trinitarian history of God. The reduction of the persons to three modes of subsistence of the one God cannot illuminate salvation history in the fullness of God's open trinitarian relationships of fellowship.[8]

The unity of the Trinity is not secured by an appeal to the absolute unity of the divine essence or mind. What Moltmann calls the "transcendent primal ground" of salvation cannot consist "in one single, homogenous divine

6. For a contemporary evaluation of different models of the Trinity, including a variety of "social Trinitarianisms," and specifically Jenson, Moltmann, Zizioulas, and Grudem, see Thomas H. McCall, *Which Trinity? Whose Monotheism? Philosophical and Systematic Theologians on the Metaphysics of Trinitarian Theology* (Grand Rapids: Eerdmans, 2010).
7. Moltmann, *The Trinity and the Kingdom* (Minneapolis: Fortress, 1993), 158.
8. Moltmann, *The Trinity and the Kingdom*, 158.

essence (*substantia*) or in the one identical, absolute subject." Instead, it lies in "the eternal perichoresis of Father, Son, and Holy Spirit." Salvation history, Moltmann argues, is "the love story of the God whose very life is the eternal process of engendering, responding and blissful love." So, the Trinity does not correspond "to the solitary human subject in his relationship to himself" (as in Augustine's psychological analogies) but to "a human fellowship of people without privileges and without subordinances."[9] This social application of the doctrine would be taken up by several liberation theologians in the twentieth century to underwrite a particular sociopolitical program.[10]

Moltmann also takes up Rahner's thesis that there is no final distinction between the immanent and the economic Trinity (see question 25), and he sees the cross of Christ as the fundamental expression of this identity. God suffers on the cross precisely as God, indeed, as the triune God: "The Father delivered up the Son for us through the Spirit."[11] Only by defining the persons as distinct centers of consciousness can we make sense of the love expressed on the cross. Only a social doctrine of the Trinity properly attends to salvation history and thus provides a Trinitarian ground for human community as well.

Analytic Social Trinitarianism

The emerging discipline of analytic theology seeks to bring the tools and sensibilities of analytic philosophy to bear on the development of Christian doctrine. The field is not uniform in its theological commitments or in its assessment to the weight of traditional doctrinal formulations. We would not want to suggest that all or even most analytic theologians operate from a social view of the Trinity. But there have been some prominent analytic theologians who do, which has sparked intense debates in the field. One such proponent of what we are calling analytic social Trinitarianism is Cornelius Plantinga. Plantinga understands the core of social Trinitarianism to be a commitment to the notion that the Father, Son, and Spirit are "distinct centers of consciousness."[12] He recognizes that this understanding of the divine persons raises monotheistic concerns, and he seeks to ward off the tritheism charge, once again, by appeal to a particular understanding of perichoresis.

9. Moltmann, *The Trinity and the Kingdom*, 158.
10. See, for example, this collection of essays, which features contributions from liberation, black liberation, and feminist theologians: Miroslav Volf, Carmen Krieg, Thomas Kucharz, eds., *The Future of Theology: Essays in Honor of Jürgen Moltmann* (Grand Rapids: Eerdmans, 1996).
11. Moltmann, *The Trinity and the Kingdom*, 160.
12. Cornelius Plantinga Jr., "Social Trinity and Tritheism," in *Trinity, Incarnation, and Atonement: Philosophical and Theological Essays*, ed. Ronald J. Feenstra and Cornelius Plantinga Jr. (Notre Dame, IN: University of Notre Dame Press, 1989), 22.

The divine persons' knowledge and love are directed toward one another in such an intimate way that it yields a "zestful community of divine light, love, joy, mutuality, and verve."[13] Plantinga makes a distinction between the generic essence of divinity, which all three divine persons share equally, and the personal essence of each person, which renders them truly distinct psycho-volitional agents.[14] He believes that the tritheism charge would only stick if social Trinitarianism was suggesting something like Arianism, which distinguishes the persons as "ontologically graded distinct persons."[15] But since the persons are equal as regards their generic divine essence, Plantinga believes social Trinitarianism can successfully defend its orthodox bona fides.

Other analytic theologians such as Richard Swinburne, William Lane Craig and J. P. Moreland, and Stephen T. Davis have also defended versions of social Trinitarianism.[16] Though we lack space to fully engage their various proposals, we note that analytic approaches to social Trinitarianism explore the logical possibilities of how three centers of consciousness can still constitute one God. Brian Leftow, an analytic critic of social Trinitarianism, suggests that there are three broad possibilities in this connection.[17] Functional monotheism understands the persons' unity in terms of their unfailing harmony of intention and action; group-mind monotheism suggests that the three divine minds somehow "emerge" into one divine mind; and Trinity monotheism maintains that only the Trinity as a whole, composed of three mutually indwelling centers of consciousness, is the proper referent for the name "God." Leftow rightly discerns the problem that attends all of these approaches: Only with great difficulty can they be said to constitute monotheism as it has traditionally been understood. Functional monotheism is perhaps the most obviously tritheistic approach. Three divine individuals who infallibly cooperate with one another remain three divine individuals. Even if one appeals to the doctrine of perichoresis (mutual indwelling), the problem remains. Three harmonious divine entities would still be three gods. In any event, perichoresis is not a stand-alone doctrine. It is rooted in a more basic theological category: the *homoousion*. The three persons interpenetrate one another because they share (or, more properly, are) the very same God, the same essence (see question 30). Group-mind

13. Plantinga, "Social Trinity and Tritheism," 28.
14. Plantinga, "Social Trinity and Tritheism," 29.
15. Plantinga, "Social Trinity and Tritheism," 34.
16. Richard Swinburne, *The Christian God* (Oxford: Oxford University Press, 1994), 170–91; J. P. Moreland and William Lane Craig, *Philosophical Foundations for a Christian Worldview* (Downers Grove, IL: IVP Academic, 2003), 575–96; Stephen T. Davis and Eric T. Yang, "Social Trinitarianism Unscathed," *Journal of Analytic Theology* 5 (2017): 220–29.
17. See Brian Leftow, "Anti Social Trinitarianism," in *Philosophical and Theological Essays on the Trinity*, ed. Thomas McCall and Michael C. Rea (Oxford: Oxford University Press, 2009), 52–88.

monotheism fails because it seems to suggest that there is a fourth entity in the Trinity, namely, the shared mind of the three persons. Leftow believes that Trinity monotheism stands the best chance to avert the tritheistic charge, but it can only achieve this benefit at great cost: If only the Trinity as a whole is to be identified as "God," then it seems that we cannot say of any of the divine persons, "This divine person is God." If we are prevented, for example, from affirming that the Son is God (or the Father or the Holy Spirit), then such a maneuver would seem too high a price to pay. The debate among analytic theologians continues, but social Trinitarians of this stripe seem to need a more robust way to affirm one of the basic commitments of historic Trinitarianism: that there is only one God.

Evangelical Social Trinitarianism

The final form of social Trinitarianism is expressed in the view, held among many evangelicals, known as eternal relations of authority and submission (ERAS) or eternal functional subordination (EFS). We discussed this position in detail in question 33, so our comments here will be brief. Evangelical theologians such as Wayne Grudem and Bruce Ware have developed an understanding of the Trinity that makes a distinction between ontological equality and functional submission in the Godhead. These categories apply not only in the economy of salvation but also in eternity past and eternity future. Indeed, in certain iterations of this approach, the divine persons are distinguished precisely by these relations of authority and submission. Sometimes proponents of this approach have even undermined or questioned the traditional way of distinguishing the divine persons, namely, the eternal relations of origin.[18]

Proponents of ERAS see this approach as providing a helpful analogy for complementarian gender roles: Just as the Father and Son are ontologically equal but functionally distinct (the Son submits the Father precisely as the Son), so also men and women are ontologically equal, even as women are called to submit to men in the church, the home, and society at large. While we agree that a biblical case can be made for male leadership in the home and the church, we believe that appealing to the Trinitarian relations as an analogy for this complementarian viewpoint is a category error. In any event, it

18. See appendix 6 in Wayne Grudem, *Systematic Theology: An Introduction to Biblical Doctrine* (Grand Rapids: Zondervan, 1994), 1234; and Bruce A. Ware, *Father, Son, and Holy Spirit: Relationships, Roles, Relevance* (Wheaton, IL: Crossway, 2005), 162 n. 3. Grudem's appendix does not appear in the second edition, and he addresses the doctrine in greater detail (293–98) than in the first edition. Notably, though, he also retains a sense of ambiguity about what exactly the doctrine affirms (298) and continues to insist on the eternal functional subordination of the Son (301–18). Both Grudem and Ware in late 2016 affirmed more openly and clearly the eternal relations of origin, but both have also reestablished their commitment to ERAS.

seems that ERAS amounts to another version of social Trinitarianism. If the Son eternally submits to the Father and the Holy Spirit eternally submits to the Father and Son, then it would seem to require a view of the divine persons as distinct centers of consciousness and will. Submission involves one will being voluntarily subjected to another. Even though this view is put to very different purposes than, say, Moltmann's social Trinitarianism, the views have this much in common: The divine persons are distinguished by mind and will rather than by relations of origin. In the traditional understanding of God's personal names, Father and Son connote paternity and filiation (that is, the eternal generation of the Son from the unbegotten Father), but in the ERAS understanding, these names connote authority and submission.

Evaluation

While we find social Trinitarianism ultimately unsatisfying from the perspective of historic Christian orthodoxy, there are several praiseworthy motivations behind these various social views of the Trinity. First, there is the admirable desire to avoid a Sabellian or modalistic understanding of the Trinity. The divine persons are truly distinct, not only in the economy of salvation but also in God's own inner life. One of the potential dangers of maintaining a numerically singular mind and will in God is a failure to account for these real distinctions. We believe that such distinctions are maintained more faithfully by means of traditional categories (eternal relations of origin, modes of subsistence), but all Trinitarians should take with utmost seriousness the theological desideratum of securing real distinctions between the eternal divine persons.

Second, and related, social Trinitarians are right to highlight the need to secure real relations of love between the divine persons. As Thomas McCall has pointed out, if theologians need to diminish or even deny the reality of intra-Trinitarian love, then something in the formulation has seriously misfired.[19] In any event, the very theologians who have espoused a single mind and will in the Godhead have happily affirmed the mutual love of the divine persons.

Third, social Trinitarianism is partially right to underscore the relevance of the doctrine of the Trinity for human relationships. We would simply suggest that the relevance is more global than local. The doctrine of the Trinity provides the transcendental preconditions for a universe characterized by relationality, personhood, and love. This is especially germane for angelic and human persons, who participate analogously in the personhood of the divine persons, with redeemed humanity being enveloped in the very love of the Holy Trinity (e.g., John 17). The application of the Trinity to specific social

19. Thomas McCall, "What's Not to Love? Appeals to Tradition in Contemporary Debates in Trinitarian Theology," *IJST* 25 (2023): 610–30.

arrangements—be they social, ecclesial, or familial—is a more precarious maneuver, given the *sui generis* nature of divine personhood. Humans are made in the divine image, to be sure, but not everything that obtains in human relationships is true of the intra-Trinitarian relations. Some opponents of social Trinitarianism may appear to stress the discontinuity too much. Steve Holmes, for example, provocatively states that the doctrine of the Trinity is, properly speaking, "useless."[20] But what Holmes has in mind is the proper end of Trinitarian theology. The Trinity is not a means to some other end (specially a social end) but is an end in itself—indeed, contemplating the unique and all-glorious Trinity is *the* end of human existence. Still, the Trinity does provide the ultimate ground of human relationality and love and may be said to serve as an analogous pattern for certain aspects of our relationship to God and others.

Despite these praiseworthy motivations, the various versions of social Trinitarianism all suffer from several fatal weaknesses as comprehensive models for the Holy Trinity. First, they tend to equivocate on the theological terms that comprise the traditional doctrine of the Trinity. In other words, they tend to import modern definitions of terms like "person" and "relation" into the traditional formulae. Person is understood in a modern psychological sense, as a distinct center of consciousness and will rather than in its creedal and conciliar sense as mode of subsistence. Relation is understood similarly as a relationship of minds or (in the case of EFS) as a relationship of volitional submission rather than in its traditional sense as a relation of origin.

Second, social Trinitarianisms tend to misread the patristic literature. The older de Régnon thesis has fallen out of fashion as scholars of early Christianity have examined the evidence with more scrutiny. While there were some interesting divergences between the Greek and Latin fathers (mainly tied to the question of whether or not the divine essence could be construed as a universal in the classical sense and, eventually, related to the question of the *filioque*), these differences do not map onto the contemporary debate over social Trinitarianism. Gregory of Nyssa could use three individual men, each participating in human nature, as an analogy for the Trinity (see question 16), but he did not utilize this analogy as a metaphysical model of the Trinity. The Cappadocian Fathers were as committed to a numerically singular divine mind and will as Augustine. Likewise, Augustine and other Latin fathers were as committed to real and eternal distinctions between the divine persons as were their Greek counterparts. The two are so similar that Stephen Holmes

---

20. Stephen Holmes, "Classical Trinity: Evangelical Perspective," in *Two Views on the Doctrine of the Trinity*, ed. Jason S. Sexton (Grand Rapids: Zondervan Academic, 2014), 47.

can suggest that Augustine was himself "the most capable interpreter of Cappadocian Trinitarianism."[21]

Perhaps the most persistent criticism of social Trinitarianisms relates to the difficulty of securing monotheism. If the divine persons are distinct psycho-volitional subjects or agents, relating to one another by mutual submission or else in a hierarchy of authority and submission, then how do they constitute one God? Leftow's analysis of the problem remains one of the most penetrating. Each of the possible solutions to the problem has its difficulties. In any event, more traditional formulations are better suited to secure both essential oneness (including psychological and volitional oneness) and relational threeness (where the relations are defined in terms of modes of being or relations of origin).

A final caution concerns the problems of "using" the Trinity. Again, Holmes has suggested that the doctrine of the Trinity is properly useless: It is not a means to some other end—whether social or otherwise—but is an end in itself. Karen Kilby has likewise warned against developing a social program based on a Trinitarian blueprint by appeal to the doctrine's incomprehensibility.[22] We might also appeal to Augustine's distinction between enjoyment and use: Created things are to be used, but God alone is to be enjoyed for his own sake. While the doctrine of the Trinity has application to our lives (see question 40), we must exercise great caution when appealing to the doctrine as justification for some other precommitment. The fact that the applications have been so varied (and contradictory) only underscores this caution.

Summary

Social Trinitarianism describes a family of views that are characterized by several elements: a tendency to view the divine persons as distinct centers of consciousness and will, an appeal to the Greek fathers as supposed proponents of this view, and the application of the doctrine of the Trinity to social concerns (whether ecclesiastical, political, marital, or otherwise). Some social views are more radical than others, but they are all bound together by these tendencies. While some Greek fathers did analogize the Trinity with reference to three human persons, they were all careful to affirm the unity of the divine mind and will. Therefore, social views run counter to the broad Trinitarian consensus that emerged in the late fourth century among both Greek and Latin theologians.

---

21. Stephen R. Holmes, *The Quest for the Trinity: The Doctrine of God in Scripture, History, and Modernity* (Downers Grove, IL: IVP Academic, 2012), 146. Also on this page, Holmes summarizes under seven headings the consensus reached by Eastern and Western fathers.
22. Karen Kilby, "Is an Apophatic Trinitarianism Possible?," *IJST* 12, no. 1 (2010): 65–77.

REFLECTION QUESTIONS

1. What are the hallmarks of social Trinitarianism?

2. What are the different varieties and proponents of this view?

3. What are some of the problems associated with social Trinitarianism?

4. If the divine persons are not distinct minds and wills, how can we affirm that they love one another from all eternity?

5. How might a more traditional articulation of the doctrine answer this question?

QUESTION 36

Are There Any Helpful Analogies for the Doctrine of the Trinity?

The doctrine of the Trinity can be taxing on the limits of human understanding. As the church has sought to interpret and synthesize the biblical teaching on the Trinity and to defend it against error, it has found the need to use technical vocabulary: essence, person, missions, processions, inseparable operations, perichoresis, appropriation, and so on. Even if we restrict ourselves to the biblical language, many paradoxes emerge. How can God be one (as both the Old and New Testaments consistently maintain) and yet each of the divine persons—Father, Son, and Holy Spirit—be equally and eternally God? How can the Son be one with the Father and yet eternally generated from him? How can the Spirit be identified as the same Lord and yet eternally proceed, or come forth, from the Father and Son? Despite the difficulty, the doctrine of the Trinity simply cannot be shelved as an interesting but ultimately unknowable theological truth that is best left to the experts. The doctrine is too important to Christian faith and practice. The Trinity is not graduate-level Christianity; it is Christianity 101. We begin our Christian pilgrimage by being immersed into the triune name (Matt. 28:19). We continue in the journey by being assured of the Trinity's saving work (Eph. 1:3–14) and by walking in a manner of our calling by one Spirit, one Lord, and one God and Father of all (Eph. 4:1–6). And we find our journey's end in the bliss of eternal life, which is to know the one true God and Jesus Christ whom he has sent through the work of the Helper who is sent from them both (John 15:26; 17:3). As one author put it, those who advance most in the Christian life are those who never leave the beginning: our baptism in the triune name.[1]

In order to explain this mystery, many well-meaning preachers, teachers,

1. Ben Myers, *The Apostles' Creed: A Guide to the Ancient Catechism* (Bellingham, WA: Lexham, 2018).

and parents have sought out analogies as a teaching tool. Is God like the water molecule, which can be present in three different states: liquid, vapor, and solid? Or like an egg, which is one thing with three different parts: the shell, the white, and the yolk? All analogies break down, and some analogies do more harm than good by yielding, however unintentionally, heretical conclusions. But if we cannot make use of analogies, how then should we teach the doctrine of the Trinity? In this chapter we will examine the limits of Trinitarian analogies, and in question 39 we explore more fruitful means of teaching this most foundational Christian doctrine.

Historic Trinitarian Analogies

As we stated above, many turn to analogies in order to explain the doctrine of the Trinity. Some analogies are better than others in explaining certain aspects of the doctrine, if not the doctrine as a whole. For example, some of the church fathers used the analogy of the sun and its light in order to explain how the Father is never without his Son. In this vein, Athanasius writes,

> So again we see that the radiance from the sun is proper to it, and the sun's essence is not divided or impaired; but its essence is whole and its radiance perfect and whole, yet without impairing the essence of light, but as a true offspring from it. We understand in like manner that the Son is begotten not from without but from the Father, and while the Father remains whole, the Expression of His Subsistence is ever, and preserves the Father's likeness and unvarying Image, so that he who sees Him, sees in Him the Subsistence too, of which He is the Expression.[2]

Athanasius opposes here the Arian notion that the Son's generation entails his creation. If the Son is eternally generated from the Father, then would this imply that the Father's essence was somehow divided or partitioned in order to produce the Son? Athanasius appeals to the sun and its radiance as an analogy. It is of the essence of the sun to produce light, and this is in no way divides the essence of the sun; rather, the essence of the sun is preserved whole and intact in the radiance such that one who sees the light of the sun sees the sun itself. In a similar manner, the one who sees the Son sees the Father from whom he is generated. We might extend the analogy to the Holy Spirit as well, if we consider that the sun's essence is also expressed in its heat. The analogy, of course, can be pressed too far, especially if used to subordinate the Son and Spirit to the Father. Still, the analogy gives us a way of conceiving

2. Athanasius, *Four Discourses against the Arians*, 2.33 (*NPNF*[2] 4:366).

the coeternality of the three persons. Something like this analogy is even expressed in the creedal line: "light from light."

Another analogy comes from Gregory of Nyssa in his important treatise, *On "Not Three Gods."*[3] Here Gregory compares the three persons of the Trinity to three human persons, who each share in the essence of humanity. The kind of essence that three human beings share is the same, but they each represent a distinct instantiation of that essence. But again, the analogy is imperfect, which Gregory readily admits (his book is, after all, seeking to demonstrate that Christians do *not* believe in three gods). The analogy to three humans breaks down because God is not, strictly speaking, one of a *kind*. The being of God is not a *kind essence* that is capable of multiple instantiations. The being of God is simply and essentially one. Three human persons share a common kind (human nature), but they do not share a common being, or substance. The three divine persons, on the other hand, share the identically same divine nature; they each are the very same being.

As we saw in our chapter on Augustine, the great North African theologian sees the image of God in man as the best place to search for a meaningful Trinitarian analogy. In his influential work *De Trinitate*, Augustine develops a series of so-called psychological analogies in order to contemplate the Holy Trinity.[4] As memory/understanding and will/love emanate from mind, so too the Son and Spirit proceed from the Father. Thomas Aquinas, Jonathan Edwards, and others follow Augustine in developing these analogies from human psychology. Augustine's analogies have the advantage of following key biblical themes. The Son is, after all, referred to in the New Testament as the Word and Wisdom of the Father. The Spirit is also closely associated with the themes of love and gift that Augustine sees entailed in the human will. But psychological analogies also break down because they are drawn from a single person, namely, a human person. Memory and will can be distinguished from mind in an individual human, but they do not constitute distinct persons. Like the sun/light/heat analogy, the psychological analogy when taken to the extreme can yield a modalistic picture of the triune God.

Popular Trinitarian Analogies

In addition to these historic analogies, Christian teachers are sometimes drawn to other, more popular analogies like the ones mentioned in the introduction to this chapter. The commonplace water analogy seems straightforwardly modalistic. Water can exist in the three states of matter under different conditions, but it is not so at the same time and under the same conditions. Indeed, most of the popular analogies tend toward modalism. Some sug-

---

3. Gregory of Nyssa, *On "Not Three Gods"* (*NPNF*[2]/5:333–36).
4. Augustine, *The Trinity*, 2nd ed., trans. Edmund Hill, ed. John Rotelle, The Works of Saint Augustine 5 (Hyde Park, NY: New City, 2012).

gest that the Trinity is like different roles that a person can have: a mother, a daughter, and a sister. But these roles describe the contingent relations of a single person, not really existing "relations of opposition" (to use Thomas Aquinas's term) that obtain eternally between the three divine persons. Other analogies reduce Father, Son, and Holy Spirit to three *parts* of a whole rather than three *persons* in the Godhead. The parts of an egg or an apple or the three leaves on a clover fall into this error. But if the divine persons are each simply a part of a larger whole that is God, then it turns out none of them is truly and fully God in himself.

Summary

In short, even the best analogies on offer in the history of doctrine break down in some important ways, and the popular contemporary analogies tend in a more obviously heretical direction. In our teaching on the doctrine of the Trinity, we often point out the deficiencies of these analogies to the Trinity. The obvious question that most students ask then ask is, how then do you explain the doctrine of the Trinity, especially to new believers, inquirers, or even to children? The next chapter explores some ways to introduce the doctrine of the Trinity in our preaching and teaching.

REFLECTION QUESTIONS

1. What analogies of the Trinity have you heard or used?
2. How do these analogies break down? What are the dangers in using those analogies in terms of heresies they might imply?
3. What are other, simple ways to explain the Trinity besides the use of analogies?
4. How do popular Christian songs and writings form our thinking about this question?
5. What are ways that considering this issue helps your prayer life?

QUESTION 37

Is the Doctrine of the Trinity Logically Coherent?

As we discussed in question 3 on theological method, reason is one of the four sides of the so-called Wesleyan Quadrilateral, which can help to guide an evangelical approach to theology. Scripture has pride of place as the sole, inspired and inerrant, written revelation of God. But tradition, reason, and experience function as guides to interpreting the Bible. "Reason" in this methodology encapsulates several different things. It can refer to philosophy more generally as the "handmaiden" of theology. Philosophy has a ministerial role in the theological task, not a magisterial one: it is the servant, not the master. All of the tools of philosophy are at the disposal of the theologian, whether they be metaphysical, epistemological, ethical, or aesthetic.. But one principle undergirding all of philosophy—indeed, all of human thought and communication—is logic itself. Theological formulation must be logical. Logic is a kind of negative test for the truth of a theological proposition. Logical coherence does not necessarily prove the truth of a particular doctrinal claim, but logical incoherence would certainly count against it. In this chapter, we will discuss what logic is, its basis in God's mind, and its application to the doctrine of the Trinity.

What Is Logic?

In simple terms, logic is concerned with the structure and principles of reason (*logikē*, "reason," from *logos*, "word/reason"). It especially deals with the criteria of inference in rational argumentation. Logic often takes the form of syllogisms: structured arguments that deduce a particular conclusion from two or more premises. Validity and soundness represent two tests for such syllogisms. An argument is valid if the conclusion follows necessarily from the premises. The argument is sound if it is valid and if its premises are true. Consider a standard example:

Major premise: All bachelors are unmarried.
Minor premise: Johnny is a bachelor.
Conclusion: Therefore, Johnny is unmarried.

This is an example of what is known as a categorical syllogism. It contains three categorical statements: All *A*s are *B*. *C* is an *A*. Therefore *C* is a *B*. In this case, the logic is valid. If the two premises are true, then the conclusion necessarily follows. As for the truth of the premises, the major premise is analytically true; it is true by definition. Suppose you know Johnny, and you know for a fact that the minor premise is also true: He is indeed a bachelor. Since the inference is valid and the premises are true, the syllogism is not only *valid* but also logically *sound*. But as a counter factual, suppose you know for a fact that Johnny is not a bachelor. Suppose he secretly eloped. In this case, the syllogism would still be valid: If the premises were true, the conclusion would necessarily follow. But since the minor premise is in fact false, the argument fails the test of logical soundness. These kinds of logical tests, though not always formalized in this way, are indispensable for all rational thought.

One of the foundational principles of logic is the law of noncontradiction. One common way of expressing the law of noncontradiction goes something like this: "A thing cannot be both *A* and not-*A* at the same time and in the same way." Something cannot be both true and not true at the same time and in the same respect. The computer I am using to type these words cannot both exist and not exist at the same time and under the same circumstances. Without this law no meaningful knowledge or communication could take place. One way to see readily why the law of noncontradiction is so nonnegotiable for rational thought and argumentation is to consider how one might go about denying the law. Try to disprove or even to disavow the law of noncontradiction without assuming the law itself. The statement, "The law of noncontradiction is false," would be meaningless were it not for the law of noncontradiction itself. Otherwise, the words of the sentence could just as easily be taken to mean that the law of noncontradiction is true. Thus, any arguments one could marshal against the law would be self-defeating.

We belabor these perhaps obvious points because many Christians seem to have the mistaken notion that logic is simply a human construct and that God himself somehow transcends logic. Some are willing to grant that the Trinity is illogical because God does not have to answer to logic. Logic is simply a human way of thinking, but God's thoughts are not our thoughts and his ways not our ways (Isa. 55:9). We will address the grounding of logic in the intellect of God below, but for now it is sufficient to note that the laws of logic are entailed by a commitment to truth. If we lose logic, we lose the very idea of absolute truth. The contrast between truth and falsity depends upon the distinction between the two and therefore depends upon the laws of logic. So, while it may seem pious to argue that God is so transcendent that he can be or do the illogical, such a move actually gives away something essential: the very truth of God.

What Is the Grounding of Logic?

In one of his Socratic dialogues, the *Euthyphro*, Plato poses an important and perennial question about the nature of moral absolutes: Is something pious because the gods love it? Or do the gods love it because it is pious? In other words, is the *Good* good in itself or is it constituted as good because the gods simply deem it to be so? Is goodness an objective moral norm that even the Greek gods must answer to? Or is it simply a description of the arbitrary whims of the gods themselves? If we were to transpose this so-called Euthyphro Problem to a Christian key, we might ask something similar: Is something good because God wills it to be so? Or does God will it to be so because it is intrinsically good? Some in the history of Christian thought have wished to say that God's will simply determines the good. This position is known as voluntarism (Latin, *voluntas*: will). But most in Christian theology have wished to accept neither horn of the dilemma. Goodness is not arbitrarily chosen by God's raw will, but neither is it some standard outside of God to which even God must answer. Instead, goodness simply is an attribute or property of the simple essence of God. God *is* good and therefore *does* good (cf. Ps. 119:68). This position has been called intellectualism (Latin, *intellectus*: understanding) because it maintains that God's mind (which is to say, his nature) determines what God wills.

What we would say about piety or goodness, we would say about all of the divine perfections and is, thus, related to our consideration about logic. The laws of logic (which, again, are entailed in a commitment to divine truth) are grounded ultimately in God's mind, not the creature's mind. When we think logically, we are thinking God's thoughts after him, to use a familiar phrase. That is not to say that human logic never makes mistakes. Because of our finitude and our fallenness, it often does. Nor is it to espouse a univocal understanding of divine predication. We would argue instead for an analogical understanding of our language about God: It is neither exactly the same as creaturely predication (univocity) nor entirely different (equivocity) but sufficiently similar (analogy). Still, if a theological proposition can be clearly demonstrated to entail a logical contradiction, that proposition would be for that very reason untrue. Why? Because God must answer to human logic? Not at all. But rather because God's self-communication to the creature's created, fallen, and redeemed intellect is true and therefore logically coherent. In short, logic itself is grounded in God.

The Trinity and Logic

So, is the Trinity logically coherent? To put the question more pointedly: Does the doctrine of the Trinity violate the law of noncontradiction? The short answer (and one that is fairly easy to demonstrate) is no. A thing cannot be both A and not-A at the same time and in the same way. But the doctrine of the Trinity never makes such an illogical claim. The doctrine of the Trinity, as we have seen, states that God is one in *essence* and three in *persons*. The doctrine does not state that God is one in *A* and three in *A*. But rather that God is one in *A* and three in *B*. Father, Son, and Holy Spirit are identical with regard to *essence* or *being* but really and eternally distinct with regard to *person* or *relation*. The Trinitarian categories developed as they did precisely in order to avoid saying something incoherent (and unbiblical!) about the oneness and threeness of God.

Summary

Let us return to the hesitancy mentioned above, namely, the unease about requiring Christian doctrine to be logically coherent. Perhaps we can allay this fear by making a distinction between illogic and mystery. A doctrine can be mysterious and still logically coherent. Francis Turretin argued that there are two fundamental but difficult questions at the heart of the Christian religion: the union of three persons in the one divine essence and the union of two natures in the person of Christ.[1] But neither of these doctrines entails anything logically incoherent. The two doctrines can be stated propositionally in ways that are logically defensible, but that is a fairly low bar epistemically. And the profundity of the mystery far exceeds the meager test of logical coherence. God remains incomprehensible, even effable and veiled from our sight. But who he is and what he reveals could no more entail logical contradiction and error or falsity.

REFLECTION QUESTIONS

1. Can God do the logically impossible?
2. Can theological truths be logically incoherent?
3. What is God's relationship to logic?
4. Why is it important to state Christian doctrine in logically coherent ways?
5. How can we defend the doctrine of the Trinity against the charge of logical contradiction?

---

1. Francis Turretin, *Institutes of Elenctic Theology*, 3 vols., trans. George Musgrave Giger, ed. James T. Dennison Jr. (Phillipsburg, NJ: P&R), 2:310.

QUESTION 38

How Does the Doctrine of the Trinity Relate to Other Doctrines?

As we've said since the beginning of the book, the doctrine of the Trinity is often seen by Christians as a kind of theological check mark—it matters that you have the box checked in order to be considered a Christian, but not for much else. For those who view Trinitarian doctrine this way, there doesn't seem to be much relation at all between one of the fundamental beliefs of the Christian faith and the rest of our core confessions. We might call this a minimalist approach to the question of this chapter.

For others, though, because the Trinity is the *sine qua non* of the Christian faith, it can and must be related in very specific ways to other doctrines. If you search "Trinitarian" on Amazon or in your library, you'll find "Trinitarian" approaches to almost every other Christian doctrine: anthropology, ecclesiology, creation, and the like. There tends to be a common theme among these approaches: They emphasize the relational and communal aspects of the doctrine of the Trinity. That is, because we can say—in some sense—that the Trinity is a divine community, or a relation between three distinct persons, we can therefore approach other doctrines from this relational or communal distinctive. To put it a bit differently, for this approach the doctrine of the Trinity is like a lens through which we see all other doctrines. We might call this a maximalist approach to this chapter's question.

We would like to present a different approach here.[1] In contrast to the minimalists, the doctrine of the Trinity matters for our daily lives because it is in the Holy Trinity that we live and move and have our being through the finished work of God the Son incarnate. It also matters for every other Christian doctrine that we confess and articulate. In contrast to the maximalists,

1. What follows has much in common with Fred Sanders's articulation in *Fountain of Salvation: Trinity and Soteriology* (Grand Rapids: Eerdmans, 2022), 11–31.

though, the doctrine of the Trinity, and especially the communal and relational aspects, do not map one to one onto any creaturely reality. In the end, the doctrine of the Trinity, and the one God who exists in three persons whom that doctrine attempts to describe, is a mystery. It is a mystery revealed in Scripture, and a coherent mystery, but a mystery nonetheless. There is nothing in all of creation that provides an exhaustive analogy to this reality that God is one in essence and three in persons. Even the analogies that we can give regarding *how* those persons relate, like the eternal relations of origin, are only stammering attempts by creatures to talk about our great God. They can only get us so far before we have to stop and acknowledge the limits of our creaturely minds and language.[2] Applying the communal and relational aspect of the doctrine of the Trinity to other doctrines, and especially in a way that does not sufficiently acknowledge this distinction between Creator and creature, seems to us to be an approach that is methodologically suspect.

The Trinitarian Shape of Christian Doctrine

Rather than there being some aspect of doctrine of the Trinity that we need to map onto every other Christian doctrine, such as "community," we suggest that there is a Trinitarian shape to every doctrine. Following along the lines of Trinitarian *taxis*, this approach notes that every *locus* of Christian theology is ultimately from the Father, through the Son, and by the Holy Spirit. As we saw in the chapter on the divine missions, this *taxis* of God's economic acts of creation and redemption is fitting given the eternal relations of origin (see question 30). Put another way, God's inner life—the eternal relations of origin—is reflected in his external works of creation and redemption. Theology as a discipline is the attempt to speak appropriately—that is, in a way that accurately reflects patterns of biblical language—about these external works of God. Thus, the shape of theology, the order of reflection, ought to reflect this order in God's life.

What does this mean for theological method, for articulating particular doctrines? It means that each theological *locus* ought to be articulated and organized according to this *taxis*. So, for instance, with respect to the doctrine of creation, we ought to show how creation is from the Father, through the Son, and by the Spirit. This is true both in terms of the *act* of creation and with respect to the *shape* or *order* of creation. For the first, God's act of creation is according to this *taxis*, such that the Father speaks his Word (the Son) in creating and his Spirit is the agent of that creation (e.g., he "hovered over the waters," Gen. 1:2).

2. E.g., Gregory of Nazianzus, "Oration 28: On the Doctrine of God," in *On God and Christ: The Five Theological Orations and Two Letters to Cledonius*, trans. Lionel Wickham, PPS 23 (Crestwood, NY: St Vladimir's Seminary Press, 2002), 37–67.

The shape or order of creation itself is again from the Father, through the Son, and by the Spirit. The statement that creation is "through the Son" is important here and reflects, for instance, Colossians 1:15–17:

> He is the image of the invisible God, the firstborn of all creation. For by him all things were created, in heaven and on earth, visible and invisible, whether thrones or dominions or rulers or authorities—all things were created through him and for him. And he is before all things, and in him all things hold together.

Not only is the Son the agent (along with the Father and Spirit) of creation—"*by* him all things were created"—but he is also the pattern and the *telos*, or goal, of creation—"all things were created *through* him and *for* him." Creation is patterned after God's Wisdom, his Son (Prov. 8:22–31), and its purpose is to reflect the Son. We see this preeminently in the fact that the pinnacle of creation, humanity, made in God's image, is designed to be conformed into the image of the Image of God, God the Son incarnate, Jesus Christ (Rom. 8:28–29; Heb. 1:1–3). Further, this transformation from one degree of glory to another (2 Cor. 3:17–18) is primarily cross-shaped. Cruciformity, the way of the cross, is the way of transformation into Christ's image (Rev. 12:7–18).

We could show this Christ-centered and cross-centered pattern along the same kinds of lines with every other dogmatic *locus*. Justification is centered on the atoning work of the Word incarnate, as is sanctification. Ecclesiology is the study of the people of God, bought through the blood of the Paschal Lamb who is also their Head and King, the Lion of the tribe of Judah. Eschatology is the declaration that the end of God's creating and saving purposes are found in the person and work of Jesus at his first and second coming.

Before we move on to other aspects of the way that the doctrine of the Trinity intersects with other doctrines, we should be clear that this Son-shaped approach is not an attempt to ignore the Father or the Spirit or to overemphasize Jesus at their expense. Instead, and again, it is simply a reflection of Trinitarian *taxis*—we know the Father through seeing the incarnate, crucified-and-risen Son who is revealed to us by the Spirit (e.g., John 14–17). And God reveals himself in this way because it reflects who he is in himself—one God in three persons, coexisting and coeternal, distinct from one another not in essence but in eternal relations of origin, the Father eternally unbegotten, the Son—Image, Word, Wisdom—eternally begotten of the Father, and the Spirit eternally proceeding from the Father and the Son. Thus, the economic missions—who God reveals himself to be in what he does for us—and the dogmatic loci that we articulate about those missions always lead us back to the eternal relations of origin, who God is in himself.

The Trinity and Inseparable Operations

A related way that the doctrine of the Trinity intersects with other doctrines is in acknowledgement of inseparable operations and appropriation (see questions 31 and 32). Every doctrine has a Trinitarian shape because every act in creation and redemption is brought about through the one triune God. There is no divine action, and thus no doctrine, that is performed by only one or two of the divine persons alone.

We often think of divine actions in this disjointed way, though. Take the cross, for example; I (Matt) often ask my students if they think the Holy Spirit was taking a coffee break while the Father and the Son hashed it out on Good Friday. This is a little facetious, and perhaps even a little sacrilegious, but the point is that we often think about divine actions as only being performed by one or maybe two of the divine persons while the others are off doing . . . what? Twiddling their (nonexistent) thumbs? Instead of this model of divine action, we need to remember that every act of God is inseparable; each action of God is performed by *God*, the triune God: Father, Son, and Holy Spirit.

Of course, we need to also remember the doctrine of appropriations here. It is right and biblical to appropriate particular divine actions to particular divine persons. Scripture does this, and so should we. But it is never done in Scripture and should thus never be done by us in such a fashion that the divine persons are separated by distinct individual actions. No, there is only one God, inseparably triune, and so there are only inseparably triune divine actions.

The Trinity and Christology

This inseparable Trinitarian shape is true of every doctrine, but the doctrine of the Trinity intersects in particular with Christology. In fact, these doctrines impact each other in such profound ways that it is difficult to speak of one without speaking of the other. In particular, the issue of God's essence in relation to the person of Jesus is of prime importance. This is true in at least two ways.

First, when we confess that Jesus is "true God and true man," we are saying that he is both 100 percent God and 100 percent man. The second part of that equation is pretty easy to articulate (although there are heretical pitfalls there, too!). It is the "100 percent God" part that is crucial to both doctrines. If Jesus isn't fully God, then suddenly the doctrine of the Trinity falls apart, because there would be no Trinity without three fully divine persons. But the intersection of these doctrines goes further than that. If we do not affirm the doctrine of the Trinity as we have summarized it in this volume—that is, as one God who exists in three persons who are distinguished from one another *only* via their eternal relations of origin—and instead posit a Trinity that distinguishes between persons based on attributes, appellations, actions, and/or adoration, then Jesus is not fully God and fully man but fully man and fully

Son. On the contrary, Jesus is fully man and fully *God*, the fullness of God united in the second person of God to a fully human nature in the one person of Jesus of Nazareth. This is vital to the doctrine of redemption since both of these aspects of the hypostatic union are essential to accomplishing the salvation of human persons.

Second, and related, when we confess that Jesus is 100 percent God, we are saying that according to his divinity he possesses the entire essence of God. All of the attributes of God are his. This includes God's will. In other words, according to Jesus's divinity, he possesses the one will of the Godhead. Of course, as fully human, he also has a human will. If he didn't, he'd be "God in a bod," or a kind of automaton, a human body operated by a divine spirit. But this is the heresy of Apollinarianism and provides us with zero hope for salvation. If Jesus doesn't have a fully human will, then how will our broken human wills ever be fixed? But on the other side of the equation, if Jesus only has one of three divine wills, then that would make three gods instead of one. Because what do you have with three divine wills, three distinct conscious choice-makers, if not three gods?

Summary

The doctrine of the Trinity is the foundational doctrine of Christian theology because the Trinity is the one, true, living God and therefore the center of all existence. Because of this fact, understanding the Trinity is imperative for understanding and rightly articulating all other Christian doctrines. In particular, if we don't get the Trinity right, then we don't get Jesus right, and then we don't get salvation right. Our entire faith hinges on the Trinity, the God who we worship and who saved us in Christ.

REFLECTION QUESTIONS

1. When you think about the doctrine of the Trinity, do you connect it with your other beliefs? Why or why not?

2. How has this book helped you "connect the dots" between the doctrine of the Trinity and the rest of your Christian faith?

3. Besides those mentioned in this chapter, what are other ways that the doctrine of the Trinity connects with other doctrines?

4. What are the dangers in getting this question wrong?

5. How do popular Christian songs and writings form our thinking about this question?

QUESTION 39

What Is the Best Way to Teach the Doctrine of the Trinity?

In question 36 we examined some of the most common historic and contemporary analogies for the doctrine of the Trinity. As we saw, all of them break down at some point, and some of them actually do more harm than good. How then do we go about teaching the doctrine of the Trinity, especially to those who may be unfamiliar with it? That is the question this chapter seeks to answer.

The Grammar of the Trinity

Schoolchildren must learn grammar before they can advance to higher levels of thought and communication. In the *trivium* of classical education (the first three liberal arts), there is a movement from simpler to more complex language skills: first grammar, then logic, then rhetoric.[1] On a pedagogical level, the first stage often involves a great deal of memorization and observation. Once the more basic skills are mastered, students can ascend to the more complex levels of analysis and argumentation. Something similar can be said about theological education. Before one can begin to articulate the more technical aspects of the doctrine of the Trinity, and to defend the doctrine against error, one must first learn the grammar of the Trinity.

One of the ways that Christians have trained initiates to the Christian faith, whether they be adults or children, is by means of *catechesis*. A catechism is simply a summary of the basic beliefs and practices of the Christian religion. It derives from the Greek word *katēcheō*, which means "to instruct orally." Catechisms have been used since the earliest centuries of the church

1. For a helpful treatment of the classical trivium, see Martin Cothran, "Classical Education Is More Than a Method," *The Classical Teacher*, April 1, 2018, https://www.memoriapress.com/articles/classical-education-is-more-than-a-method/.

to teach believers the faith, especially those preparing for baptism (known as catechumens). They are often structured in a question-and-answer format and are intended to be memorized. In the sixteenth and seventeenth centuries, the emerging Protestant traditions were prolific at producing catechisms. Martin Luther produced a Large and a Small Catechism. In the Reformed tradition, the Heidelberg Catechism on the continent and the Westminster Larger and Shorter Catechisms in Britain were especially influential. Later in the seventeenth century, the Baptists produced versions of the Heidelberg Catechism (Hercules Collins's Orthodox Catechism) and the Westminster Shorter Catechism (the Baptist Catechism, which is sometimes attributed to the Baptist pastor and theologian Benjamin Keach and is thus often called "Keach's Catechism"). Though the Baptist Catechism revised questions related to ecclesiology and the sacraments, it reproduced precisely what the Westminster Shorter Catechism says on the doctrine of the Trinity. Questions 8 and 9 address the Trinity:

> 8. Q. Are there more gods than one?
>   A. There is but one only, the living and true God (Deut. 6:4; Jer. 10:10).
>
> 9. Q. How many persons are there in the Godhead?
>   A. There are three persons in the godhead, the Father, the Son, and the Holy Spirit; and these three are one God, the same in essence, equal in power and glory (1 John 5:7; Matt. 28:19).

This is as good a place as any to begin teaching even children the doctrine of the Trinity. This is the basic grammar of the Trinity. Or, to switch the metaphor, this is the basic arithmetic of the Trinity: With regard to the divine essence, we count to one, and with regard to the divine persons, we count to three.[2]

From there we would have to spell out more clearly what exactly is meant by *essence* and *person*. The Baptist Catechism again echoes the Westminster Shorter on the divine essence:

> 7. Q. What is God?
>   A. God is a Spirit (John 4:24), infinite (Job 11:7, 8, 9), eternal (Ps. 110:2), and unchangeable (Jas. 1:17) in his being (Ex. 3:14), wisdom (Ps. 147:5), power

2. Fred Sanders, *The Triune God*, New Studies in Dogmatics (Grand Rapids: Eerdmans, 2016), 241.

> (Rev. 4:8), holiness (Rev. 15:4), justice, goodness, and truth (Ex. 34:6).

All that we say of God's essence we must ascribe equally and eternally to all three divine persons. The three are "the same in essence, equal in power and glory." They are not merely equal in essence; they are precisely *the same* in essence (cf. Nicaea's *homoousios*). And for that reason, they are equally all-powerful and all-glorious (cf. Nicaea: "I believe in the Holy Spirit . . . who with the Father and Son is worshipped and glorified").

How, then, are the three persons distinguished from one another? Their proper names already indicate their distinction: The Father begets the Son, the Son is eternally begotten of the Father, and the Holy Spirit comes forth from (is spirated by) the Father and Son. The Westminster Larger Catechism makes these distinctions explicit:

> 10. Q. What are the personal properties of the three persons in the Godhead?
> A. It is proper to the Father to beget the Son, and to the Son to be begotten of the Father, and to the Holy Ghost to proceed from the Father and the Son from all eternity.

This brief survey of some seventeenth-century Protestant catechisms yields the basic grammar of the Trinity. There is only one God. This one God exists in three distinct persons. The persons are the same in essence; they are the same God. They are distinguished by their personal names, which describe who they are in relation to one another from all eternity. There is enough in this summary to produce a lifetime of reflection, mediation, and worship. But the basic concepts are simple enough that even a child can set them to memory.

The Trinity in Proper Order

As we consider teaching the doctrine of the Trinity, there are two broad approaches we might take. We might follow the order of being (*ordo essendi*) and begin with God considered absolutely. Here, we might develop arguments that seek to demonstrate God's existence and then seek to explain his essential attributes and the eternal processions *ad intra*. Since God's being grounds God's actions in the world, there is good sense in following such a course. Here, we move from *theologia* to *oikonomia*, from theology proper to the economy, or plan, of redemption.

On the other hand, we might follow the order of knowing (*ordo cognoscendi*) and begin with God considered relatively: that is, God's actions in the world. In this approach, we might begin with God's saving acts in Jesus Christ or with the regenerating work of the indwelling Holy Spirit. We would then move back, as it were, from *oikonomia* to *theologia*, from the economy to theology proper. Since this is how we as redeemed individuals and humanity as a whole have experienced and encountered the triune God, there is good sense in this approach as well.

So which are we to choose? Depending on the audience and the purpose of the teaching, there is validity in either approach. In a seminary classroom, with educated believers preparing for ministry, there may be good reason to follow the *ordo essendi*. This is the approach we find in most works of dogmatic or systematic theology. This way of structuring the doctrine shows the ontological foundation of God's being for the history of redemption. This approach allows us to demonstrate that the processions ground the missions. In the context of a Sunday school class or a sermon series, on the other hand, there may be good reason to follow the *ordo cognoscendi*. Beginning from the experience of the faithful—their encounter with Jesus Christ and their experience of the Holy Spirit's presence—provides a point of contact that can make the more obscure parts of the doctrine more readily digestible. This approach allows us to demonstrate that the missions truly reveal the processions. In most contexts, this is perhaps the more helpful approach. After all, God's revelation of the Trinity occurred in history through God's saving acts, which were accompanied by God's authoritative words. When God determined to teach humanity about his Triunity, he did so not by giving (say, to Adam) a detailed description of his own inner life but by sending his Son in the fullness of time and by sending his Holy Spirit into our hearts (Gal. 4:4–6). In other words, there is a phenomenological and epistemological priority to the divine missions, which in turn reveal the divine processions to the contemplative eye of faith.

The Revelation of the Trinity

Even if we settle on the order of knowing, there are still multiple points of entry into the doctrine of the Trinity. And again, there is validity to more than one approach. We might begin with the Old Testament and work our way chronologically or canonically through the biblical material. We would start with hints and foreshadows of the Trinity in the Hebrew Scriptures, and then show how these are clarified in the teaching of the NT. Or we might begin with the New Testament—say, with one of the four Gospels—and explore how Jesus of Nazareth is revealed as the very Son of God, empowered by the Holy Spirit of God. We could move back from there to the Old Testament (perhaps especially the prophetic writings quoted and alluded to in the Gospel narratives) and demonstrate the OT support for the doctrine. Or again we might begin with the Pauline Epistles, the General Epistles, or even with Revelation—all of which provide legitimate entry points to the doctrine.

Again, any of these approaches would be valid. But we find the approach of Fred Sanders in his book *The Triune God* especially effective from a teaching standpoint. In Sanders's formulation, the Trinity was *revealed* in the Trinitarian missions, was *attested* in the writings of the NT, and was *adumbrated* (or foreshadowed) in the OT. Sanders's approach begins with "the work of God in salvation history and then [reasons] back to its antecedent principles in God."[3] The strength of this approach lies in its tethering of Trinitarian revelation to Trinitarian redemption. The way we come to know that God is a Trinity of persons is precisely through his saving acts, acts that reveal and unite us to the triune God. The one true God has always been a Trinitarian God. He did not become a Trinity in the incarnation of the Son or in the descent of the Spirit on the day of Pentecost. But the revelation of the Trinity was not always clear in the progress of revelation. The God who reveals himself to the Old Testament saints is undeniably the triune God, but he did not clearly reveal his triunity to the saints of old.

So, how do we come to know about the Trinity? We know that God is a Trinity of persons because in the fullness of time, the Father sent the Son. And after the crucified and resurrected Son ascended to heaven, the Father and Son jointly sent the Spirit to indwell and empower believers for holiness and witness. We know there is a Trinity because of the theophany in the Jordan. We know there is a Trinity because of the Transfiguration on Mount Tabor. We know there is a Trinity because the Father did not spare his own Son but delivered him up for us all (Rom. 8:32). We know there is a Trinity because the Son offered himself without blemish to God through the eternal Spirit (Heb. 9:14). We know there is a Trinity because "God so loved the world, that he gave his only begotten Son, that whosoever believeth in him should not perish, but have everlasting life" (John 3:16 AV).

But since the scope of the visible missions of the Son and Spirit was limited to the original eyewitnesses, God has provided a public and permanent testimony to them through the inspired writings of the New Testament. So, while the missions properly reveal the Trinity, the NT attests to this revelation. The language of attestation here should not be read in a minimalistic way. The Scriptures too are divine revelation. But what they reveal most fundamentally is God's mighty, saving acts in his Son and Spirit. The writings of the apostles lead us to consider that the God we meet in Jesus Christ and by the Spirit is not simply three in his manifestation to us; he is also three in his own inner life. God is as he reveals himself to be. The Son is *sent from* the Father in the incarnation because he *is from* the Father in his eternal generation. The Spirit is *sent from* the Father and Son at Pentecost because he *is from* the Father and Son in his eternal procession. The revelation of eternal life in Jesus Christ culminates in his glorification in the presence of the Father with the very glory he had with the Father before the world existed (John 17:5). In other words, the

3. Sanders, *The Triune God*, 20.

dramatis personae we meet on the stage of redemption have always existed in perfect union and communion with one another as the one true God.

Having witnessed the revelation of the Trinity through the divine missions attested in the NT, we are then sent back to the OT illuminated by the light of Christ. As B. B. Warfield once stated, the Old Testament is like a chamber richly furnished but dimly lit.[4] It is only in the light of Christ, which sheds its rays in all directions, that we can rightly see what was there in the Old Testament all along. It is not that we are reading into the Hebrew Scriptures something that is not really there. But we are reading it now with the proper interpretive key. "You search the Scriptures," Jesus tells the Jewish religious leaders, "because you think that in them you have eternal life; and it is they that bear witness about me" (John 5:39). The New Testament revelation gives a new Trinitarian luminosity to the entirety of the OT text: to God's creation by his Word and Spirit in Genesis 1; to the plural pronouns of Genesis 1:26; to the appearance of the three men to Abraham at the oaks of Mamre (Gen. 18); to the divine status accorded to the Davidic king in Psalms 40 and 110; to the mysterious Son of Man figure in Daniel 7, who somehow shares in the very dominion and glory of the Ancient of Days; and to many other passages besides. As Christians have been eager to maintain from the very beginning, the God of Abraham, Isaac, and Jacob is the God and Father of our Lord Jesus Christ. The God who called Abram, who appeared to Moses in the burning bush, and who manifested his glory to Isaiah is the God who is Father, Son, and Holy Spirit.

Summary

One useful strategy for teaching the doctrine of the Trinity is this: begin with the visible missions of the Son and Spirit in the economy of redemption; explore the ways that these missions are narrated and explained in the New Testament and how they accurately reveal what God is really like in his inner life; and then return to the Old Testament to see its splendor with new Trinitarian eyes. Catechesis and careful biblical exposition in this vein can help the faithful better understand not some new God that they have never encountered before but the God they already know in their redemption, in their worship, and in their prayers.

REFLECTION QUESTIONS

1. How would you teach a child the doctrine of the Trinity? What about an unbeliever or a new believer?

---

4. Benjamin Breckinridge Warfield, *Biblical Doctrines* (1932; reprint, Grand Rapids: Baker, 2003), 141–42.

2. When teaching the doctrine, is it better to begin with God's eternal being and work forward, so to speak, to his acts in redemption and revelation? Or is it better to begin with the history of salvation and work backward to God's eternal being? What are the strengths and weaknesses of each approach?

3. How do popular Christian songs and writings form our thinking about this question?

4. What are ways that considering how to teach the Trinity helps you learn how to pray?

5. In what ways has considering how to teach the Trinity helped you understand how to read your Bible?

QUESTION 40

How Do We Apply the Doctrine of the Trinity to the Christian Life?

With the rise of social Trinitarianism (see question 35), contemporary theology has exhibited a keen interest in applying the doctrine of the Trinity to human concerns. Versions of social Trinitarianism have been marshaled to underwrite various political arrangements (such as liberation theology) and to underscore a relational ontology of personhood. Theologians have appealed to a social doctrine of the Trinity in gender debates as well, with some seeing the doctrine as support for egalitarianism and others for a more traditional, or complementarian, vision for male-female relationships. This latter maneuver is perhaps especially familiar to many evangelicals. As we have explained in question 33, some evangelical theologians have argued for "eternal relations of authority and submission" (ERAS) or the "eternal functional submission" (EFS) of the Son and Spirit. This position maintains that there is an analogy from the Trinity to gender relations. In this reasoning, just as the Son is ontologically equal to the Father but eternally and functionally submissive to him, so also women are ontologically equal to men though functionally submissive to them in certain contexts. As we have seen, these social doctrines of the Trinity are out of step with the traditional formulation of the Trinity in several important respects. The traditional understanding of divine personhood rejects the notion that the persons are distinct centers of consciousness and will who interact with one another as three human agents would. Further, a hierarchy of authority is ruled out by the essential unity of the divine persons. One may still conclude (as we do) that a complementarian vision for gender relations has strong basis in biblical exegesis; it is simply a misstep and a confusion of categories to appeal to a wrongheaded social Trinitarianism to support this position.

Critics of social Trinitarianism have sometimes responded to these various social uses of the Trinity by suggesting that there is, properly speaking, no immediately obvious use of the Trinity at all. For example, Karen Kilby appeals to the apophatic mode of the traditional doctrine to suggest that the Trinity is simply too dissimilar from another other reality to serve as an adequate grounding for any creaturely social arrangement. Stephen Holmes states the matter more baldly, "The doctrine of the trinity is necessarily and precisely useless."[1] Strictly speaking, the doctrine of the Trinity is not a means to some other end. Instead, the contemplation of triune God is itself the end and goal of human existence, as Holmes goes on to underscore: "For us to see the beauty of the divine life and to respond with awestruck worship is not something that serves another, higher, end, not something of use. Instead, it is, simply and bluntly, what we were made for."[2]

While there is good reason *not* to view the Trinity as a kind of exact blueprint for creaturely relations, that does not mean that the doctrine has no application to the Christian life whatsoever. The Trinity is woven into the entire fabric of Christian belief and practice. The light of the Trinity sheds its rays in all directions, implicating the whole of creaturely existence and redeemed life. So, while we may not wish to *use* the Trinity to undergird our other commitments, there are still ample opportunities to *apply* the doctrine to the Christian life. This chapter explores some of the ways that the doctrine of the Trinity is highly relevant to Christian spirituality. We note three areas in particular: evangelism/discipleship, assurance, and prayer/worship.

Evangelism and Discipleship

A first point of application that we wish to highlight is the church's commission to make disciples of all nations. Recall that the Lord's Great Commission to his church compels us to make disciples and then to baptize them in the triune name and to teach them all that Christ has commanded. Jesus has given the church instructions not only about the mission and the message but also about the means and the method. Enrolling learners in the school of Christ is, therefore, decisively Trinitarian. The Christian life begins by being immersed into the triune name. As Ben Myers has so eloquently put it, "In discipleship, the one who makes the most progress is the one who remains at the beginning."[3] We grow outwardly by growing deeper into the fundamental mystery of the faith with which are marked and sealed in our baptism. In this sense, evangelism and discipleship are not really two things but one: When we invite sinners to repentance and faith, we are inviting them not only to receive God's free and unmerited pardon but also to begin the journey of transformation into Christlikeness through the work of the Holy Spirit to the glory of God the Father.

1. Stephen Holmes, "Classical Trinity: Evangelical Perspective," in *Two Views on the Doctrine of the Trinity*, ed. Jason S. Sexton (Grand Rapids: Zondervan Academic, 2014), 47.
2. Holmes, "Classical Trinity," 48.
3. Benjamin Myers, *The Apostles' Creed: A Guide to the Ancient Catechism* (Bellingham, WA: Lexham, 2018), xv.

So, to the degree that we are concerned with missions, evangelism, and discipleship, we should be concerned with the doctrine of the Trinity. As ministers and teachers, we are keenly aware that, for many, this claim seems counterintuitive. Many Christians tacitly pit theology against evangelism. How can we worry ourselves with fine metaphysical distinctions and obscure historical texts when there is a lost world all around us that desperately needs Jesus? In answer to this rhetorical question, we would put forth another: Just who is this Jesus we proclaim? Do we preach a merely human Jesus, even a Jesus who shows us the power of self-sacrificial love? Or do we not also preach a Jesus who is the divine and only begotten Son of the Father, who was conceived by and empowered by the Holy Spirit? Do we not proclaim a Jesus who, as both God and man, can alone mediate between God and man? Do we not share with the lost a Jesus who as God can provide an infinite atonement for sin and as man can die and be raised as humanity's representative and substitute? Do we not present Jesus as the definitive revelation of God who reveals the Father in the power of the Spirit? We believe the answers to these questions are obvious.

Does a person have to believe in the Trinity, then, in order to be saved? It depends on what one means by "believe in the Trinity." If the question is, does a person have to be trained in the technical apparatus of the doctrine of Trinity and its historical development and theological meaning, then the answer is no. Even children can understand the rudimentary truths of the gospel sufficient for faith and salvation. No advanced degrees in fourth-century controversies are required. But do we not teach our children the true identity of Jesus as both God and man? Do we not teach them that "God so loved the world that he gave his only begotten Son"? Do we not teach them that when they repent and believe in the gospel, the Holy Spirit comes to indwell them? Surely, even a rudimentary presentation of the gospel is insufficient if it makes no reference to the necessity of faith in the Father, Son, and Holy Spirit. Certainly, Christians can have developing and even erroneous beliefs about the doctrine of the Trinity at various points in their spiritual journey. But to omit mentioning the triune nature of the God of the gospel (especially if it is intentional) is a dereliction of our evangelistic duty. The gospel concerns the Son of God, not just a prophet or even a messiah, but the Son of God incarnate (John 1:14; Rom. 1:4). And, again, the first act of obedience for new converts is submission to baptism in the triune name. It is no accident, then, that early Christian catechesis followed a "rule of faith" that was explicitly Trinitarian in its form and content: "I believe in God the Father Almighty. . . . I believe in Jesus Christ his only Son our Lord. . . . I believe in the Holy Spirit."

Assurance

The problem of assurance is familiar to any believer who has traversed the Christian pilgrimage for any amount of time. Faith is often tinged with doubt. The unnamed father in Mark's gospel expresses succinctly the experience of every believer: "I believe, Lord, help my unbelief" (9:24). The pressing question of the rich young ruler expresses well our existential angst: "What must I do to inherit eternal life?" (Luke 18:18). The Westminster Confession of Faith offers a helpful summary of the Protestant doctrine of assurance. While assurance does not "so belong to the essence of faith" that it is automatic (assurance is sometimes hard-fought), it is available to all believers through the ordinary means of grace without any need for further special revelation. Especially relevant for our purposes, assurance has a decidedly Trinitarian shape; it is the indivisible work of the Holy Trinity:

> Although hypocrites, and other unregenerate men, may vainly deceive themselves with false hopes and carnal presumptions: of being in the favor of God and estate of salvation; which hope of theirs shall perish: yet such as *truly believe in the Lord Jesus*, and love Him in sincerity, endeavoring to walk in all good conscience before Him, may in this life be certainly assured that they are in a state of grace, and may *rejoice in the hope of the glory of God*: which hope shall never make them ashamed.
>
> This certainty is not a bare conjectural and probable persuasion, grounded upon a fallible hope; but an infallible assurance of faith, founded upon the divine truth of the promises of salvation, the inward evidence of those graces unto which these promises are made, *the testimony of the Spirit of adoption* witnessing with our spirits that we are the children of God; which Spirit is the earnest of our inheritance, whereby we are sealed to the day of redemption.[4]

Those who truly believe in the Son are assured by the Holy Spirit that they are adopted sons of the Father. Further, note how this statement includes both an objective ground and a subjective appropriation of this Trinitarian assurance. We see this same dynamic in the opening chapter of Ephesians when Paul erupts into praise for God's saving benefits.

What assurance does the believer have? It is knowing the love of the electing Father, the reconciling grace of the crucified and risen Son, and the sealing, empowering work of the Holy Spirit. Once again, we see in a passage like Ephesians 1 the dialectic between the doctrine of inseparable operations and the doctrine of appropriation. It is the one God who saves, but each of the divine persons is mentioned in this passage.

Where do we turn when our repeated stumbling and falling into sin leaves us wondering if God is truly for us? What hope do we have when the

---

4. Westminster Confession of Faith, chapter 18, https://www.ligonier.org/learn/articles/westminster-confession-faith. The italics indicate scriptural quotations.

memory of past sin continues to haunt us? What guarantee do we have that we will keep from apostasy in the future? All of the promises of grace in the Bible can be marshaled in answer to these questions, but those promises have a decidedly Trinitarian form and shape.

Prayer and Worship

A final application of the Christian doctrine of the Trinity concerns the life of religious devotion, prayer, and worship. The apostolic gospel brings the believer into "fellowship (*koinoinia*: participation, communion) with the Father and with his Son Jesus Christ" (1 John 1:3). As the apostle John makes clear throughout his first epistle, this communion occurs by the mutual abiding—Christ in us and we in God—made effectual by the Holy Spirit (1 John 3:24; 4:13). The goal of the gospel is to bring us into communion with the triune God, and the "chief exercise" of this communion is prayer and worship.[5]

One of the clearest triadic formulae in the NT, the Great Commission of Matthew 28:18–20, is framed explicitly in the context of worship. We are using the term "worship" here in an expansive but not endlessly elastic sense. New Testament worship is a whole-life endeavor. It includes all of the acts of obedience directed immediately toward God by believers, including both external worship (with its ceremonies and ordinances) and internal worship (both private and family worship).[6] In this sense, Jesus's final instructions to his disciples before his ascension constitute a program for worship: Make disciples, baptize them, and teach them. At the heart of this prescription is the sacramental invocation of the triune name. Disciples are immersed in name of the Father, the Son, and the Holy Spirit.

The apostolic benediction in 2 Corinthians 13:14 is also relevant for Trinitarian devotion. It is important to bear in mind what precisely a benediction is. In its OT context, a benediction is a blessing, literally a "good word," pronounced by the priest over the people of God. The standard formula for the benediction was to be spoken by Aaron and his sons:

> The LORD bless you and keep you;
> the LORD make his face to shine upon you and be gracious to you;
> the LORD lift up his countenance upon you and give you peace.
>
> (Num. 6:24–26)

---

5. John Calvin, *Institutes of the Christian Religion*, ed. John T. McNeill, trans. Ford Lewis Battles, 2 vols. (Louisville: Westminster John Knox, 1960), 2:20.
6. For a description of early Baptist worship, which had important continuities and discontinuities with the worship practices of other Separatists and Puritans, see Matthew W. Ward, *Pure Worship: The Early English Baptist Distinctive* (Eugene, OR: Pickwick, 2014).

So, a benediction is a prayer that is spoken over the people of God (not strictly directed to God himself) but in such a way that God is the one who is invoked to bring the blessing. Many of the NT epistles close with similar benedictions and doxologies. The benediction of 2 Corinthians (13:14) is relevant because it invokes all three divine persons: "The grace of the Lord Jesus Christ and the love of God and the fellowship of the Holy Spirit be with you all." The identity of the God who blesses God's people is none other than the triune God. Perhaps it is no accident that the Aaronic blessing itself invoked the name of YHWH three times.

In a similar way, many of the NT epistles begin with greetings that invoke blessings not only from the Father but from the Son as well. For example, Ephesians 1:2 reads, "Grace to you and peace from God our Father and the Lord Jesus Christ." Jesus is placed alongside the Father as the dispenser of divine grace and peace. Prayer and worship are directed to Jesus throughout the New Testament. The magi worship him, as do the disciples after his resurrection (Matt. 2:11; 28:17). Thus, the gospel of Matthew is framed—it begins and ends—in terms of Jesus-worship. The proto-martyr Stephen prays to Jesus in his final hour (Acts 2:59–60). Paul describes the church as those who "in every place call upon the name of our Lord Jesus Christ, both their Lord and ours" (1 Cor 1:2). Religious devotion—in the form of worship, prayer, sacramental formulae, invocation, and benediction—were all directed to Jesus from the very beginning of the Christian movement.[7]

What about the Holy Spirit? Is it appropriate to pray to the Spirit as well? Framing the question in terms of what is "appropriate" is apt. We recall again of the doctrine of appropriations. If the normative pattern of prayer commended in Scripture is directed to the Father (Matt. 6:9) in the name of the Son (John 16:23–24) and in the power of the Holy Spirit (Eph. 6:10), we must be careful not to draw an illegitimate conclusion from these appropriations. It is proper to pray to the Father as the ultimate origin of all things—not only the creative source of the cosmos but also the relational source of the other two divine persons. In other words, praying normatively to the Father highlights the Father's distinct personal property as the unbegotten origin of all things. Likewise, it is proper to pray in the name of the Son as the one through whom God created the world and who mediates God's redemption to us. And it is proper to pray "in the Spirit" as the one who brings the indivisible work of the Holy Trinity to its perfective end. But again, the doctrine of appropriations must be held in tension with the unity of being and the unity of external operations held in common by all three persons. The Son and the Holy Spirit, no less than the Father, are the one true God to whom we direct our prayers. Again, recall the apostolic benediction of 2 Corinthians 13:14: The divine

7. For more on this theme, see Larry W. Hurtado, *Lord Jesus Christ: Devotion to Jesus in Earliest Christianity* (Grand Rapids: Eerdmans, 2003).

blessing is invoked from all three persons. Similarly, in the introduction to Revelation John invokes a Trinitarian blessing:

> John to the seven churches that are in Asia: Grace to you and peace from him who is and who was and who is to come, and from the seven spirits who are before his throne, and from Jesus Christ the faithful witness, the firstborn of the dead, and the ruler of kings on earth. (Rev. 1:4–5)

Many scholars of Revelation interpret the "seven spirits" as a reference to the Holy Spirit, given the symbolic significance of seven as the number of perfection.[8] If that reading is correct, then we have another triadic invocation in this passage. Divine grace and peace are pronounced over the churches from the Father, the Holy Spirit, and Jesus Christ.

In short, we have good biblical and theological reasons for praying not only to the Father but also to the Son and Spirit. There are clear biblical precedents for it, and it seems to be an obvious entailment of the biblical and historic doctrine of the Trinity: that God is one being and one subject and therefore one object of our prayer and devotion. To return to Holmes's provocative claim about the uselessness of the doctrine of the Trinity, this point of application enables us to see the truth behind this claim. The Holy Trinity is the source and cause and the end and goal of everything that exists. The triune God is not a means to some other end—whether ecclesiastical, political, social, or therapeutic. He *is* the end of all our lives and all our longings. As Thomas Aquinas put it, "knowledge of the Trinity in unity is our whole life's fruit and goal."[9]

Summary

Perhaps we might want to avoid *using* the doctrine of the Trinity as a pretext for some social program, but we should seek to *apply* the doctrine to our spiritual lives. The Holy Trinity is the beginning, the middle, and the end of the Christian life. When we come to faith in Jesus, we are immersed into the triune God that he reveals and marked in our bodies with this new Trinitarian identity through the waters of baptism. When we often lose heart in our battles with sin and temptation, the work of the Trinity assures us that we are loved by the Father, redeemed by the Son, and sealed by the Holy Spirit. The fruit and end of our whole lives is to know the Trinity in unity, an intimate participatory knowledge expressed in prayer and praise, which will culminate

8. G. K. Beale, *The Book of Revelation*, NIGTC (Grand Rapids: Eerdmans, 1990), 189–90.
9. Thomas Aquinas, *Sentences Commentary*, I d.2, q.1 a.5 exposition of the text. Cited in Gilles Emery, "God the Trinity," in *The Oxford Handbook of the Reception of Aquinas*, ed. Matthew Levering and Marcus Plested (Oxford: Oxford University Press, 2021), 629.

in eternal glory and beatitude. We anticipate that heavenly glory when we sing the Gloria Patri, one of the oldest hymns of the faith: "Glory be to the Father and to the Son and to the Holy Spirit, as it was in the beginning, is now, and ever shall be, world without end. Amen."

REFLECTION QUESTIONS

1. How much of the doctrine of the Trinity does someone have to know in order to be converted to Christ?
2. How does the doctrine of the Trinity bolster your assurance of God's grace?
3. Is it appropriate to pray to the Holy Spirit? Why or why not?
4. In what other ways can we apply the doctrine of the Trinity to our lives?
5. How do popular Christian songs and writings form our thinking about this question?

Scripture Index

Proverbs

Isaiah

Jeremiah

Ezekiel

Daniel

Joel

Micah

Matthew

Mark

Luke